Canadian
Victims of Crime
Critical Insights

Canadian
Victims of Crime
Critical Insights

J. SCOTT KENNEY

Canadian Scholars' Press Inc.
Toronto

Canadian Victims of Crime
by J. Scott Kenney

Published by Canadian Scholars' Press Inc.
180 Bloor Street West, Suite 801
Toronto, Ontario
M5S 2V6

www.cspi.org

Canadian Scholars' Press Inc./Women's Press gratefully acknowledges financial support for our publishing activities from the Ontario Arts Council, the Canada Council for the Arts, the Government of Canada through the Book Publishing Industry Development Program (BPIDP), and the Government of Ontario through the Ontario Book Publishing Tax Credit Program.

Library and Archives Canada Cataloguing in Publication

Kenney, J. Scott (James Scott), 1963–
          Canadian victims of crime : critical insights / J. Scott Kenney.

Includes index.
ISBN 978-1-55130-361-1

          1. Victims of crimes—Canada—Textbooks. I. Title.
HV6250.3.C3K46 2009   362.880971   C2009-900917-X

Typeset by Jeff Zuk.
Cover design by Troupe Design.

09 10 11 12 13   5 4 3 2 1

Printed and bound in Canada by Marquis Book Printing Inc.

For Paul
(1963–1983)
and his family

I'll always remember our laughter well into the night
as our parents told us to sleep ...

||| TABLE OF CONTENTS

Preface

The story of this book began over 25 years ago. It was then, late on a sunny June afternoon in 1983, that my family was unexpectedly visited by my grandmother and aunt, who informed us of the murder of my cousin. What followed was a whirlwind of activity—visiting his parents and siblings, the funeral, the protracted grief of family, and later hearing my mother's accounts of the offenders' trial. These, plus my family's subsequent questioning of officials and key contacts in the nascent Canadian victims' movement, began to open my eyes to the experiences of—and the sociological contexts faced by—victims of crime.

Largely on the basis of these experiences, I was motivated to enter law school. I graduated, was admitted to the bar, practiced law for several years, and volunteered with a local victims' organization. Realizing the institutional restrictions built into the criminal justice system, and ultimately realizing that law was not for me, I then applied to graduate school. I spent much of the 1990s volunteering with prominent Canadian crime victims' organizations (e.g., CAVEAT), making contacts, and conducting my doctoral research on the families of homicide victims.

Successfully defending my PhD in 1998, I obtained a Social Sciences and Humanities Research Council of Canada post-doctoral fellowship to conduct research on public and community-based victim services, which by then had been developing rapidly for over a decade. Since then, I have been able to become involved in research on restorative justice, the emergence of the Canadian victims' movement, and state crime. I have also been active in university pedagogy in the areas of deviant behaviour and criminology, personally developing and teaching courses on victimology at several universities.

I have learned a great deal about crime victims since my family was suddenly initiated into their ranks in the summer of 1983. Through academic research, personal experience and reflection, determination, and persistent effort, this book represents the evolution of 25 years of experience and research—both personal and academic—on the situation of crime victims in Canada. It is a situated, critical, yet relatively broad compendium of my published and unpublished work that raises key issues and debates for criminal justice practitioners, activists, therapists, community activists, and students. It helps begin to fill a key gap in the published literature: despite victimology being a growing sub-field in criminology, there have been few Canadian texts to date.

Of course, no book can cover every aspect of Canadian victims' experiences. Indeed, I fully expect questions about some of my thoughts and findings presented here—which is a good thing. I can only respond that I would like what is contained in these pages to serve as a challenge to start debates and encourage further victimological research to test conclusions and make comparisons. If it succeeds in doing that, then I will feel this exercise has been worth the effort.

I would like to thank many individuals and institutions for their assistance over the years in the various projects leading up to this book. I thank Dawna Speers, Priscilla De Villiers, and the many other individuals I met while volunteering with CAVEAT. I thank the many, many participants who agreed to speak to me about their experiences. I thank those provincial departments of justice that enabled me to access data and participants for my research. I thank my co-authors, Donald Clairmont, Karen Stanbridge, and Alfredo Schulte-Bockholt, for their assistance and thoughtful contributions. I thank the Social Sciences and Humanities Research Council of Canada for funding those parts of my doctoral and post-doctoral research represented herein. Most of all, I thank my family, without whose support and encouragement this book would never have been possible. This one's for you, Paul.

CHAPTER 1

Introduction

This book critically considers the meanings that are presented—and that emerge—in various contexts experienced by victims of crime. These include: (1) the initial impacts of crime; (2) social dynamics encountered by victims in their families and informal social settings; (3) gender and coping attempts; (4) the justice system; (5) encounters with victims' services programs, support groups, and shelters; (6) victims' experiences in restorative justice (RJ) sessions; and (7) comparisons with the position of victims in developing countries (including the implications of this body of work and suggestions for future research).

My general thesis is that many victims—particularly victims of violent crime—are poorly understood, and the institutions and services set up to help them often have counter-intuitive, even potentially harmful impacts. This is because support services are poorly funded, provide services in line with restrictive constructions of victimhood embedded in their own institutional contexts, and are currently often built around the very limited, indeed largely powerless role of the victim in the criminal justice system. As such, many services, to a large extent, represent a public relations exercise—more of an effort to make it appear that something is being done than providing substantive programs.

METHODOLOGIES

As the chapters that follow draw upon different data, to avoid repetition I will here briefly outline the various sources of data and research methods used, concluding with a discussion of the thematic organization of this book.

Homicide Data

Large parts of Chapters 2 and 3, along with a segment of Chapter 4 (which respectively focus on the relative impact of crime, the social dynamics faced by victims outside of formal institutional contexts, and encounters with legal institutions), are drawn from my doctoral research on the families and loved ones of murder victims. While focusing on a very specific form of victimization, as will be seen, these data remain suggestive of broader implications for victims of other forms of violent and non-violent crime, relate to a broader victimological literature, and call for comparative research.

The methods underlying my doctoral research were qualitative in nature. Recognizing the difficulty of accessing highly personal information from a traumatized population, I used a wide variety of direct and indirect approaches, including extensive volunteer involvement with a prominent victims' organization, advertising for interview/survey participants with a variety of other victims' organizations, reviewing published accounts, and seeking information through the legal system. While some of these strategies were more successful than others, taken together they ultimately resulted in a large volume of rich, qualitative data falling into three categories: (1) intensive interviews with 32 individuals; (2) 22 mail-back surveys; and (3) 108 homicide files obtained through a provincial criminal injuries compensation board (CICB), including information on 145 individuals.[1] Interview and survey participants were informed in advance about the subject matter of this study and confidentiality arrangements, and were given the opportunity to ask questions before proceeding. For the homicide files, a confidentiality agreement was negotiated for transcription/content analysis of data.[2]

Subject to my ability to gain access to willing participants, efforts were made to cover an ever wider variety of individuals, as evidenced by both the literature and completed fieldwork.[3] Attempts were made to clarify and validate observations, to resolve anomalies and contradictions, and to fill in parts of the social process that had not yet been observed (Schwartz & Jacobs, 1979). Sampling was "an ongoing procedure" (Williamson, Karp, & Dalphin, 1977). Using more than one source enabled the critical evaluation of information by "checking out" each form of data against the other (Douglas, 1976).[4] This inductive, critical approach to various sources of data enabled me to gain a more rounded interpretive understanding of participants' lived experiences than would otherwise be the case (Glaser & Strauss, 1967). Sampling continued in this fashion until the point where incoming data revealed nothing new. Hence, the ultimate conclusions are less likely to carry an obvious bias toward any specific demographic group,[5] although broader generalizations must be so qualified.[6]

Data were transcribed verbatim and entered into NUD*IST software, and a systematic filing system was developed (Lofland and Lofland, 1984). Coding and analysis initially proceeded according to various common and special classes (e.g., survivor's relation to the deceased for the former; involvement with the CICB for the latter). As analysis progressed, materials were coded and re-coded into theoretical categories that emerged from the data (Berg,

1995). Throughout, emerging theoretical categories and the various sources of data were continually cross-checked against each other (Berg, 1995; Schatzman and Strauss, 1973). If inconsistencies were located, emergent ideas were either discarded or reformulated until "practical certainty" was achieved.

Victim Services Data

Extracts in Chapters 2, 4, and large parts of Chapter 6 (which respectively focus on the impact of crime, the impact of encounters with legal institutions, and the role of victim service and help agencies) are drawn from my post-doctoral research on public and private victims' services programs in Nova Scotia. Again, the methods were qualitative. After carefully reviewing local services for victims of crime—both public and private—I contacted key representatives of each, discussed my proposed research, and inquired whether they would like to participate. After some correspondence and discussion, the three most prominent organizations agreed to participate and allowed me to prepare notices to be distributed to their staff and clients.[7]

This approach ultimately resulted in qualitative data related to three groups: (1) government victim services officers and their clients; (2) members and support volunteers of an organization dedicated to combating impaired driving; and (3) staff and clients of a local shelter and outreach service for abused women. The first two groups afforded me opportunities to observe interactions between participants and their support workers/volunteers during the course of their activities, and extensive field notes were taken. In relation to the latter group, a female assistant was hired to observe and take field notes. She was carefully debriefed and we discussed and compared our observations on a regular basis. In addition, taped follow-up interviews were conducted in relation to each service with participants and staff, in which many of the observed themes were probed more deeply and later transcribed for analysis. I personally dealt with participants in all respects, with the exception of interviewing the clients of women's shelters and support services for abused women. These interviews were conducted by my assistant.[8]

All participants were informed in advance that I was doing a study of "what victim programs do," provided with assurance of confidentiality, and given ample opportunities to ask questions before proceeding.[9] Not surprisingly, given the sensitive nature of this research, there were cases where individuals did not feel comfortable with my presence or that of my assistant, and I was bound to respect that.[10] Whenever possible, however, attempts were made to query support staff and interview the participants in broad terms about either the case in question or cases like it, in order to supplement observations. While admittedly imperfect, this was all that I could do to cross-check this information in sensitive settings.

Data in relation to the first group consisted of four months (50 hours) of observational research carried out between January and May 1999, including encounters between 25 clients and five support staff in both the offices of a government-run victims' services program and the provincial courts. Field data were supplemented with interviews of 24 clients and five support staff, ranging from 45 minutes to two hours in length. This program provides contacts and support services to victims of crime who are involved in the court process, typically after a charge has been laid against the offender. Operating largely as an information provider and referral service, it provides a variety of voluntary programs and services. These include court preparation sessions, funding for counselling through criminal injuries compensation, and assistance with preparing victim impact statements. Victim services officers essentially deal with clients—either over the phone or in person—in an attempt to explain the court process. They provide emotional support, keep clients informed about their cases, pass on relevant forms and documentation, and liaise with prosecutors, other officials in the justice system, counsellors, and community organizations. My research was particularly helped by the development of a good working relationship with an experienced victim services officer who allowed me to progressively observe and document her discussions with clients, her dealings with them in court, and so on. This individual then served as a "gatekeeper," facilitating similar dealings with others.

The second group dealt specifically with victims of impaired driving. Participant observation of 23 victims and 11 support volunteers was carried out for six months (40 hours) between March and September 1999. The observed themes were explored in more detail in interviews with 12 victims and 11 support volunteers, ranging from one and two hours in length. These data related to the local chapter of a private, national organization that combines support and advocacy functions, largely operating through the use of victim volunteers rather than professional employees. Observation involved attending regular business meetings, observing the group's formal and informal support practices, advocacy, and fundraising activities, and socializing after meetings. Again, coming to know well-placed individuals made it possible to progressively observe and document encounters that may not have been possible at the outset.

Data from the third group included four months (30 hours) of fieldwork with 20 clients and all six support workers of a women's shelter/outreach service between November 1999 and February 2000—this time by a female assistant. Following discussion of these data with my assistant, these served as the basis for her to conduct follow-up interviews with 10 clients and six support workers, ranging in length from 40 to 90 minutes. This service is a shelter for abused women and an associated outreach program. This privately run organization provides a safe haven for women who have suffered various degrees of domestic violence at the hands of an intimate partner. Beyond shelter, food, clothing, and varying levels of child care, the organization offers emotional support, court support, referrals (e.g., for legal aid, social assistance, housing), counselling, and support groups. Outreach continues many of these functions for non-residents or former residents (e.g., referrals, security signalling devices), but exhibits more of a focus on education, counselling, and support groups. In these contexts, support from a well-respected "gatekeeper," along with developing relationships between my assistant and support staff, ultimately resulted in field notes covering encounters between support workers and clients.

Interestingly, clients and support workers in each group were often aware of the others' programs, providing important contrasting opinions in relation to the others' policies and practices.[11] More importantly, while retaining my status as a researcher, the multiple roles related to my—and my assistant's—dealings with these different groups sensitized me to the tensions and conflicts between the interests and needs of these organizations.

Subject to my ability to gain access to willing participants, efforts were made to cover an ever wider variety of survivors, as evidenced by both the literature and completed fieldwork. Because differing perspectives in relation to particular practices were inevitable, attempts were made to clarify and validate observations, to resolve anomalies and contradictions, and to fill in parts of the social process that had not yet been observed (Schwartz & Jacobs, 1979).[12] Sampling was "an ongoing procedure" (Williamson et al., 1977). Using more than one source enabled the critical evaluation of information by "checking out" each form of data against the other (Douglas, 1976). This inductive, critical approach to various sources of data enabled me to obtain a more rounded interpretive understanding of people's lived experiences than would otherwise be the case (Glaser & Strauss, 1967). Sampling continued in this fashion until the point where incoming data revealed nothing new.[13]

Once collected, data were transcribed and entered into NUD*IST software, and a systematic filing system was developed (Lofland & Lofland, 1984). Coding and analysis initially proceeded according to various common and special classes (e.g., one's relation to the offender for the former; involvement in court preparation sessions for the latter). As analysis progressed, materials were coded and re-coded into theoretical categories that emerged from the data (Berg, 1995; Schatzman & Strauss, 1973). Throughout, emerging theoretical categories and the various sources of data were continually cross-checked against each other (Berg, 1995). If inconsistencies were located, emergent ideas were either discarded or reformulated until "practical certainty" was achieved (Denzin, 1978).

Restorative Justice Data

Much of Chapter 7 is informed by an ethnographic study of youth RJ sessions that I conducted with Donald Clairmont in 2003–2004. These were held under a provincial program where, upon the proposal of a police officer or prosecutor, an "offender" who has "accepted responsibility" can "choose" to enter this program to avoid court. "Victims" are then contacted to see if they wish to participate. If so, the parties meet, along with a facilitator, to work out a contract resolving the matter.[14]

Between April 2003 and May 2004 we observed the dynamics of such sessions in and around a mid-sized Canadian city. Our attendance was negotiated with the non-profit community justice agencies that were running the program for the justice department and, for ethical reasons, was consented to by participants. Twenty-four of the 28 sessions each included at least two RJ facilitators (usually volunteers), an offender, victim, and at least one supporter, either of the victim or the offender. The parties were told that we were external evaluators and that our role was not to participate, but to observe, take notes, and remain unobtrusive. We noted that their collaboration was voluntary and confidentiality would extend to data storage, reporting, and publication. After taking questions, if there was not unanimous consent then we would leave before the session began. This occurred in just in one instance.

Subject to our ability to gain access to participants, sampling involved efforts to cover an ever-wider variety of sessions, as evidenced by both the literature and completed fieldwork. For a medium-sized city (population 350,000) making up 37% of the provincial population, we found that there were few victim–offender sessions scheduled and even fewer held. Although we were allowed to attend 64 sessions over 13 months, we knew that the program officials felt that certain sessions, often those involving intra-familial conflict, were too sensitive for us to attend. Thus, while we felt that we had a broad cross-section of offences, participants, and demographic characteristics,[15] our conclusions must be so qualified. Moreover, given monthly schedules, we knew of more sessions than we could attend, but these remained a small fraction of the 1,991 provincial youth who were criminally charged in 2003–2004 (Thomas, 2005).[16] Of 64 RJ sessions scheduled, 24 were complete victim–offender sessions, while 14 had a party missing and were converted into "accountability sessions" where the facilitator took over the victim's role as a shaming agent. A total of 25 sessions were cancelled when a party did not show, and one lacked consent for our observation. Absent both sides, given our topic, with four exceptions, where we observed accountability sessions we left without observing.

Field notes were transcribed and entered into NUD*IST software, and a systematic filing procedure was developed. Given our focus on the RJ process, we sorted the common verbal actions of victims, offenders, supporters, and facilitators. Narrative interrelations between base categories soon emerged (e.g., defensive rhetoric by one party following offensive claims by another) so the data were re-coded into theoretical categories representing typical interlocking, strategic, and identity claims. As these often involved lengthy narrative chains competing over the definition of the situation, the outcomes were categorized and the dynamics behind them probed. These revealed contextual factors and strategic actions by parties other than victim and offender. Theoretical categories were continually cross-checked against each other (Berg, 1995). If inconsistencies were located, emergent ideas were either discarded or reformulated until "practical certainty" was achieved.

Other Matters

While the above represent the primary data sources for this book, there are several extracts based on other forms of research. For example, one extract in Chapter 4 involves legal research that I conducted on the historical and present position—both procedural and substantive—of the victim in the Canadian criminal justice system. In addition to my homicide data, Chapter 5 contains an empirical analysis (with Karen Stanbridge) of documentary and published sources on the emergence of the Canadian victims' rights movement in the early 1980s. Finally, Chapter 8, in which I suggest an uncomfortable international comparison between Canada and Colombia in relation to victims' rights, is informed by both international surveys (e.g., the International Criminal Victimization Survey) and ongoing research with Dr. Alfredo Schulte-Bockholt, who has garnered much material on criminal victimization in Latin America.

A final consideration is that as with the study of deviance, the study of criminal victimization poses difficult methodological challenges (Gomme, 2007). While the difficulties with traditional quantitative approaches such as victimization surveys have been discussed in detail elsewhere (Gomme, 2007) and the pros and cons of qualitative methods are well known (Berg, 1995; Gomme, 2007), Appendix C highlights further specific issues faced by qualitative researchers—particularly when dealing with those suffering from emotionally upsetting forms of victimization. While qualitative researchers are able to obtain detailed and meaningful data on victims' lived experiences, great care must be taken with regard to research ethics, accessing subjects, interviewing, ethnographic observation, use of language, transcription, and analysis and presentation of results. Indeed, it is important to also consider the researchers' experiences because these sometimes reflect and shed useful light on the data encountered. I hope that my comments in this regard will encourage qualitative researchers to build on the observations, strategies, and methodological insights noted, particularly by providing accounts of their own research experiences in other qualitative analyses of more far-ranging victimological contexts.

ORGANIZATION OF THIS BOOK
This book is organized as follows.

Chapter 2 discusses the impact of crime. It includes extracts from three pieces indicating that the impact of crime is poorly understood. It begins with data from my post-doctoral research indicating that victims of various offences do not necessarily see themselves as such at the outset, raising questions about stereotypes and assumptions that are not borne out in fact. This is followed by an extract from my homicide study on individuals who do clearly see themselves as victims. This indicates the dimensions of their "loss of self" following the crime, along with when and how they articulate these dimensions interactionally.

Chapter 3 focuses on the social dynamics experienced by victims of violent crime outside of formal institutional contexts. Largely drawing upon my homicide data, I begin with an excerpt indicating how victims of crime often do not receive sympathy and support, but neglect and stigmatization from family, friends, and others—indicating that a parallel labelling process is frequently at work for victims. This is followed by a second piece that articulates the differing social dynamics underlying the grief of men and women in homicide cases, along with related "vicious cycles"—related to coping attempts—that serve to block coping. I conclude the chapter with an excerpt that considers how coping in homicide cases is both related to- and constrained by—participants' social interactions in a variety of informal and institutional contexts.

In Chapter 4, I consider the significant part played by the criminal justice system and its related institutions in the experiences of crime victims. I begin with a piece that sets out the historical construction of the victim's limited legal role, as well as its practical effects at each stage of the criminal justice process. This is followed by excerpts from both my homicide study and my post-doctoral research indicating, in victims' own words, how they felt the justice system affected their experiences.

Chapter 5 (with Karen Stanbridge of Memorial University) extracts a recent paper that discusses the role and strategic management of emotion in the context of a victim's place in the criminal justice system, in the emergence of the Canadian crime victims' movement.

Chapter 6 reviews in detail the role played by agencies that have been set up to provide services to victims of crime. I begin by reviewing and critically analyzing various responses to the traditional legal position of victims (e.g., civil lawsuits, the CICB, victims' bills of rights, and victims' services programs). Next, drawing upon my post-doctoral research, I critically consider the potentially counter-intuitive impact of encounters with victim support programs. This begins with a critical analysis of victims' and staff's comments on a provincial victims' services program. I follow this with an analysis of victims' and supporters' comments on a private victim support/advocacy group. Lastly, there are excerpts from women and service providers in relation to women's shelters and outreach services. The general theme reflected is that each group is set up to help victims in a way that is reflective of its institutional and organizational context. These privilege some matters and push others into the background. Moreover, despite formal attempts to avoid encouragement of the victim role, each group actually facilitates this role in different ways.

In Chapter 7, I provide a critical look at RJ. Since ethnographic study of RJ sessions as they happen has been sorely lacking, I present a study (with Don Clairmont of Dalhousie University) of youth RJ sessions. Our analysis calls attention to how traumatic, shaming emotions are dramaturgically mediated by the rhetorical use of the victim role—and how such micro-political shame management may serve to facilitate apparently meaningful outcomes, undermine them, or result in agreements based more on *realpolitik* than reintegration. We also call attention to the importance of the organizational context behind these sessions and of facilitator skills and practices, and suggest several possible avenues for further research. Ultimately, our findings reveal a very different picture from those seen in the frequently idealistic images in the literature, underscoring the need for further research and policy analysis in this important area of criminal justice.

Given these critical findings, Chapter 8 presents a provocative international comparison. Since much of the foregoing casts doubt upon the effectiveness of Canadian victim policy, I attempt to throw Canadian policy into high relief by comparing Canada with a developing country that exhibits high rates of criminal victimization and human rights abuses, and an ineffective criminal justice and policy response. Specifically, drawing upon papers presented at the American Society of Criminology conference in 2004 and the British Society of Criminology conference in 2005, I, together with Alfredo Schulte-Bockholt of St. Mary's University, draw uncomfortable parallels between the Canadian and Colombian treatments of crime victims. We note that both show questionable political, social, and institutional commitments to helping victims, drawing upon the discourse of necessity to manipulate the boundary between ideal and "realistic" responses in the social contexts at hand.

Finally, in Chapter 9 I briefly summarize the key results from preceding chapters, draw out common themes, and make suggestions for further research.

ENDNOTES

1. Interview and survey participants' involvement in this study averaged 6.28 and 7.56 years after the crime, respectively. In comparison, 66.7% of CICB data were collected in under three years, reflecting legislative application deadlines.
2. More detailed information on research instruments may be obtained from the author.
3. For further details of my sampling procedure, please see Kenney (2004, p. 252).
4. Indeed, at times the data from several sources provided useful contrasting information on the same individuals.
5. As the CICB data helped round out the largely white, middle-class, and organization-linked composition of the interview and survey data, the interview and survey data helped to balance the demand characteristics of the CICB process.
6. For response rates, please see Kenney (2004, p. 252).
7. Each organization was informed in writing that I was seeking to comparatively examine "what victim support programs do" in dealings with clients, and how clients respond to those programs. I indicated that my qualitative, processual approach would shed new light on "best practices" in victim support. Because I planned observational research as well as interviews, before proceeding I obtained university ethics review of the proposal and made written assurances of confidentiality to the organizations before proceeding.
8. Whenever possible, interview participants were sought among those observed, although written interview requests were later distributed more broadly among staff and clients. Interviews were not conducted until the fieldwork was concluding and I could review field notes for commonalities and comparisons. A series of probing questions was then constructed for interview sessions. These questions enabled consideration of the dynamics of a *particular* group and meaningful comparisons *between* groups, and allowed me to better cross-check observational and interview data.
9. Data were only collected from willing participants who had been informed in advance about the nature of the research. Beyond written notices to each organization, before proceeding with observations or interviews the participants were again appraised—both verbally and in writing—of the nature of the research, confidentiality, and so on. Written consent was obtained before proceeding.
10. In relation to the three sources of data, those who did not feel comfortable with having a researcher present broke down as follows: three from victims' services, four from impaired driving support, and four from women's shelters/outreach services. In these cases, I or my assistant left the setting.
11. For example, provincial victim services staff had regular dealings with seven support workers in the other two groups, who offered their considered—and critical—insights.

12. Observations began with support workers who had extensive experience in local victim organizations and clients who had previous dealings with the justice system and various victim services. I then focused on people who had dealt with the issues that I wanted to learn more about (e.g., group counselling sessions, clients' encounters with support workers when preparing victim impact statements). Follow-up interviews were also selected using this approach, supplemented with probes on topics of interest.

13. Participants were predominantly female, with the exception of about one third of both supporters and clients of the impaired driving group. While this would be expected of women's shelters, and is in line with the Nova Scotia Victims' Services Division 1999 *Activity Report*, male under-representation has been noted in studies of victimization (Blanchard, 1987; Hussey, Strom, & Singer, 1992; Janoff-Bulman & Hanson-Frieze, 1987; Roane, 1992). Support staff tended to be middle class and clients working class, although less so for clients of the impaired driving group. The data showed limited ethnic diversity, reflecting the provincial population. Most support workers were married; clients were not, with the exception of the impaired driving group. Most support staff were in the 30–50 years age bracket; clients, except in the impaired driving group, tended to be under 30 years old. The impaired driving group and the women's shelter dealt with expected offences, while victim services, in line with its statistics, dealt with family violence, sexual abuse, and stranger assaults. Clients of victim services and the women's shelter ranged from several months to two years between the crime and data collection, while the impaired driving group ranged from two to 16 years.

14. For details of the administration and general procedural format of RJ sessions under this program, see Kenney and Clairmont (2008).

15. For demographic details of RJ participants and facilitators, the offences dealt with, and session outcomes, see Kenney and Clairmont (2008).

16. Special group sessions (drug education or shoplifting) and community service orders round out this broader group, in addition to the many youth dealt with in court.

REFERENCES

Berg, B. L. (1995). *Qualitative Research Methods for the Social Sciences* (2nd ed.). Needham Heights, MA: Allyn & Bacon.

Blanchard, G. (1987). Male victims of child sexual abuse: A portent of things to come. *Journal of Independent Social Work 1*(1), 19–27.

Denzin, N. K. (1978). *The Research Act: A Theoretical Introduction to Sociological Methods* (2nd ed.). New York: McGraw-Hill.

Douglas, J. D. (1976). *Investigative Social Research*. Beverly Hills, CA: Sage.

Glaser, B., & Strauss, A. L. (1967). *The Discovery of Grounded Theory: Strategies for Qualitative Research*. Chicago: Aldine.

Gomme, I. (2007). *The Shadow Line: Deviance and Crime in Canada*. Toronto: Thomson-Nelson.

Hussey, D. L., Strom, G., & Singer, M. (1992). Male victims of sexual abuse: An analysis of adolescent psychiatric inpatients. *Child and Adolescent Social Work Journal, 9*(6), 491–503.

Janoff-Bulman, R., & Hanson-Frieze, I. (1987). The role of gender in reactions to criminal victimization. In R. C. Barnett, L. Biener, & G. K. Baruch (Eds.), *Gender and Stress* (pp. 159–184). New York: The Free Press.

Kenney, J. S. (2004). Human agency revisited: The paradoxical experiences of victims of crime. *International Review of Victimology 11*, 225–257.

Kenney, J. Scott and Clairmont, Don. (2008). Using the Victim Role as Both Sword and Shield: The Interactional Dynamics of Restorative Justice Sessions. Journal of Contemporary Ethnography (in press) published "online first" on August 23, 2008.

Lofland, J., & Lofland, L. H. (1984). *Analyzing Social Settings*. Belmont, CA: Wadsworth Publishing Company, Inc.

Roane, T. H. (1992). Male victims of sexual abuse: A case review within a child protective team. *Child Welfare 71*(3), 231–239.

Schatzman, L., & Strauss, A. L. (1973). *Field Research: Strategies for a Natural Sociology*. Englewood Cliffs, NJ: Prentice-Hall.

Schwartz, H., & Jacobs, J. (1979). *Qualitative Sociology: A Method to the Madness*. New York: The Free Press.

Thomas, J. (2005). Youth court statistics, 2003/04. *Statistics Canada—Catalogue no. 85-002-XPE, 25*(4), 1–19.

Victims' Services Division. (1999). *Activity Report: April 1, 1998–March 31, 1999*. Halifax: Nova Scotia Department of Justice.

Williamson, J. B., Karp, D. A., & Dalphin, J. R. (1977). *The Research Craft: An Introduction to Social Science Methods*. Boston: Little, Brown.

CHAPTER 2

The Impact of Crime

INTRODUCTION

The statistics on crime are compelling. In 2007, despite a 7% yearly decrease and the lowest crime rate in 30 years, uniform crime report data show that Canada still experienced 306,559 violent offences (–2.5%), 1,094,703 property crimes (–7.7%), and 901,638 other *Criminal Code* incidents (–8.6%) (Dauvergne, 2008). Comprising 13%, 48%, and 39% of recorded crimes respectively, these figures include 594 murders, 29,600 robberies, 21,449 sexual assaults, 236,934 assaults, and 230,920 break and enters, among other offences. Youth crime remained relatively stable, but violent youth crime was double the rate of 20 years ago.

Given inaccuracies in detection, reporting, and recording (Gomme, 2007), most notably that only 34% of criminal victimizations are reported (Gannon & Mihorean, 2005), researchers employ surveys to get a better picture. The 2004 General Social Survey found that 28% of Canadians reported being victimized in the previous year (vs. 26% in 1999), an increase driven largely by theft and vandalism. Household victimizations were most common (34%), followed by violence (29%) and thefts of personal property (25%). Notably, the proportion of violent offences resulting in injury had increased to 25% (vs. 18% in 1999) (Gannon & Mihorean, 2005).

Those who have been assaulted, robbed, or otherwise victimized face various potential impacts—from physical and psychological distress to financial loss (Wallace, 2007). Some argue that these may be measured through "objective" and "subjective" criteria (Kennedy & Sacco, 1998). Objective criteria emphasize material losses, calculating harm in terms of the actual monetary cost to the victim and society (e.g., valuables taken, lost days at work, medical costs of physical injuries). Subjective measures consider psychological impacts, particularly long-term emotional symptoms.

While material consequences are significant (Miller, Cohen, & Weirsma, 1996; Wallace, 2007), most researchers have focused on long-term emotional impacts. Post-traumatic stress disorder, battered woman syndrome, and the cycle of violence are common topics (Kennedy & Sacco, 1998; Wallace, 2007; Weed, 1995; Widom, 1989). Many have also sought temporal uniformities in reactions. Lindemann (1944) described the consequences of trauma in terms of impact, recoil, and recovery stages, and research has followed in relation to criminal victimization (Bard & Sangrey, 1986; Riedel, 1990; Young, 1991).

Nevertheless, conventional victimology assumes the objectivity of individuals or groups as victims without considering the interpretive, definitional processes involved in constructing this reality status (Holstein & Miller, 1990). Victims are interactionally constituted: "Describing someone as a victim is more than merely reporting about a feature of the social world: it constitutes that world" (Holstein & Miller, 1990, p. 105). Dropping this assumption enables researchers to view "victims" from a new angle, to analyze the specific interactional dynamics and the subtle "victim assignment practices" where initially confused, traumatized, and vulnerable individuals either learn to adopt or resist being cast into the victim role. By focusing on the "seen but unnoticed" (Garfinkel, 1967), much may be learned about how people become "victims."

For example, Emiliano Viano (1989) outlined four stages in the definition of victimization, centred on claims to victim status. Considering how experiences are defined by "victims" and by others, these outline a process whereby "real" victim status is assigned. At each stage, people have different perceptions of their status as "victims," which affect their behaviour and the odds of moving on.

Viano's stages are as follows: (1) the experience of harm, injury, or suffering caused by another; (2) perception of this harm by some as undeserved, unfair, and unjust, hence perception of themselves as victims; (3) attempts by some to get others to recognize the harm and validate their victim claims; and (4) receipt by some of these individuals of validation of their victim claims, thereby becoming "official" victims and potentially benefiting from support (Viano, 1989, p. 10). It is not necessarily a given that one passes from one stage to the next (there are factors that inhibit this), so analysts must always consider the dynamics of the situation.

Finally, victim status has consequences. Holstein and Miller (1990) noted that the rhetorical establishment of victim status has the micro-political consequences of deflecting responsibility, assigning causes, specifying responses and remedies, and accounting for failure (Box 2.1). These potential benefits can lead to "victim contests" over the apparent moral high ground (pp. 113–114).

I consider such issues in this chapter. My theme is that the impact of crime is poorly understood, requiring more empirical attention to definitional processes and interpersonal dynamics. My first extract shows that a significant number of "victims" (of various offences) do not initially make victim claims,

BOX 2.1:
THE MICRO-POLITICAL CONSEQUENCES OF VICTIM CLAIMS

Claims of victimization, if accepted as "fact," have the practical objectives of deflecting responsibility, assigning causes, specifying responses and remedies, and accounting for failure: (1) when trouble emerges, an "innocent" party—the object of the injury or trouble—can be specified by assigning victim status, thus exempting them from blame; (2) categorizing a person as a victim instructs others to identify the sources of harm, implicitly designating a victimizer; (3) designating victims suggests the person deserves help or compensation, while indicating others should be sanctioned or provide restitution; (4) victimization rhetoric preserves good intentions and ideals. It does not deny failure, but it invites such a conclusion while maintaining a person's integrity. A sense of competence is maintained by portraying persons as dissatisfied, yet helpless in the circumstances. Victim status may be openly negotiated, contested, even imposed, highlighting the political character of description. If "victim" is a claim about the world, then belief in its "factual" status depends on credibility, influence, and warrant for honouring one set of claims over another. Disagreements over victim status may become conflicts in which assignments are openly disputed.

Abridged from: Holstein, J. A., & Miller, G. (1990). Rethinking victimization: An interactional approach to victimology. *Symbolic Interaction 13*(1), 103–122. See pp. 108–114.

raising questions about unsupported stereotypes and assumptions. I then shift my attention to homicide, outlining dimensions in the experiences of those who *have* come to see themselves as victims, along with when and how they articulate these dimensions. Both suggest that further empirical research on the impact of crime is required.

VICTIMIZATION AND VICTIM IDENTITY

My data from three victim service and support organizations revealed no uniform response to victimization. Indeed, claims to victim identity do not necessarily follow from victimization. Both victims and support workers provided evidence for two groups of initial claims: (1) those who did not claim victim identity despite their victimization; (2) those for whom this identity was claimed to automatically emerge from victimization.

In the first group, which made up 41% of clients,[1] subjects claimed the crime did not immediately result in a victim self-image.[2] Some simply denied that they were victims: "I'm not a victim and I don't want to be treated that way" (female, field notes). Others claimed that they either did not know how to "classify" themselves (interview #1: female, age 65) or did not consider this role until much later (interview #3: male, age 29).

Others claimed to have initially interpreted the situation differently:

> "I initially wouldn't say I saw myself as a victim. I mean, previously, when I thought of a victim I thought of something happening directly to me physically. Now I see not all are physical victims. Some are emotional and indirect" (interview #10: male, age 35).

> "Actually when I was there I didn't realize I was abused. I would never have called myself an abused woman. I just thought [the offender] had a bad day, or a problem he was taking out on me" (interview #27: female, age 29).

Finally, some claimed their ongoing abilities in difficult situations as evidence that they were *not* victims. Consider a woman who had prepared to leave and then charge her abusive partner:

> "I took action, and I think it finally made him see that I'm not as stupid as he tells me, that I have a mind of my own. I can think things for myself and make smart decisions. I feel like I have been reborn. I see myself as a victor, not a victim" (interview #26: female, age 33).

Clients' claims were corroborated by support staff (Box 2.2), indicating that some clients present as victims, while others do not: "There is no typical answer" (survey #2: female, age 46).

Thus, it is clear from both clients and support staff that victimization does not necessarily result in initial claims to victim identity. While some might suggest this results from trauma and shame (Gilligan, 2003; Nathanson, 1994; Scheff & Retzinger, 2000), the interactional elements above indicate that more is at work.

The second group, comprising 59% of clients, claimed victimhood almost immediately following their victimization[3]: "I saw myself as a victim at the outset" (interview #5: male, age 57). Interestingly, unlike those above, who sometimes denied victimhood in favour of those who had been more directly victimized, these people claimed that they were victims as well: "I think that not just our daughter was a victim, but I think our whole family was as well" (interview #15: female, age 35).

BOX 2.2:
SUPPORT WORKERS' COMMENTS ON VICTIMIZATION AND INITIAL VICTIM CLAIMS

The four support workers below are commenting on the relationship between victimization and claims to victimhood. Most realized that the latter did not necessarily follow from the former. Various factors, including a client's definition of the situation, history, relationship to the offender (if any), and emotions separated these. One claimed victimhood for clients:

"Victims of assault, irrespective of severity or circumstances, don't necessarily see it as a crime (e.g., 'it was a minor incident'/'no big deal'). Some make it clear that they are not victims and don't want to be seen as such ... Some would be more inclined to describe themselves as victims, but there has been a whole lot of crisis/drama by the point I see them. Many times people will self-identify as a victim of crime, but use that word very hesitatingly. I'll ask them some questions and review services, and then they'll explain they are not really a victim, depending on the crime" (interview #30: female, age 47).

"Those clients who consider themselves/present as victims probably have been abused longer, either as kids or with a series of abused partners. Those who don't have probably been in a shorter abusive relationship or had a strong upbringing where self-esteem was more firmly established" (interview #25: female, age 42).

"Some become more and more helpless. Others, however, [get] in touch with their anger, which gives them the strength to do something. Victimization engenders fear and powerlessness, on one hand, and anger on the other. These can coincide in the same person. Which becomes predominant is a good question" (interview #8: female, age 27).

"They don't know that they're victims, but they are" (interview 11[a]: male, 47).

Source: Kenney, J. S. (1999). *Unintended Consequences: The Interactional Dynamics of Victim Service and Support Programs.* Unpublished post-doctoral research, Dalhousie University, Halifax, NS.

Some claimed that this identity flowed automatically from victimization: "I feel I am a victim as I've been victimized" (interview #28: female, age 24). Despite this, most went on to elaborate a variety of rationales. The most prominent of these was that they had somehow changed as a person. One person who had suffered an assault stated the following:

> "I changed drastically from how I was before the crime. Before I was out every night with friends and involved in lots of activities. Now, the things I enjoyed most of my life are completely taken away from me. I've been sick from the stress, stopped eating, quit my job, and want to get away from everything. I became very snappy with my parents and pushed my boyfriend away. I slept a lot, had nightmares, and started sleeping in my parents' bed. I quit school and stopped socializing completely. I won't stay home alone or it makes me sick to my stomach. I've thought of suicide" (interview #20: female, age 17).

Indeed, many such clients expressed the impact on their sense of self more generally. In particular, those subjects who had a loved one who had been killed noted that they had lost a part of themselves (interview #4: female, age 52), including the deceased's future activities in the family (interview #5: male, age 57). All of these statements relate to "metaphors of loss" (Kenney, 2002).

Many clients linked their victim claims to the actions of the offender. Consider individuals who lost loved ones to impaired driving: "Once I heard about the offender hiding his car, I felt like a victim right away" (interview #2: female, age 48).

Similarly, consider the following woman who had been sexually assaulted by a once-trusted friend: "I feel betrayed (by the offender). I never really believed it is the person closest to you. I'm scared, but feel the urge to physically hurt him because he causes me so much pain when I see him" (interview #20: female, age 17).

Others linked their victim claims to what can be termed "concomitants of victimization," such as low self-esteem, fear, and helplessness:

> "For the longest time I lived in fear, and didn't leave because [the offender] threatened to kill me if I did. Since I left, he has threatened to kill me and follows me still. I see myself as a victim. I live in fear and don't even go outside. Every person I'm around I'm nervous. I feel that I do things wrong. I feel that I can't tell the truth. I get anxiety attacks. I had to quit my job. This is a big change. Now I can't do nothing. I just can't" (interview #31: female, age 28).

BOX 2.3:
VICTIMS' SUFFERING

"I felt like a light bulb and there was no electricity or light in it. All my emotions were cut off. Every once in awhile I would have a very intense, deep pain where I thought my heart and lungs were going to explode and I would stand in my kitchen and cry. My husband used to get scared and leave. In fact, if I could have walked away from myself I would, because I used to frighten myself. I used to think I was going to die. I wanted to die. I was mentally like a jigsaw puzzle where everything is scattered, but you've got to find the piece so you can make a little bit of sense of your world. I wasn't even aware how much time was passing. Your world is like someone has taken glass, smashed it on cement and you've got to put all the pieces back together again to make that window or that mirror. You're shattered, hurt as much as you can be" (interview 11[b]: female, 43).

Source: Kenney, J. S. (1999). *Unintended Consequences: The Interactional Dynamics of Victim Service and Support Programs.* Unpublished post-doctoral research, Dalhousie University, Halifax, NS.

Many subjects pointed to a loss of freedom as justification for their victim identity:

"I saw myself as a victim. I went from being a totally resourceful, healthy person to being unable to work [had a stroke]. Things I took for granted have now become obligations [taking care of deceased's children]. I've not only lost my freedom, but my own children are fearful that they will lose me too. The crime has certainly changed my life and many lives around me. The effect of the crime has been a chain reaction" (interview #14: male, age 38).

Finally, subjects pointed to their suffering (Box 2.3). Besides physical injuries and physical manifestations such as loss of sleep, loss of appetite, and declining physical health, subjects emphasized fluctuating feelings of shock, numbness, guilt, anger, rage, fear, and depression, accompanied by cognitive difficulties with concentration and memory.

Clients' rationales were backed up, in some cases, by support workers, particularly with regard to the link with the offenders' behaviour and concomitant factors:

> "Women who have been abused suffer a loss of power, control, and self-esteem, recurring nightmares and emotional damage. The effects of abuse are accumulative. There is much guilt, fear, and self-blame. Victims also have left home and everything behind in many cases and are totally fragmented" (interview #9: female, age 39).

However, support staff, aware not all clients considered themselves victims, were less likely than clients to automatically make this link: most, as noted earlier, saw that concomitant factors could exist without victim identity.

Summing up, clients in this study who had suffered criminal victimization did not necessarily claim to be victims of crime from the outset. Rather, they broke down into two groups: (1) those who did not initially claim victim status; and (2) those who immediately considered themselves as victims. Support workers' comments were found to support each of these groupings. Several important themes emerged. One was the importance of clients' initial definition of the situation, which emerged in both claims of why they did not consider themselves to be crime victims, and rationales of why they did. Combined with these were the concomitant factors of victim identity, including variations in self-esteem, fear, and helplessness, cutting across categories.

Of course, this was a relatively simple exercise. Some may consider clients' verbal claims to victim status to be less significant than others, and defer to associated factors as evidence of an "objective" crime victim identity despite clients' claims. This is implicit in writers who emphasize shame (Gilligan, 2003; Nathanson, 1994; Scheff & Retzinger, 2000). Others, given individuals disavowing an initial victim identity in response to a specific question, may consider this of greater importance. In relation to the former, I note the problem of "experts" claiming to know more about someone's experience than they know themselves, and who can be wrong in interpreting contexts (Rosenhan, 1975). From the other position, issues of impression management become problematic (Goffman, 1959). Hence the focus on claims. Such issues draw attention to the reality status of victims, make us think about what constitutes a "real" victim, lend credence to the work of Viano (1989) and Holstein and Miller (1990), and suggest further research on the social construction of victims.

DIMENSIONS OF IMPACT AND THEIR RHETORICS

In this section, I report results from a 4.5-year study of individuals bereaved as the result of homicide ("survivors"). Unlike the above, these individuals *definitely* claim victim status, and the task is to explore that further. Following a review of the relevant literature, I present data on a series of "metaphors of loss": pragmatic, situated expressions illustrating various dimensions of victimhood. After analyzing their gender dynamics, I review the interactional contexts in which these are strategically used.

Murder and the Self

When considering the significance of homicide for self, three positions can be taken. First, the developmental perspective, which stresses the formation of self in taking the role of others (Herman & Reynolds, 1994; Mead, 1934; Meltzer, 1994; Prus, 1996), raises the question of what parts of the self are lost when one of them dies. Second, the existential perspective suggests that self is revealed in emotional states (Adler, Adler, & Fontana, 1994; Denzin, 1985; Fontana, 1984). Third, Plummer (1995) focused on "storytelling," pragmatically checking the consequences of how parties collectively reassemble a sense of self and identity, build communities, educate, and encourage change, or provide a sense of order in the world (pp. 172–179).

Each position may be found in literature on victimization, self, and bereavement. Several authors have addressed the first approach, speaking of the damage to the self in "victims" as the result of violence (Bard & Sangrey, 1986; Casarez-Levison, 1992; Hagemann, 1992). In addition, others have outlined assumptions about self and the world that are violated by bereavement (e.g., trust, autonomy, ideals, continuity, competence, control, and future) (Attig, 1996; Charmaz, 1980; Janoff-Bulman, 1985; Klass, 1988). In contrast, existentialist studies focus on the emotional meanings that emerge as the victimized self struggles to incorporate new experiences into its evolving reality (Johnson & Ferraro, 1984). Finally, Rock (1998) discussed how alienated homicide survivors sometimes band together, engaging in a project to "remoralize the universe, an attempt to alleviate pain and suffering by seeking coherence in meaning through belief" (p. 116), building a "creative mythology which gives pattern and purpose to the survivor's new life" (p. 128).

In what follows, I expand upon these earlier insights and systematically delineate how self is impacted through the murder of a loved one. I review both potential self losses and the deep emotional meanings that may emerge—not in simple terms of truth or falsehood, but in terms of their practical interactional consequences—for respondents and for their interaction partners. I outline specific dimensions of self that may be impacted after the murder of a loved one and how these are expressed, reconstituted, and utilized in specific interactional contexts. Like Harold Garfinkel (1967), who "made trouble" to examine the "seen but unnoticed" aspects of social life, I examine an extremely troubling and unexpected social situation to shed light on the foundation and enactment of selfhood.

Gender and Emotion Management

First, it is important to consider gender. It has been widely noted that men are underrepresented in the literature on victimization (Blanchard, 1987; Broussard & Wagner, 1988; Hussey, Strom, & Singer, 1992; Roane, 1992). Similarly, most information on parental bereavement comes from mothers, not fathers (Lister, 1991; Staudacher, 1991). This suggests that a broadening focus can be achieved through gender analysis.

Since gender schemas are an important part of self-concept, inasmuch as self-relevant assumptions on gender are challenged, one might expect decreased self-esteem in victims (Janoff-Bulman & Hanson-Frieze, 1987). However, as research indicates that men are far less likely to report or disclose victimization, women are more likely to engage in social withdrawal, and men are more prone to later behave aggressively, it has been claimed victimization does not so much challenge women's assumptions about themselves as it does their faith in others. Men, on the other hand, question their male identity.

While the bereavement literature focuses on differential reactions to loss (Forrest, 1983; Raphael, 1984; Wilson et al., 1982), controversy over differences in the intensity of grief by gender (Cook, 1988; Littlewood, 1992; Sobieski, 1994) and variations in coping strategies (Clyman et al., 1980; Littlewood, Hoekstra, & Humphrey, 1990; Littlewood et al., 1991; Mandell, McAnulty, & Reece, 1980) has prompted some to comment about the interplay of gender and self. Lister (1991) argued that individuals are socialized, directly or indirectly, to perceive and experience death and loss and express grief in particular ways. W. H. Schatz (1986) claimed that socialization in traditional male roles (e.g., competitor, protector, provider) means that men experience loss as a "failure," while Sobieski (1994) emphasized that men experience bereavement as a "test of masculinity." This contrasts with women, who experience a pervasive loss of a relationship throughout their social context (B. D. Schatz, 1986).

Finally, beyond the emotion-management literature focusing on gender and self in the expression and management of emotion (Hochschild, 1983; Thoits, 1990), Clark (1987, 1990) articulated useful models of distinguishing sympathy worthiness[4] and various emotional tactics to enhance place.[5] Given the greater leeway for emotional expression in female roles, this suggests a differential use of such tactics.

All of this suggests the need for a gender analysis of loss and emergent meaning, and of the ongoing struggles and pragmatic consequences surrounding such expressions. Together with bracketing the essential truth claims of the developmental and existentialist approaches, and using their insights as "sensitizing concepts" (Blumer, 1969), the following synthesizes such insights and Plummer's (1995) pragmatic approach to analyze survivors of homicide.

BOX 2.4:
EMOTIONS AS MICRO-POLITICAL PLACE MARKERS AND PLACE CLAIMS

People assemble place (i.e., interpersonal position) with the glue provided by emotions. Constructing a sense of relative place involves self-evaluation and comparison, and those activities evoke feelings (e.g., pain, shame, and belittlement, or pride, pleasure, and empowerment). Sending a place message can evoke some of those feelings in others, plus information about the social ranking system: (1) emotional place markers relay messages to self about one's place in an encounter, reminding when they evoke emotions; (2) emotions may be used interpersonally as place claims. People may actively and intentionally instigate emotions in each other and themselves ... to shape definitions of situations and of self. They want affirmation of their standing [rather than] feeling "out of place," or negotiate their place, trying to move (usually up, sometimes down), reminding and counter-reminding each other of their proper places with "emotion cues"; (3) people sometimes act manipulatively, targeting emotions at each other to enhance their power.

Abridged from: Clark, C. (1990). Emotions and micropolitics in everyday life: Some patterns and paradoxes of place. In T. D. Kemper (Ed.), *Research Agendas in the Sociology of Emotions* (pp. 305–333). New York: SUNY Press. See pp. 308–314.

Metaphors of Loss

Despite disclaimers that there were "no words" to describe the murder of a loved one, survivors quickly went on to articulate a rich series of metaphors to illustrate its impact, which I term "metaphors of loss." These attempt to convey, insofar as words can, the effect of homicide on those close to the deceased. They constitute the typical ways that survivors express their perceived loss of self, the existential meanings emotionally disclosed to them, and attempts to pragmatically control the definition of the situation.

The single most common metaphor used asserted a generalized *loss of self*. Subjects generally claimed they had "lost part of themselves" when the deceased was killed.

> "I feel that someone has taken part of me when [my son] died. I loved him so much it hurts ... To me, my children mean the world. For someone to take one of them is like taking part of me." (criminal injuries compensation board [CICB] #93: female, age 52).

Sometimes, this was expressed in terms of an "amputation" or having one's "heart torn out"; at other times in terms of being "half gone." In still

BOX 2.5:
THE "RIPPLE EFFECT"

"Violent crime victimizes everyone, sort of like a pebble in a lake. The closer you are to the pebble, the more that it seems to victimize you. But nobody escapes. Even the general public become victims of crime. You feel the anguish, the agony, the grieving, the feeling of heartache and loss yourself personally. But even those other people have lived a loss. They are not quite as free and carefree as they once were" (interview #13: male, age 46).

Source: Kenney, J. S. (2001). Metaphors of loss: Murder, bereavement, gender, and presentation of the victimized self. *International Review of Victimology 9*, 219–251. See pp. 229–230.

other cases, it was expressed in terms of emptiness, using terms such as "void," "vacuum," "a hole," "blackness," having an "empty heart," and feeling "hollow." Finally, it was asserted in terms of death: "It's a death of yourself inside. You die a little slower each day" (interview #10: female, age 60).

Such metaphors, as accomplished meanings emerging from profound emotional experiences, claim the loss of a loved one is experienced as a loss of part of one's "self." As identity "announcements" during role-taking and role-making (Hewitt, 2000; Stone, 1981) or as emotional "place markers and place claims" (Clark, 1990), these indicate the role that the speaker intends or wants to enact in a situation (Box 2.4).

In an interaction where the subject of victimization comes up, if one's response "places" the speaker into the announced victim role, a situated victim identity is constructed—further reinforcing the speaker's social and personal identities. This is precisely what happened. In the interviews I was struck by the sympathy I frequently expressed in response to the interviewees' comments. Even in the CICB data, officials in direct encounters often tried to address respondents' upset, thereby responding to this announced role—even when the respondents did not ultimately get what they wanted.

The political nature of these metaphors is further illustrated in that they were generalized beyond the survivors alone (Box 2.5).

While this generalized "loss of self" was the root metaphor most frequently asserted by respondents, they were quick to add a series of variations where different dimensions were articulated.

The next most frequent type of metaphor claimed that survivors had suffered a personal *loss of future* that was, by its very nature, permanent. With regard to the first aspect, one woman stated:

"It's as though your life is going along in one direction, and then something happens and it takes a right angle turn, and your whole future is just sliced away. And it's totally an unknown path in front of you" (interview #2: female, age 51).

As for persistence, survivors indicated that their loss was both irreversible and permanent. Some claimed it "will always be with me forever," that their lives had been "irrevocably changed," and several that they were "stuck" at the point at which they heard of the murder. This relates to the work of Mead (1932), who claimed that the future is an integral aspect of the present. Essentially, survivors claimed that they could never recover totally because, once an important future aspect of their self-identities had been cut away, all that they could foresee was a future darkened by its loss: "It's a horrible, aching thought that never will we ever feel perfectly happy again. It just won't happen because a very big part of our life is missing and we can't get it back" (interview #31: female, age 46).

Yet, one must not reify these claims; more may be happening than is signified by the literal meaning. These may serve to buttress claims to victim status, assert the respondent's control over the definition of the situation, and certainly serve to encourage sympathetic responses.

While the first two metaphors may be applicable to other types of bereavement, the third most common metaphor has particular resonance for homicide. Survivors frequently asserted that they: (1) felt personally violated by the murder; and that this (2) left behind a devastation that penetrated to the very core of their being.

With regard to this first aspect, survivors typically compared the impact to "being murdered myself," often referring to feeling physically "wounded" deep in their "heart." Words such as "violation," "assault," and "trauma" were abundant: "I felt like when they shot my son, they shot me. I felt such an emptiness. They killed my boy, and they killed me inside" (survey #19: female, age 45).

Secondly, a penetrating devastation was frequently expressed. Survivors used a variety of terms illustrative of destruction, damage, and "ruined" lives. One woman stated: "It's like sinking in quicksand, but never quite suffocating and dying oneself" (survey #20: female, age 53). Another commented: "What more can they do to me? They destroyed me. I mean, I'm still alive, but how much? Not the way I was. They took my daughter away, what are they going to do? Kill me?" (interview #23: male, age 49). Another woman said:

"My spirit, life, and physical body [are] weakened by what I am forced to go through ... My life is no longer my life. It is an

BOX 2.6:
PERSONAL CHANGES AND THE EVERYDAY WORLD

"What once was accepted, familiar, even taken for granted, has suddenly been put in question. Familiar places are suspect: they may contain dangers we had never thought about. Familiar people are perhaps not the same. The crime of one person puts the fidelity of the whole human race in doubt. Person by person, like an electrical system after a power failure, our relationships have to be checked out and rendered operative again. Until then, an invisible barrier exists between us and our fellows, which can easily over time harden into stone" (survey #5: male, age 63).

"My whole life just changed after. I don't have the same interests or do the same things, and I never will. I didn't have interest in going back to work. I just stopped doing practically everything, being involved in things. It's like, all of a sudden, you lose your taste buds and food doesn't taste the same. It's all the same food you ate before, but if you can't taste it, there's nothing to it. That's the way, to some extent, my life was after. It took quite a while, and, to some extent, it's still that way" (interview #23: male, age 49).

Source: Kenney, J. S. (2001). Metaphors of loss: Murder, bereavement, gender, and presentation of the victimized self. *International Review of Victimology 9*, 219–251. See pp. 232–233.

existence from day to day. Each day brings tears and all-consuming sadness—memories that haunt me, 29 years of memories. I drag myself through each day, hour by hour. There's no one [who] can ease the pain in my heart, no caress can ease it, no voice can please it" (interview #10: female, age 60).

Without a doubt, such claims have profound micro-political significance, considering that the interactional results included attentive, sympathetic listening and support, buttressing respondents' compensation claims for "pain and suffering" and, in some cases, encouragement of political action to "see that justice is done."

The next most frequent metaphor is most interesting for self: *"I'm a different person now"* (interview #9: male, age 48). Survivors asserted that, since the murder, they had become different people referring to "personality changes" they had noticed. Indeed, one woman asserted that she felt "like a change was going through my whole body" after learning of the murder (CICB #14: female, age 60). In many cases, survivors claimed newfound difficulties with concentration and memory; others said they had become unusually cautious. Other subjects spoke of having different and diminished interests, goals, priorities, and involvements (Box 2.6).

These claims were often corroborated by others. Thus siblings and partners, in expressing their own changes, noted how significant others had become more "reclusive" and "emotionally detached." Doctors and psychiatrists noted that their patients exhibited diminished interests, goals, and "enthusiasm for life." Such interactional corroboration—particularly by intimates and authority figures—further ratified respondents' micro-political claims to victim status as the controlling definition of the situation.

Going hand in hand with these other losses is the fifth metaphor: *loss of control*.

> "I'm a victim because my life has been irrevocably changed. The choice of what I want to do with my life has been changed. The expectations of my future have been changed. You know, I've really, in a sense, been held captive because I sit and watch my family suffer, and there is nothing I can do about it! ... You know, the thing that's hurt my family, I can't control. So, I've had a lot of my freedoms taken away. A lot of the choices in my years to live. What do I do now?" (interview #11: male, age 57).

Here we see the paradoxical nature of victimization in its fullest expression. While, on the one hand, this respondent is claiming loss of control in various areas of his life, he is simultaneously attempting to control the definition of the situation by buttressing his claim to victim status. Irrespective of the essential truth or falsity of his claim, its micro-political nature is plain. Moreover, the intensely emotional delivery of this statement, like many others, left little room to respond but in agreement.

Lastly, there is the metaphor of *lost innocence*, which underlies radical changes in survivors' perceived sense of reality. This appeared in several variations. First, there was survivors' shock that such a thing could happen: "We lived in a good area. We taught our kids to do unto others. So, I mean, for someone just out of the blue to do something like this for no reason is just horrifying" (interview #25: female, age 45).

Lost innocence was also expressed in relation to the cherished characteristics of the deceased as a person—as in "the loss of an innocent" (survey #20, female, age 53)—and in relation to the effect of the murder on surviving children whose "childhood has been stolen" (interview #13: male, age 46). Finally, it was expressed in relation to ideals of justice:

"I've always believed in justice. That ... you know, an accused has a right to a fair trial. You've got the right to be presumed innocent. I've got no argument that. That's the way it should be. But when you see the trickery going on, we've lost the principle of law—and a lot of that's been taken away" (interview #11: male, age 57).

Indeed, one man, who throughout the offender's trial had professed faith that justice would be served, collapsed in a "nervous breakdown" when the verdict was read and the offender convicted of a lesser offence (interview #23: male, age 49). He expressed how he had changed, along with much bitterness and depression, punctuated by bouts of anger at himself, the system, and the offender. Beyond "emotionally drained," he said he felt "destroyed" and, without this faith in justice to sustain him, claimed that a key component of his self had been undermined. His interview exhibited profound lost innocence on his part. In addition, in retrospect, his unpredictable outbursts effectively gave him control of the dialogue—cementing his victim status in interaction.

Gender

Going hand in hand with the expression of these metaphors was their interrelationship with gender.[6] This relates both to their differential expression and what gendered individuals are trying to say about themselves.

There were a number of striking similarities across gender lines. Regarding the root metaphor, both genders emphasized losing a "child," even though the deceased was often an adult. Many felt that they had lost a "friend" as well. As for loss of future, both considered loss of their future lineage as important. Being a "different person" was expressed by each in terms of becoming more reclusive, emotionally detached, and exhibiting diminished goals, interests, and enthusiasm for life. Indeed, the frequency of lost innocence was equal across gender lines.

Despite these similarities, each gender viewed the feelings of the other as different. Some men perceived a qualitatively different bond between mother and child that was reflected in their style of suffering (interview #24: male, age 47). Women emphasized how, rather than view parenting activities as a way to define themselves, the loss of a child and the status that affords it is the "supreme loss of ego for a man" (interview #17: female, age 50). This may partially explain why it is difficult for some couples to relate to each other after the loss of a child, and the high incidence of misunderstanding and conflict in these relationships. In cases with more similarities than differences, survivors perceived one another in stereotypical terms.

BOX 2.7:
MALE ANGER

"I was afraid of what I'd do without thinking [in court]. I'll tell you, I just wanted to grab [the offender], and rip his head off. You know? Or just go through his chest, take his heart out and show it to him, and say 'This is what you did to us. You have taken our hearts out of our bodies and crumpled [them] in your hand!'"(interview #20: male, age 37).

Source: Kenney, J. S. (2001). Metaphors of loss: Murder, bereavement, gender, and presentation of the victimized self. *International Review of Victimology* 9, 219–251. See p. 237.

There were, however, some gender differences. Despite the relatively balanced sample,[7] metaphorical expression showed a marked imbalance in favour of women and "non-traditional" men.[8] These groups expressed four of the six metaphors in ratios of at least 2:1 over traditional men, with the exception of loss of control, where the ratio reversed.[9] This presumably reflects traditional female roles in promoting emotional expression, and male roles of quiet strength and stoicism.

Beyond quantification, two matters stood out. First, men adhering to traditional roles tended to emphasize their actions in relation to them (e.g., "failing" as protectors, as providers, or in handling their emotions). They felt unable to achieve goals (e.g., plans with the deceased) and threw themselves into work. Traditional women, in contrast, emphasized damaged interrelationships (e.g., loss of companionship, being unable to attend a child's wedding, not having grandchildren).

Second, traditional women were both more emotionally expressive than their male counterparts and their metaphors exhibited a more passive, victim-oriented tone. For example, in expressing the metaphor of violating devastation, one woman compared it to being "stabbed at the same time as she was" (interview #1: female, age 47). Another commented "I cannot imagine ever being more violated—not even by rape" (interview #2: female, age 51). Men tended to be more prone to an active, angry tone (Box 2.7).

Such differences may reflect that victimization challenges basic background assumptions of the male gender schema (Janoff-Bulman & Hanson-Frieze, 1987), yet openly expressing this may represent a personal failure under various male roles (Schatz, W. H., 1986; Sobieski, 1994; Staudacher, 1991). Indeed, the angry, violent imagery could reflect a tendency to behave in a "super-masculine" manner to compensate (Janoff-Bulman & Hanson-Frieze, 1987). Metaphors expressed in this fashion may thus serve as gendered, micro-political "place claims" for such men (Clark, 1990).

Next, gender differences facilitated interpersonal conflict. "Traditional" men, who more often continued working, were particularly upset by the ongoing depression of "traditional" women. One man struggled to remain working, and bemoaned his wife's long depressive episodes, continual nervousness, hours spent crying, and inability to engage in any of their previous activities (CICB #46: male, age 54). Emphasizing both "protector" and "provider" roles, such men felt pressure to "remain strong" and keep working for others (interview #30: male, age 64). Their partners often interpreted this as "uncaring" and "getting on with their lives" (survey #21: female, age 56). Men felt that they were not being given credit for their efforts and became less "tolerant," punctuating their emotional repression with bouts of anger. Women felt that their male partners did not understand their grief, and became more upset and angry in turn. These interactions between sharply contrasting gender identities developed into "victim contests" (Holstein & Miller, 1990), and often influenced the direction in which interpersonal relationships evolved. Notably, in families with less sharply defined gender identities, such conflict was less evident.

Finally, there is the issue of behavioural responses to and uses of these metaphors in the external world. Most traditional females became fearful and reclusive, corroborating the concept that victimization undermines women's assumptions about others (Janoff-Bulman, 1985). Some did not want to go out for fear of offenders (CICB #14: female, age 60). Others talked of becoming "paranoid" as "the whole world turns nasty and you don't trust anybody" (interview #2: female, age 51). In contrast to traditional males, who generally kept busy and occupied in their jobs (survey #5: male age 63; interview #30: male, age 64) or, in several cases, either attempted to, or would have liked to personally confront the offender (interviews #12, #26, and #32), traditional females often became beset with fear, particularly when they discovered that the justice system would not protect them (interview #8: female, age 45).

Interestingly, however, a minority of women responded by banding together to fight for change. Indeed, all of the victims' organizations that I contacted for my homicide research were predominantly comprised of women.[10] These "non-traditional" women took their losses as a rallying cry for activism, and used these metaphors as the ground in which to nurture a new identity. In the words of one activist, referring to her daughter: "Her eyes have been closed. Ours have been opened" (interview #1: female, age 47).

Metaphorical Context

Simply describing survivors' typical metaphors of loss and their articulation by gender tells us little without elaborating on their social contexts. Most survivors expressed these metaphors in response to specific questions or during certain types of interactions with CICB officials. Metaphors of loss were largely expressed in relation to interview/survey questions that asked respondents: (1) how they would describe losing a loved one in this way; and (2) whether they now saw themselves as victims. In answering both of these questions, women articulated approximately twice as many metaphors as men and showed a greater variety of metaphors, with an emphasis on violating devastation. Indeed, traditional females expressed metaphorical illustrations of their spouses' reactions twice as frequently as men reciprocated.

In each context we can see the micro-political use of these metaphors as "place markers" and "place claims" to victim status (Clark, 1990; Holstein & Miller, 1990). Such gender differences are noteworthy, given the argument that victim status does not challenge traditional female-gendered identities (Janoff-Bulman & Hanson-Frieze, 1987).

However, unlike traditional males, many traditional females also expressed the various metaphors in relation to their feelings when they first heard of the murder, referring to articles or speeches they wrote to educate others, or in justification of their disproportionate involvement in victims' rights work. Taken together, these suggest that female gender roles may more readily facilitate the expression and sharing of the deep emotional meanings that are inherent to these metaphors, lending themselves to micro-political displays. Indeed, these contexts relate to Plummer's argument that telling such stories serves to reassemble a sense of self, provide a sense of order in the world, build communities, educate, and encourage reform (1995, pp. 172–179).

Turning to the CICB data, metaphors were primarily expressed in response to requests for documentation, official scepticism, or unfavourable rulings. Many appeared on CICB questionnaires asking applicants to describe how the murder affected their lives, or in consultations with mental health professionals preparing psychological assessments. They also appeared in letters accompanying subjects' applications, notes documenting conversations with applicants, and in response to letters requesting documentation. Yet respondents also expressed metaphors in response to unwelcome interactions. Some were expressed in response to letters indicating that to receive compensation for pain and suffering, applicants must have experienced "nervous shock" over and above what the average individual would experience in the circumstances. Others were expressed in personal letters responding to scepticism from CICB officials, sometimes in testimony before the CICB, sometimes in response to rulings denying or mitigating their claims, and sometimes in support of requests for an extension of benefits. Indeed, metaphors were sometimes expressed in newspaper articles or lawyers' letters quoting subjects' comments on the unresponsive CICB These metaphors were used as micro-political "place markers" and "place claims" to rhetorically underscore the validity of their victim claims and the legitimacy of their positions (Clark, 1990).

Interestingly, while the expression of particular metaphors by gender showed little discernible pattern in these interactions with the CICB, women expressed them more often when faced with scepticism or upsetting encounters. This suggests that women may be both more metaphorically expressive and more prepared to micro-politically use metaphors in contests over victim status (Holstein & Miller, 1990; Loseke, 1993).

This leads to a related question: how do survivors use metaphors? From the above data, we can see that metaphors were used in two ways. First, survivors used metaphors to express the inexpressible—to convey, as far as possible through words, their pain, loss, and the meanings disclosed in their lives. Indeed, initial disclaimers, apparent confusion, and long pauses often preceding the metaphor lend credence to this—further buttressing Plummer's claim that telling such stories serves to reassemble a sense of self, provide a sense of order, build community, educate, and encourage change (1995, pp. 172–179). Second, when survivors' victim status was questioned, they enunciated metaphors to reinforce it. This was particularly notable in the CICB data. Here, metaphors were used as a tactic to achieve control over the definition of the situation when something was at stake. In this respect, metaphors of loss intersect with and elaborate our understanding of the presentation of self (Goffman, 1959). This may be significant more broadly, considering that many respondents had affiliations with victims' rights organizations.

Finally, it appeared that metaphors were disproportionately expressed by bereaved parents: 79.3% of the metaphors were expressed by this group, despite their making up, on average, only 65.2% of the sample. This corroborates claims that parental bereavement is the most severe loss, but may not be well conceptualized (Fish and Whitty, 1983; Rando, 1986). These metaphors add to our understanding of parental bereavement, elaborating how it has a more profound impact on self than other losses, which, with the possible exception of siblings, did not show this imbalance.[11] This suggests that more intimate familial ties result in both greater loss and deeper meanings emerging for self—and others.

Ultimately, each metaphor has at least two fundamental aspects. First, metaphors can constitute existential meanings, disclosed in emotion, shedding light on various fundamental dimensions of the self. Metaphors may signify the loss of a subject's relationship with the deceased, along with integral aspects of his/her prior identities, and express the structure of a self struggling to make sense of itself in a world where people get murdered.

Second, metaphors serve a pragmatic purpose in social interaction, acting as announcements in the process of role-making and role-taking (Hewitt,

2000; Stone, 1981), plus emotional place markers and place claims (Clark, 1990). They assist individuals in rhetorically controlling the definition of the situation, particularly when claims to victim status are involved.

Inasmuch as the first approach is valid, the metaphors relate to yet empirically expand the literature on victimization and self. Where previously there were either passing, vague theoretical references to the impact of a homicide on victims' "entire self" (Casarez-Levison, 1992, p. 49) or references to "important assumptions" such as trust and a sense of autonomy (Bard & Sangrey, 1986; Hagemann, 1992; Janoff-Bulman, 1985), these metaphors specifically elaborate the dimensions in which background assumptions may be violated, and give clear expression to the emotional experiences of those whose selves have been impacted.

Similarly, these metaphors empirically elaborate the positions on bereavement and loss of self taken by Charmaz (1980), Klass (1988), and Attig (1996). In considering their rational, developmental focus on what was lost, these metaphors move beyond earlier abstractions to systematically delineate dimensions that were previously implicit or discussed in a fragmentary fashion.

Finally, each metaphor may be seen as expressing how, instead of being shattered, the existential self incorporates experiences into its evolving reality through emotional struggle. These metaphors, found in subjects' attempts to "express the inexpressible," may be the emotional lenses through which the "victimized self," as an "organizing perspective," presently interprets or reinterprets all other aspects of its reality (Johnson & Ferraro, 1984).

CONCLUSION

In this chapter I have highlighted several key issues about the initial impact of victimization that bear further investigation. On one hand, this assessment reveals that the impact of victimization is still poorly understood. Contrary to commonsense assumptions (indeed, those of some therapists, activists, and academics), individuals suffering from criminal victimization often do not claim victim identity. Rather, much depends upon their definition of the situation in specific social contexts. I feel that these preliminary findings call out for comparative research in relation to a greater diversity of offences, victim backgrounds, and offence contexts to see whether these findings hold, and to what extent they may be qualified empirically. Indeed, these findings highlight the difficult question of what, in fact, constitutes a "real" victim found in the work of Viano (1989) and Holstein and Miller (1990). They also call for researchers to find innovative ways to move beyond unhelpful terms such as "objective" and "subjective" measures—and the corresponding pitfalls of prevailing "expert" knowledge and "victim" impression management—by highlighting the construction of reality, and its pragmatic implications, occurring in the social context.

In this chapter I have also highlighted the lived experiences of individuals who experienced—and took on—the identity of victim. The survivors of homicide victims elaborated various losses of self: existential meanings, disclosed in emotion, shed light on various fundamental dimensions of the self that may be impacted by crime. These can signify a loss of subjects' relationships with the deceased, with various integral aspects of their prior identities, and express the structure of a self struggling to make sense of itself in a world where people get murdered. Elaborating on prior literature on victimization and self, bereavement and self, and gender, future research should emphasize the evolution both of those aspects of the self that remain following the impact of crime and how they evolve in interaction. While I attempt to do this in the case of homicide in the next chapter, I strongly urge future researchers to study these issues—and how they may be elaborated upon, varied, or discounted—in other victimization contexts (e.g., violent vs. property crimes), in other bereavement contexts (e.g., terminal illness, car accidents, suicide), and in the experiences of individuals in the throes of other life crises (e.g., divorce, bankruptcy, terminal illness).

Finally, in this respect, metaphors of loss often serve a pragmatic purpose in social interactions, acting as announcements in the process of role-making and role-taking (Hewitt, 2000) and as emotional place markers and place claims (Clark, 1990), assisting individuals to rhetorically control the definition of the situation when micro-political claims to victim status are in question. Again drawing attention to both the question of what constitutes a "real" victim and the pragmatic construction of victimization in interaction, I call upon researchers to compare how metaphors are used in other kinds of victimization (e.g., domestic violence, fraud) and in other types of micro-political interaction (e.g., spousal relationships, office politics). Researchers should also move beyond the micro-political realm described here and examine how these metaphors are used in the political process of constructing social problems more generally. This may be significant, considering that a sizable number of interview respondents had affiliations with victims' rights organizations with a political agenda.

In the next chapter, I continue with the construction of victimization—this time with attention to the social reactions experienced, and actions taken, in various contexts.

ENDNOTES

1. This breaks down further to nine of 24 victim service interview clients, five of 12 people from the impaired driving group, and five of 10 women from women's shelters.

2. Shelter workers were particularly insistent that victimization does not necessarily result in victim claims.

3. This breaks down further to include 15 of 24 victim service interview clients, seven of 12 people from the impaired driving group, and five of 10 women from women's shelters.

4. Clark's theoretical model distinguishes individuals who receive sympathy from those who are blamed via the concept of the "sympathy margin" (i.e., the amount of leeway one has to be ascribed sympathy). Anyone ascribed this margin has the right to sentiment, empathy, and a display of sympathy. Margins are not static, but are continually negotiated through adherence to norms (1987, pp. 303–313).

5. Clark (1987) identified five strategies: (1) expressing negative other-emotions; (2) expressing positive other-emotions indicating own inferiority or equality; (3) controlling the balance of emotional energy; (4) eliciting obligation; and (5) expressing positive other-emotions indicating own superiority.

6. In this part, gender is not seen as a binary opposition between totally masculine males and utterly feminine females. Rather, "adherence" to traditional gender roles was determined by the presence or absence of behaviours identified in the literature as indicative of conformity to either typical male or female gender roles. "Flexibility" to traditional gender roles was determined by the absence of such patterns, along with the presence of behaviours that are traditionally indicative of the opposite gender.

7. The sample broke down as 53.5% female to 46.5% male.

8. Overall, 65.2% of respondents were parents of the deceased. Most (77.5%) were between the ages of 35 and 65 years, while most of the deceased (65.2%) were between 15 and 30 years. Thus, there was possibly greater adherence to "traditional" gender roles than would be found among other demographics.

9. Lost innocence was expressed equally by gender.

10. This was explained by respondents in terms of men's disproportionate employment obligations and better wages, women's emotional expressiveness and ability to interact regarding such matters, and simple self-interest in the face of predominantly male aggressors.

11. While making up, on average, 11.3% of the sample, bereaved siblings expressed 13.4% of the metaphors.

REFERENCES

Adler, P. A., Adler, P. , and Fontana, A. (1994). Everyday life sociology. In N. J. Herman & L. T. Reynolds (Eds.), *Symbolic Interaction: An Introduction to Social Psychology* (pp. 407–423). New York: General Hall.

Attig, T. (1996). *How We Grieve: Relearning the World.* New York: Oxford University Press.

Bard, M., & Sangrey, D. (1986). *The Crime Victim's Book* (2nd ed.). New York: Brunner/Mazel.

Blanchard, G. (1987). Male victims of child sexual abuse: A portent of things to come. *Journal of Independent Social Work 1*(1), 19–27.

Blumer, H. (1969). *Symbolic Interactionism.* Englewood Cliffs, NJ: Prentice-Hall.

Broussard, S. D., & Wagner, W. G. (1988). Child sexual abuse: Who is to blame? *Child Abuse and Neglect 12*, 563–569.

Casarez-Levison, R. (1992). An empirical investigation of the coping strategies used by victims of crime: Victimization redefined. In E. C. Viano (Ed.), *Critical Issues in Victimology: International Perspectives* (pp. 46–57). New York: Springer.

Charmaz, K. (1980). *The Social Reality of Death: Death in Contemporary America.* Reading, MA: Addison-Wesley.

Clark, C. (1987). Sympathy biography and sympathy margin. *American Journal of Sociology 93*(2), 290–321.

Clark, C. (1990). Emotions and micropolitics in everyday life: Some patterns and paradoxes of "place." In T. D. Kemper (Ed.), *Research Agendas in the Sociology of Emotions* (pp. 305–333). Albany, NY: State University of New York Press.

Clyman, R. I., Green, C., Rowe, J., Mikkelsen, C., & Ataide, L. (1980). Issues concerning parents after the death of their newborn. *Critical Care Medicine 8*(4), 215–218.

Cook, J. A. (1988). Dad's double-binds: Rethinking father's bereavement from a men's studies perspective. *Journal of Contemporary Ethnography 17*(3), 285–308.

Dauvergne, M. (2008). Crime statistics in Canada, 2007. *Statistics Canada—Catalogue no. 85-002-X, 28*(7).

Denzin, N. K. (1985). Emotion as lived experience. *Symbolic Interaction 8*(2), 223–240.

Fish, W. C., & Whitty, S. M. (1983). Challenging conventional wisdom about parental bereavement. *Forum Newsletter: Forum for Death Education and Counseling 6*(8), 4.

Fontana, A. (1984). Existential sociology and the self. In J. A. Kotarba & A. Fontana (Eds.), *The Existential Self and Society* (pp. 3–17). Chicago: University of Chicago.

Forrest, G. C. (1983). Mourning the loss of a newborn baby bereavement. *Care* 2, 4–5.

Gannon, M., & Mihorean, K. (2005). Criminal victimization in Canada, 2004. *Statistics Canada—Catalogue no. 85–002-XPE, 25*(7).

Garfinkel, H. (1967). *Studies in Ethnomethodology.* Englewood Cliffs, NJ: Prentice-Hall.

Gilligan, J. (2003). Shame, guilt, and violence. *Social Research 70*(4), 1149–1180.

Goffman, E. (1959). *The Presentation of Self in Everyday Life.* Garden City, NJ: Doubleday.

Gomme, I. (2007). *The Shadow Line: Deviance and Crime in Canada.* Toronto: Nelson.

Hagemann, O. (1992). Victims of violent crime and their coping processes. In E. C. Viano (Ed.), *Critical Issues in Victimology: International Perspectives* (pp. 58–67). New York: Springer.

Herman, N. J., & Reynolds, L. T. (1994). *Symbolic Interaction: An Introduction to Social Psychology.* New York: General Hall.

Hewitt, J. P. (2000). *Self and Society: A Symbolic Interactionist Social Psychology.* Boston: Allyn and Bacon.

Hochschild, A. R. (1983). *The Managed Heart.* Berkeley, CA: University of California Press.

Holstein, J. A., & Miller, G. (1990). Rethinking victimization: An interactional approach to victimology. *Symbolic Interaction 13*(1), 103–122.

Hussey, D. L., Strom, G., & Singer, M. (1992). Male Victims of Sexual Abuse: An Analysis of Adolescent Psychiatric Inpatients. *Child and Adolescent Social Work Journal, 9*(6), 491–503.

Janoff-Bulman, R. (1985). Criminal vs. non-criminal victimization: Victims' reactions. *Victimology 10*, 498–511.

Janoff-Bulman, R., & Hanson-Frieze, I. (1987). The role of gender in reactions to criminal victimization. In R. C. Barnett, L. Biener, & G. K. Baruch (Eds.), *Gender and Stress* (pp. 159–184). New York: The Free Press.

Johnson, J. M., & Ferraro, K. J. (1984). The victimized self: The case of battered women. In J. A. Kotarba & A. Fontana (Eds.), *The Existential Self and Society* (pp. 119–130). Chicago: University of Chicago Press.

Kennedy, L. W., & Sacco, V. F. (1998). *Crime Victims in Context.* Los Angeles: Roxbury.

Kenney, J. S. (2002). Metaphors of loss: Murder, bereavement, gender, and presentation of the "victimized" self. *International Review of Victimology 9*, 219–251.

Klass, D. (1988). *Parental Grief: Solace and Resolution.* New York: Springer.

Lindemann, E. (1944). "Symptomatology and Management of Acute Grief," *American Journal of Psychiatry 101*, 141–148.

Lister, L. (1991). Men and grief: A review of research. *Smith-College Studies in Social Work 61*(3), 220–235.

Littlewood, J. (1992). *Aspects of Grief: Bereavement in Adult Life*. London: Tavistock/Routledge.

Littlewood, J., Cramer, D., Hoesktra, J., & Humphrey, G. B. (1991). Gender differences in parental coping following their child's death. *British Journal of Guidance and Counselling 19*(2), 139–148.

Littlewood, J., Hoekstra, J., & Humphrey, G. B. (1990). *Child Death and Parental Bereavement*. Groningen, The Netherlands: University Hospital.

Loseke, D. (1993). Constructing conditions, people, morality, and emotion: Expanding the agenda of constructionism. In J. Holstein & G. Miller (Eds.), *Constructionist Controversies: Issues in Social Problems Theory* (pp. 207–216). New York: Aldine.

Mandell, F., McAnulty, E., & Reece, R. (1980). Observations of parental response to sudden unanticipated infant death. *Pediatrics 65*, 221–225.

Mead, G. H. (1932). *The Philosophy of the Present*. Chicago: Open Court.

Mead, G. H. (1934). *Mind, Self, and Society*. Chicago: University of Chicago.

Meltzer, B. N. (1994). Mead's social psychology. In N. J. Herman & L. T. Reynolds (Eds.), *Symbolic Interaction: An Introduction to Social Psychology* (pp. 38–54). New York: General Hall.

Miller, T., Cohen, M., & Weirsma, B. (1996). *Victim Costs and Consequences: A New Look*. Washington, DC: US Department of Justice.

Nathanson, D. (1994). *Shame and Pride: Affect, Sex, and the Birth of the Self*. New York: W. W. Norton.

Plummer, K. (1995). *Telling Sexual Stories: Power, Change, and Social Worlds*. London: Routledge.

Prus, R. (1996). *Symbolic Interaction and Ethnographic Research*. Albany, NY: State University of New York.

Rando, T. A. (1986). Parental bereavement: An exception to the general conceptualizations of mourning. In T. A. Rando (Ed.), *Parental Loss of a Child* (pp. 45–58). Champaign, IL: Research Press.

Raphael, B. (1984). *The Anatomy of Bereavement: A Handbook for the Caring Professions*. London: Hutchinson.

Riedel, K. (1990). *The Victim's Guide to the Canadian Criminal Justice System*. Toronto: Centennial College Press.

Roane, T. H. (1992). Male victims of sexual abuse: A case review within a child protective team. *Child Welfare 71*(3), 231–239.

Rock, P. (1998). *After Homicide: Practical and Political Responses to Bereavement*. Oxford: Clarendon.

Rosenhan, D. (1975). On being sane in insane places. In T. J. Scheff (Ed.), *Labeling Madness* (pp. 54–74). Engelwood Cliffs, NJ: Prentice-Hall.

Schatz, B. D. (1986). Grief of mothers. In T. A. Rando (Ed.), *Parental Loss of a Child* (pp. 303–314). Champaign, IL: Research Press.

Schatz, W. H. (1986). Grief of fathers. In T. A. Rando (Ed.), *Parental Loss of a Child* (pp. 303–314). Champaign, IL: Research Press.

Scheff, T., & Retzinger, S. (2000). Shame as the master emotion of everyday life. *Journal of Mundane Behaviour 1*(3), 303–324.

Sobieski, R. (1994). *Men and Mourning: A Father's Journey through Grief.* Toronto: MADD Canada.

Staudacher, C. (1991). *Men and Grief.* Oakland, CA: New Harbinger.

Stone, G. P. (1981). Appearance and the self: A slightly revised version. In G. P. Stone & H. A. Farberman (Eds.), *Social Psychology through Symbolic Interaction* (2nd ed.). New York: Wiley.

Thoits, P. A. (1990). Emotional deviance: Research agendas. In T. D. Kemper (Ed.), *Research Agendas in the Sociology of Emotions* (pp. 180–203). New York: State University of New York Press.

Viano, E. C. (1989). Victimology today: Major issues in research and public policy. In E. C. Viano (Ed.), *Crime and Its Victims: International Research and Public Policy Issues* (pp. 3–14). New York: Hemisphere.

Wallace, H. (2007). *Victimology: Legal, Psychological, and Social Perspectives.* Boston: Allyn and Bacon.

Weed, F. (1995). *Certainty of Justice: Reform in the Crime Victim Movement.* New York: Aldine de Gruyter.

Widom, C. (1989). The cycle of violence. *Science 244*(4901), 160–166.

Wilson, A. L., Fenton, L. J., Stevens, D. C., & Soule, D. J. (1982). The death of a newborn twin: An analysis of parental bereavement. *Pediatrics 70*, 587–591.

Young, M. (1991). Survivors of crime. In D. Sank & D. Caplan (Eds.), *To Be a Victim: Encounters with Crime and Injustice* (pp. 27–42). New York: Plenum.

CHAPTER 3

Social Dynamics in the Wake of Crime

INTRODUCTION

Victimization does not necessarily end with the initial impacts of crime. A multi-faceted and complex phenomenon, it may play itself out in subjects' social interactions for some time, emerging in ways that they—and many in society—might not anticipate. It is to this social evolution of the victimization experience that this chapter speaks.

Focusing on social dynamics largely outside of formal institutional contexts, I begin by examining the social reactions experienced by those left behind by homicide ("survivors"),[1] —revealing a parallel labelling process for victims. Next, I articulate differing social dynamics underlying male and female grief, along with related "vicious cycles" that serve to block coping. Finally, I consider how human agency is both related to—and constrained by—social interactions in various contexts.

SOCIAL REACTIONS AND VICTIM LABELLING

Crime creates problems for people. Early research, particularly from the labelling perspective, largely focused on offenders (Becker, 1963; Lemert, 1951). However, victims often experience labelling as well (Taylor, Wood, & Lichtman, 1983). By delineating social reactions and consequences, I broaden the labelling perspective consistent with its interactionist roots.

In my studies, varying social responses were found to interactionally shape survivors' experiences, strongly suggesting differential labelling dynamics in relation to: (1) extended family and friends; (2) acquaintances, strangers, and the community; and (3) survivors' responses.

Extended Family and Friends

A minority (less than 20%) of survivors experienced widespread, ongoing support from extended family and friends.

41

BOX 3.1:
THE SOCIOLOGICAL DYNAMICS OF SYMPATHY

Victims may be either considered "sympathy worthy" or "blamed" for their plight (Clark, 1987, p. 298). Clark distinguished these categories through the concept of the "sympathy margin" (i.e., the leeway a person has for which he/she can be granted sympathy and not blamed). While factors such as age, social class, sex, and type of problem are key for strangers (Clark, 1987, pp. 291, 298, 300–301), those in close relationships are obligated to create wider margins. However, anyone who has been ascribed a sympathy margin has the right to sentiment, empathy, and a display of sympathy. Margins are continually negotiated and may be "increased, decreased, replenished, or used up entirely" (p. 302).

In tough times people may cash-in "credits" built up throughout their "sympathy biography," but should not drain the account completely or they will have to look for sympathy elsewhere. Significant here is adherence to "sympathy etiquette," which includes not making false claims, not claiming too much, claiming some sympathy in appropriate circumstances, and reciprocating to others (Clark, 1987, pp. 303–303). Otherwise a person becomes a "deviant sympathizer," who either "underinvests" by not recognizing others' right to sympathy, or "overinvests" by giving sympathy to those whose plights are seen as socially unworthy (pp. 313–316).

Source: Clark, C. (1987). Sympathy biography and sympathy margin. *American Journal of Sociology* 93(2), 290–321.

> "I've always had people really look after me. I've never been left to do this alone—and that made a huge difference. My family and friends were there morning, noon, and night for at least two years, which made me feel good—to know that they were there for me" (survey #19: female, age 45).

Such individuals reported a number of "helpful" responses, such as visiting and staying, providing ongoing emotional support, and handling responsibilities, and the ability to pick up subtle cues regarding when and how to offer support.

These survivors were considered "sympathy worthy" (Clark, 1987). As family and friends were relatively close, they may have built up or felt it necessary to extend a wider "sympathy margin" (Box 3.1) than others, at least initially.

As a minority response, this may also involve survivors adhering to norms of "sympathy etiquette" (Clark, 1987) by "appropriately" reaching out. Both are interrelated with "victim" status. In some instances, extended helpful responses suggest that the murder of a loved one *prima facie* constitutes, for such sympathizers, a "legitimate" sympathy claim, and the victim label lengthens its acceptable expression.

This may also involve accommodation to deviance (Rubington & Weinberg, 1987). As homicide grief is often extreme and persistent (Klass, 1988; Knapp, 1986; Rynearson & McCreery, 1993), family and friends who respond helpfully attempt to make adjustments to accommodate survivors' powerful emotions without explicitly labelling deviance. If anything, it is the situation that is unusual, not the survivors' reactions, which are considered normal for victims. Hence, victim labels may both play a role in accommodation to deviance and serve as the entry point to a parallel labelling process surrounding the word "victim." Accommodation in one sense is thus interchanged by labelling in another.

However, stigmatization of victims and the labelling of emotional deviance generally proceeded when accommodation quickly broke down, or never began. These were the most common patterns. Survivors who reported ongoing lack of support from extended family and friends felt that this worsened their experience. Indeed, some felt "ostracized" (interview #14: male, age 54). Others stated the following:

> "I was alone—all the time. Nobody came around. My family hasn't been supportive. None of them have come, and *that hurt* ... It's been two years, and I think you are the third person that's been in this house" (interview #10: female, age 60).

> "This was a time for me to find who my real friends were, and it *hurt a lot* to see your friends are not always the ones you had considered" (survey #3: female, age 58).

"Unhelpful" responses included no initial support, rapidly disappearing support (e.g., after the funeral), "inappropriate" attention, widespread avoidance by others, communication problems such as "stock" responses and attempting to identify with feelings, and, in some cases, overt conflict. These reflect negative feelings, uncertainty, and misconceptions about responding to suffering (Wortman & Lehman, 1983).

Interestingly, some considered such responses the result of being labelled as victims, others the result of being labelled as deviants. Survivors' rationales were instructive in separating these.

Some claimed that extended family and friends were afraid to do or say anything that might upset them further, and thus avoided contact. This involved ascriptions of sympathy worthiness and labelling as victims, but uncertainty as to the appropriate response:

> "I know my family just damn well didn't know how to cope and how to deal with me [sounds angry]. They were scared. In fact we talked about it ... They really didn't know how, and were afraid to even phone me [sounds tearful]" (interview #15: female, age 49).

> "My friends shy away ... I had a few people I've bumped into, and I've said: 'You haven't been around.' 'Well, it's not that we didn't want to. We just don't know what to say, and didn't want to say the wrong thing and hurt your feelings'" (interview 21: female, age 45).

Avoidance was exacerbated where family and friends were so upset themselves that seeing the "victims" evoked unpleasant feelings all around:

> "I think the reason why some of them were standoffish was because they couldn't handle it themselves. I figure that because they knew [the deceased] personally, they just couldn't handle it. It was too close to reality for them, so they kind of backed off. I was a little bit taken aback by that and I was very hurt. It's been difficult because you really do need them at a time like that" (interview #1: female, age 47).

Such responses were particularly notable among those who had previously been close to the respondents.

Some survivors, who were initially labelled as victims, noted that sympathetic responses eventually gave way to others urging them to "get on with your life." This signifies a breakdown in ascriptions of sympathy worthiness and emerging stigmatization as "helpless victims" via a key sympathy norm: do not claim too much for too long.

> "We had some very close friends who came out to visit us, but after a while their recommendation was, 'You've got to put this in the past, like, bury this right now.' [Sarcastically] The closest friends we had! He'd say to me '[name], you've got to put this behind, get back to work, and you've got to get on with your life.' You know, 'You've got to maintain your business, you've got to ...' and I'm not thinking any of this!" (interview #14: male, age 54).

Indeed, this was the entry point for an underlying tone of shame (Gilligan, 2003; Nathanson, 1994; Scheff & Retzinger, 2000).

Thoits (1990) said, "just as behaviour sometimes deviates from norms, so [do] many feelings and emotional displays" (p. 181). Thus, some survivors came to feel that they were stigmatized as emotional deviants due to "inappropriate" behaviour in public:

> "They started changing the subject a lot, so we would just pick up on it that 'Ok, we won't talk about this any more.' We caught the vibes, right? Bad vibes. Some pulled back from us, and this continues right up to the present" (interview #8: female, age 45).

> "I think if I'm showing signs of emotion, I mean showing tears or emotional stress to others, they don't feel very comfortable, because they don't know how to handle it. It drives people away" (interview #5: male, age 50).

Finally, some individuals were simply stigmatized as deviants: "The rest of my relatives were worthless and acted like a stigma attached to us, like something about us caused us to have a murder victim" (survey #7: female, age 38).

Such individuals felt blamed, or that they were seen as contributing to their plight. In some cases this referred to ostensibly "questionable" circumstances (e.g., the murder of drug dealers or women who remained with abusive partners). However, in cases where such circumstances were not readily apparent, stigmatization may reflect the belief that "people get what they deserve" (Lerner, 1980). Essentially, survivors were perceived to break another sympathy norm: not making "false claims" to sympathy.

The result of such interactions, regardless of the rationale, was that survivors became socially isolated when they needed support. Moreover, while this often upset them further, many chose to withdraw themselves because "people in general don't understand" (interview #29: female, age 37).

Summing up, survivors who indicated broad support from extended family and friends, along with few insensitive comments and avoidance behaviours, reportedly fared better—congruent with the social support literature (Klass, 1988). This relates to accommodation, but also to the sensitive, overt construction of sympathy worthiness associated with the victim label.

However, most survivors experienced unhelpful interactions. These survivors generally reported faring worse than those with perceived long-term support. Indeed, they experienced additional losses. These provided more reasons to be upset, while accumulated indignities were interrelated with

BOX 3.2:
SOME POSSIBLE TRAJECTORIES OF LABELLING

Lemert (1951, p. 120) distinguishes primary from secondary deviance. While various reasons may lie behind an actor's original (primary) deviation, "when a person begins to employ his deviant behaviour, or a role based upon it, as a means of defence, attack, or adjustment to the overt and covert problems created by the consequent societal reaction to him, his deviation is secondary." Secondary emotional deviance combines this with Thoits' (1990) concept of emotional deviance (i.e., continuing to display "inappropriate" emotions, or a role based on them, as a defence, attack, or adjustment to problems created by social reaction). Finally, Taylor et al. (1983) distinguished primary victimization (i.e., the initial victimizing circumstances) and secondary victimization: based on negative social reactions. "Some victimizing attributes are exaggerated in non-victims' minds to encompass capacities not affected by the victim's situation ... Once a person has been labelled, others may over-interpret all that person's behaviour as resulting from the labelled attribute, and the victim may begin to think of self the same way" (pp. 232-234).

Sources: Lemert, E. (1951). *Social Pathology*. New York: McGraw-Hill.
Taylor, S., Wood, J., & Lichtman, R. (1983). It could be worse: Selective evaluation as a response to victimization. *Journal of Social Issues 39*(2), 19–40.
Thoits, P. (1990). Emotional deviance: Research agendas. In T. D. Kemper (Ed.), *Research Agendas in the Sociology of Emotions* (pp. 180–203). New York: State University of New York.

various labels (Wortman & Lehman, 1983). In some cases behaviours were associated with uncertainty, unexpressed or inappropriately manifested sympathy, and the label of victim; in others with stigmatization as "helpless" victims or deviants; and in still others with stigmatization as "emotional deviants" (Thoits, 1990). Regardless of the label, such survivors were avoided, stigmatized, and encountered difficulties in communication and/or conflict. Moreover, their resulting social and emotional isolation, commonly employed as a defence or reaction, could be evidence of "secondary victimization" (Taylor et al., 1983), "secondary deviance" (Lemert, 1951), or "secondary emotional deviance" (Lemert, 1951; Thoits, 1990), depending on the emphasis (Box 3.2).

Acquaintances, Strangers, and the Community
Surprisingly, respondents often noted receiving remarkable support from mere acquaintances. This included many of the practices discussed earlier, but especially emotional support:

"It was really strange because you found out who you could lean on. You know, and sometimes it's the people you least expect" (interview #16: female, age 56).

"We found some friends that we considered to be close friends never showed up again. Yet, there were other people that came out that we had sort of considered acquaintances, and we became very close" (interview #24: male, age 47).

It is possible that acquaintances who labelled survivors as victims considered them as legitimately sympathy worthy as did sympathetic friends and family, but the expression of sympathy was not as often blocked by familiarity and personal grief.

Interestingly, survivors also occasionally noted a groundswell of support from strangers in the community. Strangers sometimes volunteered to search for missing persons (whom, it was later discovered, had been murdered). They sent cards, flowers, or food, raised money, erected memorials, organized petitions, and urged survivors to take action. Two factors were associated with this: First, either the deceased or their survivors were well known, had much prior community involvement, or both:

"[The deceased] had a lot of friends. She was a very popular girl, and I was very active in the community ... So, I mean, there were a lot of people that it stunned too. Then, as the trial went on, they were reading the newspaper and were getting upset with what was being said, and most of the people got together and wanted to do something" (interview #23: male, age 49).

Second, there was widespread media coverage sympathetic to the survivors:

"The local paper did a good story, and people started coming to the door then, and we had literally hundreds of total strangers just arriving at our door in tears, very upset. It was obviously that their prayers were with us. Food started arriving in trays, flowers, baskets of fruit, it was just incredible. From 10 am to 10 pm there was just a steady stream of traffic, and probably 30 to 40 people at all times" (interview #31: female, age 46).

Indeed, it appeared that several respondents were cast into the role of victim advocates:

> BOX 3.3:
> ## MORE POSSIBLE TRAJECTORIES OF LABELLING
>
> "Tertiary victimization" is a compound term inspired by the work of Taylor et al. (1983) and Kitsuse (1980). As negative labelling of victims may affect their identities, positive labelling may foster identities emphasizing the moral, socially efficacious side of the victim role by encouraging "confrontation, assessment, and rejection of the negative identity imbedded in secondary deviation, and the transformation of that identity into a positive and viable self conception" (Kitsuse, 1980, p. 9). The concept of "tertiary emotional deviance" adds Thoits' (1990) ideas, referring to the manipulative use of emotions—often defined as awkward, disturbing, and so on—to press home counter-definitions of behaviour for personal or political ends (e.g., victims who have become advocates for victim rights).
>
> **Sources:** Kitsuse, J. (1980). Coming out all over: Deviants and the politics of social problems. *Social Problems 28*(1), 1–12.
> Taylor, S., Wood, J., & Lichtman, R. (1983). It could be worse: Selective evaluation as a response to victimization. *Journal of Social Issues 39*(2), 19–40.
> Thoits, P. (1990). Emotional deviance: Research agendas. In T. D. Kemper (Ed.), *Research Agendas in the Sociology of Emotions* (pp. 180–203). New York: State University of New York.

"I went on the radio [to thank the community search teams]. A policeman phoned in and said 'I searched for [the deceased], now what are you going to do?' And that's how I started. I wrote a petition, and this whole thing kept going and kept going. So that is how [this victims' rights group] happened. People just kept coming to us and saying 'what are you going to do?' There was never a day when the phone didn't ring 30 times" (interview #17: female, age 50).

Such widespread community support was sometimes the genesis of enduring victims' rights organizations, where survivors, cast into the role of advocate, used the victim role as a sword to fight for change. Such labelling contained the potential social basis for "tertiary victimization" (Kitsuse, 1980; Taylor et al., 1983) or "tertiary emotional deviance" (Kitsuse, 1980; Thoits, 1990), where the victim role is converted into something positive, meaningful, and socially efficacious (Box 3.3).

However, where the deceased and/or survivors were not well known, sympathy was lessened. In addition, where interactions with the media did not go well or if there was little interest in the story or an unfavourable portrayal, the affect on sympathy, community support, and survivors was magnified: "Why isn't our daughter being talked about?" (field notes: female, age 50). Another woman said: "The publicity made it worse. The fact that the murder had to do with drug dealing made it much worse, as there was no sympathetic community support. It was almost like AIDS" (criminal injuries compensation board [CICB] #91: testimony of female, age 46).

Aside from a generalized lack of sympathy, such circumstances frequently increased the potential for stigmatization. Three types of negative interaction followed. First, there was harassment:

> "Like, we got obscene phone calls to the house. The minute we became public, I got calls that 'If you and your family had belonged to the right religion, these horrible things wouldn't happen. God is punishing you.' We'd get calls like that. One day this guy phoned and asked if I was the mother of one of these children that had been murdered. I said I was, and he says 'Well, would you stay on the line while I masturbate?' And like this is for real! This is going on like every hour around here!" (interview #15: female, age 49).

Secondly, there was blaming, particularly in a context of ongoing speculation, innuendo, and gossip. One mother commented:

> "One young girl came to the funeral home. I think when you have that type of thing, some come just to be nosy. She had just come with these other girls, and said 'Well, the little slut got what she deserved.' People had to hold us back!" (interview #21: female, age 45).

Finally, notoriety resulted in uncomfortable interactions in public:

> "You know, you're a bit of a freak for a while. People point you out. When they hear the name, they say, 'Oh, are you *the* [respondent's name]?' ... I kind of lose it there" (interview #16: female, age 56; emphasis in original).

> "We went on a cruise. When we'd come down to dinner, everyone's laughing having a good time. Whatever table we'd pick, whew! Dead silence" (interview #26: male, age 61).

Survivors who reported such responses claimed they were faring worse. Indeed, it could be argued such encounters lead to "secondary victimization" (Taylor et al., 1983).

Summing up, these findings are intriguing, particularly insofar as, contrary to Clark (1987), acquaintances, strangers, and community members often responded more sympathetically than extended family and friends. Of further interest is the potential for popular protest, fed by the media, to inculcate positive new role identities (e.g., "victims' advocate") indicative of tertiary victimization (Kitsuse, 1980; Taylor et al., 1983). More negative interactions re-victimized survivors, adding to the secondary labelling process discussed above.

Survivors' Responses

Following a homicide, survivors faced one major decision: whether to attempt to deal with the homicide primarily on their own or seek out help from other individuals, groups, and institutions. Responses generally involved an interplay between a gendered orientation toward seeking help and a variety of interactional incentives and disincentives.

The first strategy was common among men, who often avoided seeking help from medical professionals, self-help, and/or "victims'" groups. Women reported greater levels of seeking out medical and psychiatric care, involvement in victims' and self-help groups, and support from social services when unable to work. Indeed, one survivor, who is also a victim therapist, noted that her clientele was approximately "one quarter men, the rest women." (interview #6: female, age 46).

Survivors also faced a variety of incentives and disincentives related to the labelling process. Frequently, there was a link between support and help-seeking behaviour: those with support were less inclined to seek out help than those without.

> "We didn't require counselling. We've got good family around" (interview #24: male, 47).

> "I did go to a psychiatrist on a regular basis, because [sighs] after a while your friends don't want to hear about it any more. They just don't want to talk about it, or they're uncomfortable talking to you about it" (interview #16: female, age 56).

> "If it wasn't for the group, I would be so isolated, and I wouldn't have ... soul companions. Because our families won't let us talk about it" (interview #19: female, age 53).

This illustrates how sympathetic labelling as victims can accommodate survivors, while isolating stigmatization as victims, deviants, or emotional deviants can increase the chance of contact with subcultures (such as support groups) or more formal agents, potentially applying medical labels.

In some cases, others tactfully and altruistically encouraged survivors to seek help:

> "I have a friend who lost his son—I guess it was some sort of cancer. Well, because of his loss, he had sought help with [a self-help group]. So, knowing what had happened to us, he says 'I'd like to talk to you for a minute.' We talked a bit, and he went on to tell me about the group. He told me about himself, and how his grief had been helped. He highly recommended it, saying that he wouldn't have survived without them. It was interesting, so I approached my wife" (interview #4: male, age 56).

Others, however, appeared to resent such "interference" and avoided seeking help. These were most often men, suggesting that gender also plays a role.

Finally, there was the element of choice. Consider the following woman, who joined a support group after unsupportive interactions during the funeral and avoidance thereafter:

> "I had people there who I could talk to, and that was good for me. In fact, right or wrongly, I made the *decision* that would be the only place I'd ever talk about this. I would not talk to my friends or family unless I had to. But fortunately, you know, *a survivor will find a way—and that's exactly what I did.* I felt 'Hey, who needs them?'" (interview #18: female, age 55; emphasis added).

Theorists note that labelling can have both adaptive and maladaptive consequences (Plummer, 1979). Here, informal labelling was important in either directing survivors to therapy and self-help or "forcing" them into further social withdrawal. A breakdown in perceptions of sympathy worthiness, and the corresponding aspect of the victim label, undermines accommodation. This results in either a shift to the stigmatized, "helpless" side of the victim label or the labelling of individuals as "deviant," in this case "emotionally deviant." Indeed, when not initially perceived as sympathy worthy, victims can be blamed as deviants. All of these outcomes may significantly impact self-identity (Rubington & Weinberg, 1987). In such cases, the concepts of secondary victimization (Taylor et al., 1983) and "secondary emotional deviance" (Lemert, 1951; Thoits, 1990)—in which survivors begin employing victimization, "deviant" behaviour, or roles based on them to defend or adjust to problems created by social reaction—are suggested.[2]

Importantly, both within and outside their respective subcultures (Rubington, 1982), survivors sometimes embraced and at other times distanced themselves from these roles, or aspects thereof (Goffman, 1961). It appeared that a form of impression management (Goffman, 1959) was sometimes used, which I term "volitional gerrymandering" (e.g., the same advocate stridently using the victim role as a sword to fight for change, and later stressing emotional trauma as a shield to fend off criticism).

Ultimately, survivors' help-seeking orientations were rooted in gender, social incentives, and social disincentives. The perceived level of support, coupled with gender, the relative maintenance or breakdown of accommodation by others, and individual coping choices contributed to the odds of survivors moving beyond the "unofficial" sphere to more "formal" helping agents. The labelling process appeared to be at work (Lemert, 1951; Plummer, 1979), reflected in both secondary and tertiary victimization (Kitsuse, 1980; Taylor et al., 1983) and corresponding aspects for deviance (Kitsuse, 1980; Lemert, 1951; Thoits, 1990). Either way, survivors employed these roles to defend or adjust to interactional problems. While all can impact an individual's self-concept, particularly when a "deviant identity" is being inculcated (Rubington & Weinberg, 1987), one must also consider potential impression management through "volitional gerrymandering."

I now turn to more intensively consider the gender dynamics in survivors' experiences.

GENDER ROLES AND GRIEF CYCLES IN HOMICIDE CASES
In this section, I consider: (1) gendered coping attempts; (2) grief cycles; and (3) the impact on health.

Gendered Coping Attempts
The data revealed that survivors' experiences were shaped by gendered coping strategies. Broadly, those who engaged in strategies enabling them to balance the focus between their own and others' pain and activities enabling them to compartmentalize their thoughts and deal with them a bit at a time felt that they were somehow "coping" with their experience. Those who continually emphasized their pain, or engaged in simple avoidance strategies, claimed more difficulty.[3]

Survivors who expressed difficulty frequently focused on their pain. This was expressed in, for example, suicidal ideation, drinking, and drug abuse:

"Life seems so worthless that the best thing may seem to us to end it all. It is a dangerous state that can pour over us in waves, and may persist for years. The suicide may indeed take place—or we may kill the pain we feel instead with drugs and drink, which doesn't help in the end" (survey #5: male, age 63).

Often this was accompanied by a tendency to engage in social withdrawal:

"We hid. We thought we were just the poorest parents that lived because we allowed a daughter to get involved with a man that was a psychopath. My wife wouldn't talk to anybody. I wouldn't talk—it took me six to eight months before I could even talk to my own family. If we thought we saw someone we knew, we'd immediately backtrack and go the other way for fear they'd want to say something to us. We went inward. We went home. We shut our doors, and as much as said 'Let's wait our turn to die'" (interview #26: male, age 61).

There were four gender differences in those who reported difficulties with coping. First, such men were more likely to increase their alcohol intake than women[4] (Lister, 1991; Sobieski, 1994). Second, men showed greater irritability and aggressiveness (Schatz, 1984, 1986), which manifested in their taking their frustration out on others. Third, such women more often became dependent on prescription medication than men (Cleary, 1987).[5] Finally, women more often engaged in social withdrawal than men (Janoff-Bulman & Hanson-Frieze, 1987). This largely related to the traditional provider role of men, which limited their ability to engage in such withdrawal.

Conversely, survivors who reportedly "coped" engaged in strategies with distinct characteristics. First, they exhibited a less exclusive emphasis on self, instead helping others or achieving goals:

"I coped with the grief because my husband and some of the siblings were having a most difficult time. You heal by helping others heal or understand" (survey #13: female, age 60).

"I've become more focused in what I'm trying to do, and I think I owe it to my daughter and to the memory of other victims to do the best I can to bring about changes to the justice system" (field notes: male, age unknown).

Second, such survivors perceived that they had choices in dealing with their grief:

> "I don't think grief is a stage, I think it is a process, and I think it's very personal. I think how you react, and in how you grieve, I think that you can make choices and decisions that can help you personally" (interview #29: female, age 37).

Third, such survivors balanced between focusing on themselves and their grief and attention to outside activity:

> "Like, I'm in the car all day long ... When you're in the car, you're by yourself. Sometimes I'm driving down the road crying my eyes out. But when you're going into a customer, you had to straighten up like that [snaps fingers]. I was able to pretty well control things during the day, 'cause I knew I had to go to the customers. That gave me a lot of relief" (interview #30: male, age 64).

> "*I could deal with it in reasonable chunks.* I find—and I still find—going back and forth to work in the car is when I would bawl my eyes out. I like opera, and I took every tragic aria that I could. I cranked it up loud and cried my eyes out. But I got it out" (interview #2: female, age 51; emphasis added).

Essentially, these survivors worked through their grief a bit at a time as they felt necessary. Indeed, recognizing their varying moods, they learned what actions worked best at the time:

> "You are up, you are down, and, they gradually lengthen so your highs are longer and your lows are a little shorter. And now, you might get like three months, maybe four months where things are fairly decent. But then, you'll crash for maybe like three days, and you'll just sit there and just cry, cry, cry, cry, cry. And there's nothing you can do about it. You have to work through it and just accept that's the way it's going to be. If you try and fight it, and the longer you try and push this off, when that low point hits, it's worse. So it's better to just go with the flow" (interview #25: female, age 45).

Finally, there was often a practical element to such strategies: "Mrs. _____ was feeling very frightened living alone and had ordered a guard dog for protection" (CICB #88: psychiatrist's letter re: female, age 68).

Thus, regardless of gender, survivors who engaged in this second group of strategies characterized them as *balancing* between active involvement in grief and pulling back; focusing on themselves versus focusing on individuals, activities, and goals. They did not exhibit heavy alcohol and medication use, displacement of anger, or suicidal ideation as frequently as survivors who did not engage in these strategies.[6] Indeed, such strategic alternation enabled them to avoid the twin pitfalls of a (1) continual emphasis on grief, and (2) emotional repression.

Grief Cycles

Some survivors experienced gendered "grief cycles." Inextricably related to traditional gender roles, these reflected responses to grief facilitating the repetition of painful patterns. Those whose circumstances, reactions, and coping strategies led them into these "traps" invariably claimed difficulty coping.

MALE GRIEF CYCLES

Men who experienced this pattern spoke of being dominated by guilt, apparently rooted in a feeling of "failure" in their traditional "protector" role:

> "The pain, guilt and 'what ifs' will always be with me forever. I'm always wondering what I could have done" (CICB #41: survivors' response to board questionnaire: male, age 41).

> "The true impact that this savagery has had on me could never be adequately described. My role as family protector has been violated. No matter how old a son or daughter is, Dad is there to protect" (interview #10: male, age 57).

However, they felt it necessary to repress their upset (Wilson et al., 1982), remain strong, and refrain from overt displays of sadness (Littlewood, 1992; Sobieski, 1994):

> "I think fathers feel that they're the father. They have got to be *strong* for not only his wife, but for all the other kids. So, you'd better not be letting down too dang much, 'cause they're going to be going now. *You've got to be up there all the time*" (interview #30: male, age 64; emphasis added).

Repression often involved men throwing themselves into work or other activities (Lister, 1991; Littlewood et al., 1991). However, this could only take them so far:

> *"Night is hard because you're not busy.* You have time to think. You lay down in your bed, you've had an exhausting day, 10–12 hours, and you lay down and you relax—and then you realize you got nothing to do. You're just laying there and *then the thoughts start coming"* (field notes: male, approximately age 45; emphasis added).

Essentially, these men appeared to become dominated by the situational dissonance between the male gender prescriptions to "protect" and to "be strong." The inability to protect the deceased led to disproportionate guilt and upset, yet expressing this upset, and possibly upsetting others, represented a further failure on the gender prescription to be strong.

In response to these "failures," men reported overwhelming anger: one strong emotion traditionally allowed for men. One commented on its dynamic nature: "You can stay in that stage fluctuating between hate and grief, hate and grief forever. You're all the time in a *vicious circle"* (interview #12: male, age 61; emphasis added).

Indeed, this man, the former leader of a victims' rights group, added that he has seen men stuck in this "vicious circle" for 30 years.

Finally, guilt, repression, and anger led many men to recurring depression. One, who could not continue repressing his thoughts, became so angry that he could not function. This "failure" then repeatedly sent him into depression:

> "I went into deep periods of depression and would then have to miss work because I was so deeply depressed about the death of my son. This led to an inadequate income while I was not able to work, and I had to buy groceries and other necessities on credit, until I suddenly found I could not pay off my creditors" (CICB #11: survivor's letter to board: male, age 35).

This leads to factors that feed back into men's guilt and restart the cycle, all linked to traditional gender roles (Box 3.4).

Essentially, men adhering to strict gender roles got caught in the nexus between guilt over not being able to protect the deceased, repressed grief over their loss, anger over what had happened, and depression over finding it hard to remain strong, protect, and provide for their families—which simply fed back into guilt to begin the process again. This

BOX 3.4:
FACTORS FEEDING BACK INTO MEN'S GUILT

"My remaining children are denied the protection I would like to give them. I can do very little to ease their pain or the pain of my wife. The mental trauma and stress often leaves me at a loss for words. I sit and watch my family suffer, and there is nothing I can do about it! I couldn't protect [the deceased], and I can't protect my family now. Because, the thing that's hurt my family, I can't control [respondent becoming angry]" (interview #11: male, age 57).

"When I couldn't keep it in anymore, I put stress on my family. They came under the stress of their loss and what I was going through as well. Everybody was walking around with kid gloves. Any kind of problem magnified itself through what kind of crap you can cause. I mean, boy, you can really dish it out when you want to. I was very, very angry for numerous things, and the anger that came out in me was really unbelievable—and *then I'd I feel awful about that too*" (interview #32: male, age 47; emphasis added).

Source: Kenney, J. S. (2003). Gender roles and grief cycles: Observations on models of grief and coping in homicide cases. *International Review of Victimology, 10*(1), 19–47.

guilt–repression–anger–depression dynamic typically became cyclical in these men, and formed a block to coping:

"You have so many emotions that are hard to control. You are like a rollercoaster. One minute, you are ... sad, and in tears, and the next minute you are angry. I'm afraid of myself, in the sense of what I might do. I find myself getting angry a lot of times, because I can't handle ... because of the whole failure. Not just losing her, but my failure ... I'm sorry. That can be a real hard thing. I don't think I'll ever get over it" (interview #23: male, age 49).

The ultimate response to this frustrating emotional deadlock was either to turn anger *outward* at the offender and/or others, or *inward* and to consider suicide:

"Anger is too mild a word. It can be described better as raging fury. It can be directed against rational objects—the criminal, the police, the justice system—though the intensity is likely to be out of proportion to the fault. It can stretch further, against neighbours, family members, the press, the church, God himself" (survey #5: male, age 63).

"You do beat yourself up. When you're feeling a lot of anger and depression, you'll want to hurt yourself. Suicide's not a problem. You're not worried about that. Like, you can get to the point where you want to hurt yourself so much" (interview #32: male, age 47).

Ultimately, men expressing difficulty coping tended to adhere to traditional gender roles and experience a guilt–repression–anger–depression dynamic, often remaining stuck for extended periods. This grief cycle is implied in the literature written by survivors, suggesting that traditional roles require men to use much of their energy to control emotions evoked by grief (Schatz, 1986)—indeed, that men see controlling emotions as a test of masculinity (Sobieski, 1994). It is implied, but never elaborated, in "double binds" between cultural and professional demands for expression and traditional gendered demands for repression, as outlined by Cook (1988). Yet this goes further, identifying the dynamic, central mechanism through which men's grief becomes blocked after homicide.

This cycle also differs from gender-neutral, psychological models, whether based in "stages" (Casarez-Levison, 1992), "tasks" (Klass, 1988; Worden, 2001), or "disorders" (Walker, 1992) in that: (1) it is specifically linked to survivors' gender roles; (2) is empirically grounded in this form of bereavement; (3) it reflects the culmination of social interactions, rather than decontextualized observations of individual behaviour; and (4) unlike the relative passivity of stage models and psychological disorders (Attig, 1991, 1996), it illustrates the impact of various activities in inhibiting coping.

FEMALE GRIEF CYCLES

Female gender roles traditionally allow far more flexibility in emotional expression: "I think it's more acceptable for a mother to just break down whenever" (interview #25: female, age 45).

This potentially results in a different blockage: continually focusing on what they have lost.

"I spend my days wanting him back desperately. I want to hug him, to say goodbye, to tell him how much I loved him. Will this ache inside never go away? My constant tears never seem to dry up. I have his picture on the wall with the rest of the

BOX 3.5:
FEMALE EMPHASIS ON LOSS AS FEEDBACK

"Actually, you die a little slower each day. It gets worse with time. The first year is bad, but you go back to the year before and think about everything that you did with your child. Say ... July, you did this and this. August, OK, we went camping, etc. ... The second year, you've got the year before. OK, you had the funeral, you had all the court time, and all the frustrations you deal with there. You've got nothing to look back to last year, apart from pain and anger. The third year ... I found even worse 'cause you've got nothing to relate to, sort of like 'Did I really have a child?'" (interview #25: female, age 45).

"I never slept. I didn't eat, just cried, cried, cried, and was angry. I kept trying to think 'Well, how can we get it right? We should be able to do something ... We should be able to do something.' And you get thinking ... 'You just cannot be unaccountable' and *end up very similar to the reaction when the policeman came and told us of the murder. It just starts all up again*" (interview #10: female, age 60; emphasis added).

Source: Kenney, J. S. (2003). Gender roles and grief cycles: Observations on models of grief and coping in homicide cases. *International Review of Victimology, 10*(1), 19–47.

family pictures. Sometimes late at night I stand in front of them and talk to him. He doesn't answer me but somehow I never give up hope. Maybe one morning I will wake up and find it has all been a horrible nightmare. It is a nightmare and it is neverending" (CICB #13: survivor's letter to board: female, age 48).

Indeed, some related this to the traditional nurturing role: "I feel betrayed by my own *devotion* to carrying out the plan of parent" (interview #10: female, age 60).

In addition, these women repeatedly reviewed emotionally upsetting events of the murder. This practice not only prolonged their upset but intensified it, with a feedback loop developing due to a concentration on events in previous years (Box 3.5).

Indeed, these women began to feel hopeless that things would ever be any different:

> "I have feelings of powerlessness over any negative attitudes I feel, desperate longing to have life back as it was, and a need to seek unscathed pastures of peace. I feel agonized that my golden years will not be as I expected, that my heart and soul will ache with longing until my dying day. I don't want to live with this agony to a great age. The screams from my heart are silent screams taking many forms of behaviour, many outbursts of denial to myself, even to punishing myself for giving in to self-pity, and no interest in life around me. How can my very being mend?" (interview #10: female, age 60).

Finally, these women emphasized the victim role:

> "Just let us sit and just vegetate, because, boy, as victims, that's exactly what you want to do. You don't want to do anything. You just curl up and die, really … [becoming emotional]" (interview #8: female, age 45).

Indeed, such women were typically beset with fear—a corollary of the victim role. Some women spoke of becoming "paranoid," how "the whole world turns nasty, and, you don't trust anybody" (interview #2: female, age 51). Others feared for their children's safety (CICB #1: female, age 32). In addition, there was fear of the offender:

> "Every woman in this family is terrified of meeting [the offender]. There's a lot of tears. Since we went to his parole hearing and got to listen to him, *we don't doubt for one second when he comes out he's going to hurt somebody else.* The guys don't feel the fear the same because, unless he's coming with a gun or something, they've got a chance. We have the same [chance the deceased] had [starts to cry]." (interview #8: female, age 45).

All such emphases served to block coping. Not only did such women remain depressed and preoccupied with the deceased (Clyman et al., 1980) and the crime, these feelings intensified through continued concentration on the events of prior years until the women expressed powerlessness over this feedback dynamic, their "victim" status and fearfulness.

ADHERENCE TO GENDER ROLES
Here, I must consider the relative flexibility or rigidity of gender roles, because this made a difference to an individual's ability to avoid the grief cycles noted

above. "Adherence" to traditional gender roles was determined by the presence of behavioural patterns that have been identified in the gender and bereavement literature as indicative of conformity to either typical male or typical female gender roles (e.g., men repressing upset and remaining strong; women expressing upset openly). Conversely, "flexibility" was determined by the absence of such patterns, coupled with behaviours noted as traditionally indicative of the opposite gender (e.g., men expressing upset openly and publicly; women "taking charge" and remaining strong for others).

Notably, men who adhered to more flexible gender roles did not become dominated by the dissonance between the male gender prescription to "be strong" and "to protect," largely because they were able to express their upset more openly:

> "I cried, we all cried. I cried to make them [the respondent's parents] cry, or not to make them cry, but, I cried *with them* so that they would feel better, get it over with. It was a good way to deal with it" (interview #3: male, age 24; emphasis in original).

> "The differences we've heard, e.g., 'big boys don't cry' were true a generation ago, but less now ... Dad cried a lot at first ... Healing for him came in the form of sharing and listening at [a victims' organization] and a men's support group" (survey #14: male, age 35).

Such men short-circuited the male grief cycle by removing the element of continual repression that is necessary for it to continue. Moreover, they learned consistent ways to understand their guilt, and developed strategies to control the hatred and anger flowing from it (Box 3.6). No longer eaten up by their alleged "failures," they were able to begin working through their grief.

Women who reportedly fared better also did not adhere to rigid gender roles. By not allowing themselves to become dominated by helplessness, they refused to be treated as helpless. As one survivor, the crusading head of a victims' rights organization, bluntly stated: "I hate the word 'victim'" (interview #17: female, age 50). Instead, by engaging in a proactive orientation toward their experience, they got in touch with energy in their anger and used it. Thus, some directed their energy into changing the justice system:

> "I have a direct approach. I write [the deputy prime minister]. I write [the provincial attorney general]. I write the solicitor general—whoever I could write. I mean, why am I going to just sit there? I couldn't take that" (interview #23: female, age 46).

BOX 3.6:
CRITICAL UNDERSTANDINGS AND COPING STRATEGIES

"There is only one person guilty here: the guy that did it" (interview #24: male, age 47).

"You've got to channel something. You've got to do something out there and try to help other people, your mate, your children, your grandparents, somebody. Otherwise, you're in a vicious circle going from vengeance to grief to vengeance, and never getting out of the guilt stage. You can control the hate and vengeance, but you can't control the grief, the sorrow, the disbelief, and the 'what ifs.' That will always be there, as they're natural feelings. Hate and vengeance are not natural to us. That's why they are the ones that you can get rid of more easily. You can control the hate and the vengeance, and the best way is to fix in your mind 'I'm not going to allow myself to be victimized by a person from prison. He's not going to keep me as his victim" (interview #12: male, age 61).

Source: Kenney, J. S. (2003). Gender roles and grief cycles: Observations on models of grief and coping in homicide cases. *International Review of Victimology, 10*(1), 19–47.

Finally, the concept of *balance* must be reiterated. While survivors who avoided grief cycles tended not to adhere to traditional gender roles, others went to the opposite extreme. Some women repressed their grief and tried to get on with lives until their anger exploded, or threw themselves into activity to the point of exhaustion. Some men openly emphasized their grief until they collapsed into depression. It was those who flexibly blended gender roles in a balanced way who were most likely to claim they were "coping."

Impact on Health

Both grief cycles often culminated in health problems. Indeed, there were apparent relationships between each and the illnesses experienced. Men were generally observed to experience heart problems and sudden deaths, related by health professionals to their repression of grief (Box 3.7).

Women more typically reported mental health problems:

"I was in a psychiatric ward for three weeks. Is that normal? I wasn't in a psych ward for my Mom or my Dad or my sister. I could handle it. I didn't dream. I didn't wake up and see my parents standing in the front room. But I do wake up seeing my daughter standing there. I hear her walking upstairs. I see

> ## BOX 3.7:
> ## MALE HEALTH PROBLEMS
>
> "Well, the grandfathers in six or eight cases died almost immediately ... fathers that are in their late 50s to early 60s, usually their health will start to fail. All of a sudden they will get a heart problem. I don't know that many women that ever had a heart attack, but I know men I've met. This is what I notice all the time" (interview #18: female, age 55).
>
> "[The survivor] became withdrawn and depressed, slept poorly and never talked about the loss. Presumably, the only way that [he] could cope emotionally with his son's murder was to suppress thinking about it to such an extent that he did not wish to talk about it. There was a gap of about five months between the loss and the onset of his illness. [The survivor] suffers from coronary artery and heart muscle disease, asthma and the side effects of the treating drugs. He has been extremely sick and many people would have been permanently disabled. He has an unusually determined personality and has been able to rehabilitate himself and return to work. His prognosis is poor, and the probability of dying during the next few years is high" (CICB #29: doctor's report re: male, age 53).
>
> **Source:** Kenney, J. S. (2003). Gender roles and grief cycles: Observations on models of grief and coping in homicide cases. *International Review of Victimology, 10*(1), 19–47.

her walking across from one room to the other. So, if I'm nuts, I guess I'm nuts" (interview #21: female, age 45).

This partially reflects the greater involvement of women with mental health professionals (Butler, Giordano, & Neren, 1985; Cleary, 1987), as well as the predominance of heart disease among men. Given these caveats, these patterns are in line with the literature. Furthermore, women experiencing grief cycles suffered physical health problems, particularly when they were already in a sensitive physical condition:

"I would think that the close proximity between the husband's death, his funeral, and the miscarriage, does suggest a causal relationship" (CICB #57: doctor's letter re: female, age 20).

"Her poor emotional state has affected her prior physical condition and worsened it. She suffers from diabetes mellitus,

> ## BOX 3.8:
> ## FEMALE HEALTH PROBLEMS
>
> "After five years, she is still obsessed by the death of her son—he is still the centre of her conversations and of her attention. On family occasions she has an empty chair and a place setting for him. This is far from being the normal grieving process. She has been unable to overcome the shock. She still wavers on the borderline of a psychotic state. She sees her son on the bingo cards—she thought that the accused was watching her house..." (CICB #8: psychiatric nurse's letter to lawyer re: female, age 52).
>
> "The applicant has brought on herself severe emotional problems leading to chronic angina and anxieties, brought on by the tensions of the various trials, learning of the brutality of her son's death, and her understanding of the questionable circumstances that evening" (CICB #12: extract from board order re: female, age 56).
>
> **Source:** Kenney, J. S. (2003). Gender roles and grief cycles: Observations on models of grief and coping in homicide cases. *International Review of Victimology, 10*(1), 19–47.

hypothyroidism, and peptic ulcer. Since her daughter's death she has had frequent admissions to [hospital]. Her ulcer has bled" (CICB #64: psychiatrist's report re: female, age 50).

Women's health problems were related to activities that emphasized the horror of events (Box 3.8).

Ultimately, both men and women who adhered to traditional gendered coping styles experienced health problems, but did so in differing ways, suggesting that further epidemiological research is required.

Issues of coping have been key in this section. However, these are intimately entwined with the next issue I will address: victims' agency.

HUMAN AGENCY REVISITED: THE PARADOX OF VICTIMS

Victims often complain of feeling powerless. In some respects this represents a psychological after-effect of the crime—something was done to them that they were unable to prevent or stop. However, emphasizing psychological after-effects overshadows the effect of subsequent social and institutional interactions on coping ability. Moreover, despite the relatively powerless position of victims in both legal institutions (Kenney, 1995) and the therapeutic literature (Attig, 1991, 1996), my data reveal that, depending on their social situation, many survivors were capable of some control over their grief.

Thus, in this section I reframe the issue in terms of the interplay between survivors' social and institutional interactions and their coping ability. Their experiences in various social contexts have much to teach us about institutional influences, therapeutic ideologies, and human agency.

The social context of survivors' agency will be outlined with regard to three principal matters: (1) encounters that increased or decreased their upset; (2) information they encountered about coping; and (3) coping strategies that emerged. These are illustrated with representative examples of dealings with: immediate family; extended family and friends; acquaintances, strangers, and the community; self-help groups; other victims; therapeutic professionals; and legal institutions.

Encounters That Increased or Decreased Upset

Social encounters offered survivors various reasons to be more or less upset. Those encounters that subjects reported as being unhelpful often further victimized them, leading to additional reasons for being upset and ongoing damage that impeded reconstitution of the self as a functioning agent. Some experienced conflicting emotional reactions from their immediate family:

> "People assume that because you've come through something very traumatic and tragic, that you're all going to come together. But, because everyone grieves in his or her own way, and goes about it differently, it loses its cohesiveness in a very short time. That takes its toll" (interview #18: female, age 55).

Some were upset by the avoidance of others:

> "It was an eye opener. Like, walking through a grocery store, walking down the aisle, I'd see somebody that I knew, and, before, they would talk to me. When they saw me coming, they turned their cart around and went the other way" (interview #32: male, age 47).

Such individuals lost more of a sense of themselves, often taking on stigmatized, isolated identities. Interpersonal difficulties with self-help and "victims'" groups had similar results:

> "Unfortunately, a lot of victims' worst victimizers are other victims. That's what causes so many victims to fall out of the victim movement. They come in, and they're victimized by other victims, and strike out" (interview #12, male, age 61).

> ### BOX 3.9:
> ### PROBLEMATIC INSTITUTIONAL ENCOUNTERS
>
> "You have to feel to heal. To do that, you need to move towards your grief, not move away from it. If you try to hide from it, bury it, or push it away, the longer your reconciliation will take. If you move towards your grief, then you will heal faster. If the medical profession turns it into an illness that you can prescribe drugs for, that is really moving away from your grief" (interview #2: female, age 51).
>
> "I had a real hard time because, on the one hand, I had RCMP, Crown, etc., telling me to keep trying to remember details, and, on the other hand, I had Criminal Injuries, doctors, friends, family, and counsellors trying to help me forget and get on with some semblance of a normal life. How can you do this and stay sane?" (survey #6: female, age 37).
>
> **Source:** Kenney, J. S. (2004). Human agency revisited: The paradoxical experiences of victims of crime. *International Review of Victimology, 11*(2/3), 225-257.

Finally, upset was evident surrounding problematic encounters with therapeutic and legal institutions where survivors' voices were neglected (Box 3.9).

Such survivors often came to see themselves as more victimized and more helpless than ever.

Conversely, those perceiving "helpful" interactions, such as a large amount of familial and community support, had fewer additional reasons to feel victimized, hence fewer ongoing impediments to functioning. Some spoke of a relatively active synchronization of reactions in their immediate family such that those who most needed support at the time were able to receive it: "We kind of leaned on each other, 'cause when one was up the other one was down and vice versa" (interview #1: female, age 47). This could be complemented when extended family and friends offered ongoing support:

> "There was an overwhelming response from our family and friends, which is wonderful, absolutely wonderful. I mean, the friends that we had stayed with us, and supported us, and continued to support us afterwards. Every one of them is still there today, as strong as they were then. The support, you know, the support that you were looking for was always before anything. It was natural. It was there from their heart" (interview #4: male, age 56).

Indeed, some noted how previous acquaintances became very supportive; others that their community rallied around them, providing letters, cards, meals, volunteers, and campaigning for justice on their behalf.

Such encounters could be further buttressed by supportive self-help and victims' groups:

> "It wasn't until I found solace in the group that the healing pro-
> cess began. I found a place to unload my anger, fears, and frus-
> trations. Healing starts with the opportunity to share intense
> emotions with others who've experienced the same. I can come
> here, and we can dump on each other without criticism" (CICB
> #87: female subject quoted in newspaper article, age 65).

Similarly, survivors could find supportive encounters with therapeutic professionals:

> "We went to marriage counselling, and, I tell you, it saved my
> marriage. The counsellor said 'Part of the problem is people
> have to learn to communicate.' 'Cause we weren't talking. We
> weren't doing nothing. He says 'You've got to learn to com-
> municate.' The, the other part was doing little things for each
> other. Those little things sure made a big difference" (inter-
> view #21: female, age 45).

Finally, such survivors had minimal or no involvement with the justice system:

> "We both discussed that we didn't want to get involved with
> the court case. I see in so many cases, and with the support
> groups, that if you do get involved in any of the court cases,
> you're emotionally involved, and you can't get on with your
> grief. So, when I think back, I think that was a wise thing to do"
> (interview #5: male, age 50).

Ultimately, subjects' encounters in various social and institutional contexts either provided reasons to be upset in addition to the murder, or somehow helped to offset or mitigate their sufferings on that account.

Information That Subjects Encountered about Coping

Interactional contexts also involved information on how to deal with subjects' experiences. While some found such information more useful than

others, awareness of coping strategies undoubtedly impacted both coping choices and ability to function. Thus, some learned by observing immediate family members:

> "I think that one reason why our family has dealt with it this, well, what I consider successfully after I've seen some other families, is because there is openness in our family. There is support ... but there is also a respect for everyone else's space. Basically, if one of us is having a bad day and the other one is reasonably OK, we kind of take turns and take the slack for each other. I guess we read each other well, so it really helps" (interview #24: male, age 47).

Such subjects both learned coping strategies and avoided the evolution of further upsetting family dynamics (e.g., blame, taking others' anger personally, and taking one's upset out on others). Survivors also noted suggestions that made them aware of coping choices, such as tactful recommendations to explore support groups (interview #4: male, age 56). Indeed, at times, widespread community responses encouraged respondents to form groups where they worked their grief out through activism (interview #17: female, age 50).

Conversely, subjects who encountered conflicting family reactions, adherence to rigid gender roles, poor communication, and lack of synchronization typically found themselves hemmed in. When these encounters were reinforced by social isolation and/or notoriety in other contexts, they could either focus on how these evolving problems further upset them personally or find ways to cope on their own. In many cases, they perceived this as an overwhelming burden, simply choosing to avoid others and deal with their grief themselves (e.g., avoiding social contact, withdrawing from prior involvements, installing security systems, taking trips, or moving). Others, however, perceived more room to manoeuvre within this framework and innovated more interactional strategies in various contexts (e.g., "floating trial balloons" to put others at ease, gauge potential reactions, or give others tacit permission to speak, changing the subject when uncomfortable, denying their identities in public, warning others about "inappropriate comments," or expressing anger). In such cases, "taking the role of the other" provided a framework within which they could creatively innovate various interactional coping strategies.

Finally, information often contained an ideological element, most notably in encounters with some self-help, "victims'" groups and therapeutic professionals. Sometimes this encouraged the reconstitution of the self in

BOX 3.10:
MEDICALIZATION AND ITS DISCONTENTS

Conrad and Schneider (1980) discussed implications of the increasing characterization of social problems in medical terms. While noting a general humanitarian aspect, where blame is reduced, there are downsides to this. These include: (1) implicitly removing responsibility from individuals in favour of their "disorder," creating a "dual-class citizenship" and "dependence on the fully responsible nonsick"; (2) medical language veiling ongoing negative judgments under "the guise of scientific fact"; (3) expert control removing informed discussion from the public realm; (4) medical social control, where things can be done that could not otherwise be considered; (5) the individualization of social problems; (6) depoliticization, where we are prevented from seeing behaviour as a possible repudiation of existing arrangements; and (7) the exclusion of evil, where it is alleged that actions are caused by sick bodies or minds and we are thus prevented from confronting the inhumanity in each other.

Source: Conrad, P., & Schneider, J. (1980). *Deviance and Medicalization: From Badness to Sickness*. Columbus, OH: Merrill.

a passive mould, with a corresponding effect on coping ability. Thus, some found themselves recast as victims and encouraged to continually rehash their upset. They often reported "cross-contamination": subtle—and sometimes less than subtle—suggestions regarding how they should feel and in light of others' experiences, and having half-digested psychological ideas about grief presented as gospel when they felt vulnerable to suggestion:

> "You go to a group and you start listening [to] how other people feel and you think 'That's the way I'm supposed to feel.' You take on—especially when you're hurting—you look for something that makes sense. That can do more harm than good" (interview #6: female, age 46).

Indeed, some groups distributed brochures outlining the passive "stage models" of grief, which inhibit active coping (Attig, 1991), suggesting that problems in the medicalization of deviance may be fostered by support groups (Box 3.10).

Similarly, in many cases where survivors reportedly coped poorly, therapeutic professionals initially viewed them as limited, weak, and incapable of coping, identifying the problem within the individual (e.g., biological changes in brain functioning). When therapy did not go well, they focused on individual-level factors as an explanation, such as "insufficient response" to treatment (CICB #13: female, age 48). Conversely, improvements were typically credited by professionals to drug treatment, "psychotherapeutic intervention," or both (CICB #96: male, age 60). Given this individualistic orientation, subjects were often officially labelled as suffering from a psychological disorder (CICB #55: female, age 36). Such professionals typically recommended long-term treatment:

> "My psychiatrist told me that I would have to go and see him for a good length of time. I asked how long, and he said that he did not know—but said he wanted to see me every three weeks instead of six" (CICB #2: female, age 45).

Moreover, many such professionals felt that survivors would "never fully recover" (CICB #13: female, age 48). Such an orientation affected perceptions of subjects' problems, and this definition of the situation shaped constructions of appropriate coping strategies (e.g., long-term treatment).

However, there were countervailing ideological elements in various contexts, such that individuals were afforded the opportunity to learn active coping strategies. Thus, some victims' groups had an active ideology that helped to restore a sense of direction and control.

> "If enough people get together maybe something, someday will be done. But, if we don't fight, we might not get anything. Working as part of a group to change the justice system makes you feel like you are doing something about it. At least you aren't sitting around doing nothing" (CICB #1: female, age 32).

Moreover, by getting involved, such subjects reported that they could share skills, dividing up tasks in a functional, efficient way and enabling them to accomplish more. They reported making important contacts, obtaining information and support in their dealings. Some victims' groups helped survivors to learn and assert their rights, guided them through the justice system, let them know what to expect, suggested strategic actions, helped obtain information about their case, and lobbied on their behalf (e.g., against the offender's parole). Some were thus advised of the CICB, provided letters in support of compensation applications, and given emotional support at hearings. In addition, victims' groups helped survivors to deal with the media and find appropriate counselling, and gave advice on forming their own organizations. All of this is potentially useful information that facilitates coping choices.

Similarly, there were therapeutic professionals who had a broader orientation than those described above. Despite their patients initially exhibiting severe upset, rather than strongly emphasizing individual factors they frequently located the problem in survivors' situation[7]: "In essence we have a case of a well-adjusted, family-oriented woman whose home life has been tragically upheaved by the shock of the tragic events that have befallen her" (CICB #56: female, age 57).

Such professionals did not emphasize long-term medical treatment. Focusing on making subjects aware of their options, they frequently offered brief, practical assistance and suggestions to help subjects deal with environmental problems (e.g., decision-making or dealing with family conflict). Perceiving situational problems as just as significant as individual ones, they often made suggestions or wrote supportive letters to employers, landlords, creditors, politicians, Members of Parliament, and even the parole board. They interceded with the CICB beyond required medical reports. They often gave a good long-term prognosis despite survivors' severe initial upset. Their broader orientation, reflective of a "task-oriented" approach, coupled with an implicit belief in survivors' abilities, differentially impacted professionals' interactions with subjects, and subjects' orientations toward active coping.

Ultimately, subjects encountered a variety of information regarding how to cope, whether observationally, by being given specific advice, innovating in specific interactional frameworks, or through the presence of ideological elements in various institutional contexts.

Coping Strategies That Emerged

Finally, there were strategies that, depending on subjects' past orientations and subsequent encounters, they chose, learned, or innovated in various contexts. Sometimes these varied by gender, rooted in unquestioned adherence to traditional gender roles. Such choices raised tensions:

> "It's tough going out to work. For a long time I never said a word. I just tried to go in and do my job. I'd leave the house with a wife that is so frustrated, so down crying, that, when you left to go out to work, you thought 'Oh shit, is it even worth going?' But I'd go. Then, I'd go upstairs when I came home. Bang! It would start again. She'd start at me again. It's been tough" (interview #26: male, age 61).

In other cases there was no gender difference. Many chose to avoid traditional repression or emphasis on their grief by balancing times of activity and time for grieving; time for others and time for themselves:

"My husband and I are very close, and I would see that, of course, he was in a huge amount of pain, so I would try to be strong for him, which meant I have to hold off, OK? Give him a turn, and then he would hold off and give me a turn. With us, it just happened that we were able to support each other at a time when we needed each other" (interview #2: female, age 51).

Indeed, sometimes individuals integrated time for "grief work" into their daily routines. Both genders spoke of how they innovated by doing their crying in the car on the way to and from work, such that they could "get it out" as necessary, but also focus their thoughts elsewhere for part of the day. Learning about their emotions from their own (or others') experiences, such individuals did not push either their "grief work" or their other activities too hard. Instead, they learned to balance these in a flexible way that enabled them to work through their grief a bit at a time in more easily digestible "chunks."

There are numerous examples of gendered coping strategies that subjects chose, learned, or innovated in particular social contexts. Some, faced with avoidance, innovated by seeking out others in a similar situation for support (women) or discovered that briefly talking about their grief at work put co-workers at ease (men). Many women utilized self-help and victims' groups as an "outlet" for a time, but withdrew once it began re-intensifying their upset. Many women who were faced with counsellors who did not meet their needs either "hedged" by remaining emotionally unavailable, or simply left and found another counsellor. Finally, more women, compared to men, who experienced difficulties with the justice system found innovative ways to fight back, such as lobbying politicians, using the press, or hiring lawyers to pressure the prosecutor.

Subjects were insistent that coping is not going back to the way that they were before the murder, instead referring to an ability to live their lives "around it" and "go on" despite this permanent life change. They noted that this ability to function in their daily lives required a great deal of effort— effort that one has to want to exert to "deal with it in your own mind." This suggests both an element of choice and agency.

While some reflexively chose, learned, or innovated strategies to cope, others almost automatically chose to follow pre-established patterns, such as repressing or emphasizing their emotions. Hemmed in by their unquestioned adherence to these, they generally assumed that their social environments left them no choices.

Considering that various social contexts permeate the choices made, the tactics learned, and the strategies innovated, it is useful to view the social construction of agency in terms of a corridor with many doors (Figure 3.1).

FIGURE 3.1:
SOCIAL INTERACTIONS AS A CORRIDOR AFFECTING SUBJECTS' AGENCY

COPING / "LIVING WITH IT"

1. Interactions provide fewer additional reasons to be upset
2. Awareness/availability of information on coping strategies
3. Strategies chosen, learned, or innovated

Family	Friends	Acquaintances	Strangers Community	Self-Help Groups	Victims Survivors	Medical Profs.	Legal Institutions

DIFFICULTY COPING

1. Interactions provide many additional reasons to be upset
2. Less awareness of coping strategies available
3. Unquestioned, pre-patterned coping responses

Source: Kenney, J. S. (2004). Human agency revisited: The paradoxical experiences of victims of crime. *International Review of Victimology*, 11(2/3), 225–257.

Each door represents a different type of encounter, such as with family, friends, the community, self-help and "victims'" groups, therapeutic professionals, and legal institutions. Over time, individuals can choose to "knock" at particular doors while avoiding—or not noticing—others. Sometimes they find a welcoming response, other times not and choose to move on. Sometimes they are initially welcomed in, but later choose or are forced to leave. Other times, once inside, they have difficulty leaving (e.g., witnesses). Each person's unique accumulation of encounters serves as the interactional framework underpinning both his/her choices and his/her ultimate coping ability.

Within this framework, each encounter offers subjects several elements that impact on agency. First, encounters contain various reasons to be more or less upset. Encounters that were reported as unhelpful often further victimized the subject and led to additional reasons to be upset, ongoing damage, and impediments to reconstituting the self as a functioning agent. Conversely, subjects who reported helpful interactions in these contexts had fewer additional reasons to feel victimized and fewer ongoing impediments to functioning. Next, these contexts involved information on how to deal with their experiences. While finding this useful in varying degrees, awareness of such strategies undoubtedly had an impact on both coping choices and ability to function (e.g., ideological information and passive/active approaches). Finally, there were the actual strategies that subjects, depending on their past personalities and subsequent encounters, chose, learned, or innovated in these contexts, sometimes varying by gender and sometimes not.

The variety of coping strategies suggests that the relevant question is not whether active coping takes place, but rather, what are the social conditions most conducive to it? Indeed, a great irony emerges: to some extent, the degree and form of agency that subjects employed in attempting to cope in the wake of murder was itself partly a product of social interaction. It was not socially determined, but the coping choices individuals made, and were consciously aware of, were at least partially shaped by the people, situations, and ideas encountered in different settings. These constituted the framework in which coping choices were made. While subjects in similar situations frequently had coping choices, some made these choices while others did not. The relative extent of one's engaged agency thus appears to be socially influenced by a combination of the self one brings to the interaction, the content of the interaction itself, and how reflective, active individuals, by taking the role of the other, actively synthesize these into either innovative or largely pre-patterned responses.

Thus, it would be absurd to assert a radical free will theory of agency irrespective of social context. Yet, the variety and innovation shown challenge a strict social determinism. Mead's (1934) conception of the self helps to resolve this dilemma. It is composed of two elements: the internalized attitudes of society (the "me") and the impulse that individuals contribute to the formulation of unique responses in interaction (the "I"). The "I" allows for consideration of agency in action. In any encounter, the individual must interpret what is said by the other and formulate a response. These depend on the self assessing the "generalized other." Yet, particularly in formulating a response, the "I"—in interaction with the "me"—produces novel or creative responses.

Depending on an individual's past socialization, and how it is utilized in current interactions, it may be that some individuals will draw more heavily on past, socialized patterns of response that are more characteristic of the "me." Thus, some grieving survivors drew on traditional gender-based coping styles, while others adopted a more balanced approach. Either could reflect the predominant influence of internalized social attitudes. Similarly, some appeared to internalize and incorporate, without judgment, what they encountered in interactions, such as conceptions of grief from therapists. Others, however, reported the active synthesis of new ideas or coping strategies with past experiences and/or the creation of new and (for them) original ways of acting. Naturally, the frequency and type of subjects' interactions with family, friends, the community, legal institutions, and help agents play a part, as do the coping ideas they bring to these interactions.[8]

My data suggest that such an extension of the Meadian perspective is a useful way to balance evidence of social influences on the grief experience and data showing individual initiative and originality in coping. Indeed, they suggest that human agency, and the form it takes in coping choices, is socially constructed by interactions between: (1) reflexive, self-aware individuals faced with options; (2) various "tried and true" choices available in the "me" portion of their selves, dominated by the "generalized other"; and (3) interactional choices presented by specific stressor(s) and individuals in the unique context of the current encounter. These are synthesized by the individual into a new "I" response that is incorporated into the individual's sense of self, which may or may not be helpful. Some will be more reflective of past socialization and uncritical internalization of interactional content; others will evidence an original individual synthesis regarding how to cope under particular circumstances.

Finally, it must be noted that perhaps the best evidence of this contrast was in how subjects ultimately related to the victim role. Some, due to past inclination or subsequent encounters, simply refused to call themselves victims, rejecting the implicit connotations of weakness and helplessness. Others emphasized distinct aspects of this role. Some used the victim role as a shield to deflect criticism and justify their present inability to engage in some responsibility (e.g., when aware of another survivor's criticism of "neglecting" her remaining children during the trial, one woman quietly noted she was "under professional care," fending off further comment). Others used the victim role as a sword to achieve goals in various situations, such as fighting for change to criminal justice institutions.[9] Indeed, there was evidence that some subjects alternated between these two characterizations as the situation demanded (e.g., the above woman also happened to be a high-profile lobbyist for victims' rights). I term this micro-political, impression management strategy "volitional gerrymandering," where different facets of the victim role are situationally played up to the agent's advantage.

CONCLUSION

In this chapter I have built upon victims' "loss of self" noted in Chapter 1, revealing how the social self is reconstructed—and struggles to reconstruct itself—in various social contexts. These include, but are not limited to, a parallel victim labelling process, socially organized gender dynamics and grief cycles, and the construction of human agency to cope in varying social and institutional contexts. Corroborating and extending literature on labelling, social responses to life crises, gender, victimization, bereavement, and agency, this chapter has revealed that the social world inhabited by homicide survivors, along with unquestioned assumptions, can often be as problematic—if not more—than the crime. It has also revealed a variety of matters—both helpful and harmful—that may be of interest to support groups, victims' organizations, and counsellors. These findings call for comparative research in other victimization and bereavement contexts (e.g., are grief cycles found in all types of bereavement or just in those where death is sudden and violent? Is some element of intention also necessary, such as in suicide? Do grief cycles vary on the basis of victim relationship or by culture? What is their relationship to the diagnosis of "mental disorders"? What are the epidemiological patterns?)

This chapter has also demonstrated the potential for human agency. Given the horrific violence of homicide, with both legal institutions and many medical, psychiatric, and counselling approaches emphasizing passive approaches, the fact that some evidence of human agency can be found here means that it can probably be found anywhere. Indeed, the various strategies chosen, learned, or innovated, survivors' ability to emphasize different aspects of the victim role as needed, and some survivors' comments about helping agents such as therapists and support groups lend credence to doubts about some common approaches to counselling victims (Fattah, 2000). They echo Conrad and Schneider's (1980) discussion of the implications of the medical model, and emphasize the need for further comparative research in differing victimization contexts and beyond. Beyond these matters, further focused, observational studies of "volitional gerrymandering" by various types of victims in differing social contexts would be most illuminating.

In the next chapter, I turn to a key element in the construction of many victims' experience: interactions with legal institutions.

ENDNOTES

1. Overall, 74.8% of cases involved the murder of the respondents' children, followed by siblings (9.3%), parents (4.1%), friends (2.3%), nieces/nephews (2.1%), and spouses (2.1%). The victims were more distant relations in 5.3% of cases. While one cannot generalize to other violent crimes, some of the dynamics outlined in this chapter may occur more broadly.
2. While labelling has a significant effect on self-identity and subsequent behaviours, whether survivors are more likely to be victims of *future* crimes is beyond these data.
3. Survivors were asked whether they felt that they were "coping" or "not coping." The nature of the data does not allow for any completely "objective"

measurement of who ultimately fared better or worse—even medical professionals with standardized psychological tests often provided differing diagnoses for the same survivor. The common thread throughout the data was the comparative words of survivors about their lived experiences, particularly their expressed coping abilities by gender. These were linked to various interactions that they perceived as either helpful or unhelpful—including their self-interactions.

4. In total, 55.8% of men reported increased alcohol consumption compared to 20.4% of women.

5. In total, 35.2% of women and 2.3% of men were initially prescribed medication. Similarly, 49.1% of women and 8.1% of men used some type of drug (excluding alcohol) to cope over time.

6. Those who considered themselves to fit into the "coping" group made up 31% of the sample versus 69% who expressed difficulties. Heavy alcohol use was evident in 63% of those who expressed difficulty but in only 6% of the "coping" group, who largely followed their previous drinking patterns. Indeed, 23.3% of the "coping" group reported efforts to avoid alcohol. Heavy drug use—prescription or otherwise—was evident among 21.4% of those who expressed difficulty, but only 9.6% of those who were "coping." Displacement of anger was evident among 34.6% of those who expressed difficulty, but only 12.3% of those who were "coping." Finally, ongoing suicidal ideation was noted among 37.4% of those who expressed difficulty, but in none of those who were "coping"—although 15.5% admitted suicidal thoughts at some point.

7. The outcome of encounters with therapeutic professionals were the result of an interplay between: (1) the ongoing severity of survivors' upset; and (2) professionals' general orientations to survivors and their problems. While the former had a wide variety of influences, varying professional orientations were observed to be at the root of many reported aggravating and mitigating interactions influencing both survivors' assessments of the care they received, and their coping abilities. While it might be claimed that survivors reportedly faring worse might have done so anyway, the data do not allow for any completely "objective" measurement of this. Indeed, therapeutic professionals with standardized psychological tests provided differing diagnoses of the same subject. The only common thread running through the varying data sources were the words of subjects regarding types of interactions in particular contexts that they found helpful or harmful—which is the focus here anyway. Careful triangulation and negative case testing between the sources of data enabled the demand characteristics of the CICB to be offset by subjects outside this context, particularly considering that these files were generally used only when related patterns were observed elsewhere. As

such, once data became saturated with repetitive codes, "practical certainty" was achieved to the extent possible.

8. While subjects who are facing more stressors may make different choices to others—and, indeed, may have fewer options—this does not mean that they have no choices. Even subjects who withdraw totally and allow their emotions to take over still make this contextualized choice on an ongoing basis.

9. These themes clearly reflect Holstein and Miller's (1990) four practical consequences of being accepted as a victim.

REFERENCES

Attig, T. (1991). The importance of conceiving of grief as an active process. *Death Studies 15*, 385–393.

Attig, T. (1996). *How We Grieve: Relearning the World*. New York: Oxford University Press.

Becker, H. (1963). *Outsiders: Studies in the Sociology of Deviance*. New York: The Free Press.

Butler, T. M., Giordano, S., & Neren, S. (1985). Gender and sex-role attitudes as predictors of utilization of natural support systems during personal stress events. *Sex Roles 13*(9/10), 515–524.

Casarez-Levison, R. (1992). An empirical investigation of the coping strategies used by victims of crime: Victimization redefined. In E. C. Viano (Ed.), *Critical Issues in Victimology: International Perspectives* (pp. 46–57). New York: Springer.

Clark, C. (1987). Sympathy biography and sympathy margin. *American Journal of Sociology 93*(2), 290–321.

Cleary, P. D. (1987). Gender differences in stress-related disorders. In R. Barnett, L. Biener, & G. Baruch (Eds.), *Gender and Stress* (pp. 39–72). New York: The Free Press.

Clyman, R., Green, C., Rowe, J., Mikkelsen, C., & Ataide, L. (1980). Issues concerning parents after the death of their newborn. *Critical Care Medicine 8*(4), 215–218.

Conrad, P. , & Schneider, J. (1980). *Deviance and Medicalization: From Badness to Sickness*. Columbus, OH: Merrill.

Cook, J. A. (1988). Dad's double binds: Rethinking father's bereavement from a men's studies perspective. *Journal of Contemporary Ethnography, 17*(3), 285–308.

Fattah, E. A. (2000). Victimology: Past, present, and future. *Criminologie 33*(1), 17–46.

Gilligan, J. (2003). Shame, guilt, and violence. *Social Research 70*(4), 1149–1180.

Goffman, E. (1959). *The Presentation of Self in Everyday Life*. Garden City, NJ: Doubleday.

Goffman, E. (1961). *Encounters: Two Studies in the Sociology of Interaction*. Indianapolis: Bobbs-Merrill.

Holstein, J. A., & Miller, G. (1990). Rethinking victimization: An interactional approach to victimology. *Symbolic Interaction 13*(1), 103–122.

Janoff-Bulman, R., & Hanson-Frieze, I. (1987). The role of gender in reactions to criminal victimization. In R. Barnett, L. Biener, & G. Baruch (Eds.), *Gender and Stress* (pp. 159–184). New York: The Free Press.

Kenney, J. S. (1995). Legal institutions and victims of crime in Canada: An historical and contemporary review. *Humanity and Society 19*(2), 53–67.

Kitsuse, J. (1980). Coming out all over: Deviants and the politics of social problems. *Social Problems 28*(1), 1–12.

Klass, D. (1988). *Parental Grief: Solace and Resolution*. New York: Springer.

Knapp, R. (1986). *Beyond Endurance: When a Child Dies*. New York: Schocken.

Lemert, E. (1951). *Social Pathology*. New York: McGraw-Hill.

Lerner, M. (1980). *The Belief in a Just World: A Fundamental Delusion*. New York: Plenum.

Lister, L. (1991). Men and grief: A review of research. *Smith-College Studies in Social Work 61*(3), 220–235.

Littlewood, J. (1992). *Aspects of Grief: Bereavement in Adult Life*. London: Tavistock/Routledge.

Littlewood, J., Cramer, D., Hoesktra, J., & Humphrey, G. B. (1991). Gender differences in parental coping following their child's death. *British Journal of Guidance and Counselling 19*(2), 139–148.

Mead, G. H. (1934). *Mind, Self, and Society*. Chicago: University of Chicago Press.

Nathanson, D. (1994). *Shame and Pride: Affect, Sex, and the Birth of the Self*. New York: W. W. Norton.

Plummer, K. (1979). Misunderstanding labelling perspectives. In D. Downes & P. Rock (Eds.), *Deviant Interpretations* (pp. 85–121). Oxford: Martin Robertson & Company.

Rubington, E. (1982). Deviant subcultures. In M. Rosenberg, R. Stebbins, & A. Turowetz (Eds.), *The Sociology of Deviance* (pp. 57–60). New York: St. Martin's.

Rubington, E., & Weinberg, M. (1987). *Deviance: The Interactionist Perspective* (5th ed.). New York: MacMillan.

Rynearson, E. K., & McCreery, J. (1993). Bereavement after homicide: A synergism of trauma and loss. *American Journal of Psychiatry 150*, 258–261.

Schatz, W. (1984). *Healing a Father's Grief*. Redmond, WA: Medic.

Schatz, W. (1986). Grief of fathers. In T. A. Rando (Ed.), *Parental Loss of a Child* (pp. 293–302). Champaign, IL: Research Press.

Scheff, T., & Retzinger, S. (2000). Shame as the master emotion of everyday life. *Journal of Mundane Behaviour 1*(3), 303–324.

Sobieski, R. (1994). *Men and Mourning: A Father's Journey through Grief.* Toronto: MADD Canada.

Taylor, S., Wood, J., & Lichtman, R. (1983). It could be worse: Selective evaluation as a response to victimization. *Journal of Social Issues 39*(2), 19–40.

Thoits, P. (1990). Emotional deviance: Research agendas. In T. D. Kemper (Ed.), *Research Agendas in the Sociology of Emotions* (pp. 180–203). New York: State University of New York.

Walker, L. (1992). Traumatized populations: Role and responsibilities of professionals. In E. C. Viano (Ed.), *Critical Issues in Victimology: International Perspectives* (pp. 37–45). New York: Springer.

Wilson, A. L, Fenton, L. J., Stevens, D. C., & Soule, D. J. (1982). The death of a newborn twin: An analysis of parental bereavement. *Pediatrics 70,* 587–591.

Worden, W. (2001). *Grief Counselling and Grief Therapy* (3rd ed.). New York: Springer.

Wortman, C., & Lehman, D. (1983). Reactions to victims of life crises: Support attempts that fail. In I. G. Sarason & B. R. Sarason (Eds.), *Social Support: Theory, Research, and Applications* (pp. 463–489). Boston: Martinus Nijhoff.

CHAPTER 4

Victims and Legal Institutions

INTRODUCTION

Legal institutions play a major role in constructing victims' experiences (Klass, 1988). Since the early 1980s the literature has grown on the victim's place in the criminal justice process (Davis, Kunreuther, & Connick, 1984; Hagan, 1985; Kenney, 1995, 1998). Unfortunately, much of this has been largely focused around specific issues such as the "rape shield" law, victim impact statements, restorative justice, and the like (Grossman & Kane, 2004). What is needed is a brief, concise account of Canadian criminal procedure and its impact on victims' experiences.

To this end, in this chapter I outline the traditional, limited legal position of victims in the Canadian criminal justice system, the many institutional restrictions that they face, and the practical effects at each stage of the criminal justice process. Next, I present excerpts from both my post-doctoral research and my homicide study indicating—in victims' own words—how they felt the system affected them.

VICTIMS' LEGAL POSITION

Victims' institutional experiences of victimization may be traced to the guiding metaphor underlying the Canadian criminal justice system: the "legal fiction" that crime is a matter between the *state* and the *accused*. This position has been constructed through a lengthy historical process (Box 4.1) and, at present, a criminal proceeding is an adversarial process between *only* these two parties.[1]

The victim is not a party and has no legal capacity to dispute decisions of the Crown prosecutor. The prosecutor works for the state and is not the victim's lawyer. The victim has only two roles to play: to call the police to report the crime and to act as a witness for the prosecution if called.[2]

This "legal fiction" has real consequences in the interactional construction of victims' experiences at each stage of criminal proceedings (Holstein &

> BOX 4.1:
> ## THE HISTORICAL CONSTRUCTION OF
> ## THE VICTIM'S LEGAL POSITION
>
> "In the early days of the development of English law there was no
> distinction recognized between public wrongs and private wrongs.
> All were treated as private wrongs. It was the responsibility of the
> victim or his family to proceed against the offender, and it was the
> victim who stood to benefit from any court order ... The state played
> no role in the process. Around the twelfth century, however, the
> notion of a crime as being something different from a civil wrong
> began to take shape. There emerged certain matters which were
> considered to be offences against the King's Peace [and these]
> gradually expanded. It was in the name of the King that offences
> against the King's Peace were prosecuted, and it was on behalf of
> the King that fines were extracted or other forms of punishment
> imposed. The victim could pursue his private remedy against the
> offender in a separate civil action, a claim in tort. It has evolved there
> is a different standard of proof for criminal proceedings. With the
> sharpening distinction between crime and tort, the victim's role in
> the criminal process has become increasingly a secondary one."
>
> **Source:** Dickson, B. (1984). The forgotten party—the victim of crime. *UBC Law Review 18*, 320.

Miller, 1990; Loseke, 1993; Schneider, 1985; Sebba, 1992). Setting the parameters like this means that victims have lost control of the process: "The state
owns the conflict and the roles left to victims are: (1) to supply the system
with raw material; (2) to give the evidence the system requires; and (3) to
serve as a 'ceremonial' or symbolic presence" (Clarke, 1986, p. 32).

I now outline the consequences of this formulation, both in lack of legal
rights and in victim's encounters with the justice system, step by step through
the legal process. I trace the interactional construction of victims' experiences
from the complaint and through the police investigation, the charging process,
bail, arraignment, the preliminary hearing, trial, sentencing, and parole. Policy
responses and programs to deal with these issues are covered in Chapter 6.

VICTIMS IN THE CRIMINAL JUSTICE PROCESS

The Complaint

Most criminal proceedings begin with a complaint. In our system, unless a
police officer directly observes or has "reasonable" grounds to believe that

an offender has committed a crime, it is incumbent upon the victim to notify the authorities (*Criminal Code*, 1985, s. 495; Goff, 2004). Yet, by notifying police—which many victims choose not to do (Bard & Sangrey, 1986; Canadian Centre for Justice Statistics, 1999; Goff, 2004; Minister of Supply and Services, 1982; Sacco & Johnson, 1990)—many embark on the road to "secondary victimization" by the criminal justice system (Canadian Federal-Provincial Task Force, 1983; Karmen, 2001).

The Police

Three factors have been cited as evidence of secondary victimization by the police, particularly prior to the victims' movement of the 1980s: (1) police response to initial victim complaints; (2) their treatment of the victim during the investigation; and (3) their methods of informing victims of the death or injury of a loved one.

First, victims have been frustrated by police failure to respond to complaints, either by dispatchers screening out "minor" incidents, instructions to call back if "private" arguments are not resolved, or vague assurances that matters will be "looked into" (Canadian Federal-Provincial Task Force, 1983, pp. 36–37; Karmen, 2001, pp. 152–153; Walker, 1994). While much of this involves management systems to prioritize responses (Goff, 2004), perceptions of "emergency" vary depending upon which end of the telephone one is on. Moreover, when the police do respond, at least until recently, they made arrests in only a minority of interpersonal disputes (Karmen, 2001; Smith & Klein, 1984). This may be frustrating, demeaning, or downright dangerous for victims.

Secondly, during investigations, victims have complained about insensitive questioning shortly after the crime (Bard & Sangrey, 1986; Karmen, 2001; Provincial Secretariat for Justice, 1984); initial failure to inform of support services (Canadian Federal-Provincial Task Force, 1983; Walker, 1994); sudden, inconvenient, and emotionally disturbing demands to identify suspect(s) (Canadian Federal-Provincial Task Force, 1983); delays in responding to requests for information (Canadian Federal-Provincial Task Force, 1983); placing the victim or their family under investigation (Provincial Secretariat for Justice, 1984); holding victims' property for investigation; public revelation of unwelcome information; and returning upsetting items to survivors (Provincial Secretariat for Justice, 1984).

Finally, until the 1990s many police forces did not have standard procedures for informing families of the death of loved ones, which sometimes resulted in families being informed by telephone or by the press, or in an insensitive, matter-of-fact manner (Amernic, 1984; Karmen, 2001; Walker, 1994).

Many of these problems have been reduced by the widespread introduction of police victims' services programs since the 1990s.

The Charging Process

If the police investigation has succeeded and the offender identified, the next step is for the appropriate charge to be laid. Once this is done, there may be communication between the Crown prosecutor and defence counsel, and a decision to increase, decrease, or withdraw charges may be made without consulting the victim. The victim has no legal capacity to compel prosecution, contest decisions, dismiss or reduce charges, or accept plea bargains (Dickson, 1984). While the Crown is ostensibly under a duty to consider the impact of the offence on the victim, consultation is rare (Canadian Federal-Provincial Task Force, 1983; Karmen, 2001). There are many instances where charges have been reduced or withdrawn or an "inadequate" sentence agreed without proper consideration of the evidence available (Canadian Federal-Provincial Task Force, 1983). This is especially upsetting to victims (Karmen 2001).

Pre-trial Release Practices

It is relatively uncommon for the accused to be remanded pending trial. While victims may wish to see the perpetrator arrested and held until trial, our system has evolved alternative measures to prompt attendance, such as issuing an "appearance notice," a "promise to appear," or a "recognizance" involving a monetary obligation (*Criminal Code*, s. 515). The *Criminal Code* directs that the officer in charge "shall" release the accused except in limited circumstances (s. 515[10]). In addition, if not released, the *Criminal Code* requires that a bail hearing be held very shortly thereafter, where the prosecution must "show cause" for continued detention (s. 515). Generally, the Crown succeeds only if detention is necessary to ensure the accused's appearance in court, if necessary in the "public interest," or for the protection and safety of the public (Canadian Federal-Provincial Task Force, 1983, p. 44).

From a victim's viewpoint, several aspects of this are disturbing. First, the mandatory language and burden on the Crown ensures that at least some dangerous individuals will slip through. Second, except in exceptional cases, no money has to change hands. Third, before 1999, Canadian law left little place for the victim to participate in hearings (Glendon et al., 1982; Provincial Secretariat for Justice, 1984) and, while the authorities are now required to consider victim safety (*Criminal Code* (s. 515(10)(b)), the active participation of victims remains at the discretion of the Crown. Finally, until the introduction of victims' services programs, victims were often not informed of the accused's release, experiencing frustration, confusion, and fear upon encountering him or her (Walker, 1994):

> "In many instances the victim is unaware that the issue of
> the accused's pre-trial release has been considered and has

had no opportunity to express his concern ... The victim has played little part in any of those decisions and may not even be informed by the police that this has occurred" (Canadian Federal-Provincial Task Force, 1983, p. 45).

Court

Assuming the victim has made a complaint, the police an arrest, charges have been laid and not withdrawn, the accused has pleaded not guilty, and there has been no referral to a pre-trial diversion or settlement program, then next come a series of court hearings that can possibly culminate in trial. A criminal trial is an adversarial process between the state and the accused, where the defence need only raise a reasonable doubt about the accused's guilt. The victim is not represented *per se*, is relegated to the role of witness, and has none of the procedural and substantive rights granted the accused (Waller, 1985).

The accused's first appearance is in a provincial court for arraignment, where charges are read and he or she is asked to enter a plea. If the accused pleads guilty (whether prompted by a plea bargain or not) then the matter proceeds to sentencing, either immediately or after the preparation of a pre-sentence report. The victim may be given no information, and may learn of this first court appearance from the media. Moreover, if previously asked to be a witness, a guilty plea has traditionally meant that victims are no longer required—and therefore have no chance to tell their story.[3]

If, however, the accused pleads not guilty, a trial date will be set by agreement of counsel. Rarely do counsel consider the convenience of victim-witnesses, and the date may be weeks or months away. Indeed, the only notification a victim may receive may be a subpoena to appear (Canadian Federal-Provincial Task Force, 1983; Karmen, 2001; Provincial Secretariat for Justice, 1984). The delays in this process are frustrating to victims (Bard & Sangrey, 1986; Dickson, 1984; Karmen, 2001; Sebba, 1992), and this frustration is often exacerbated by adjournments (Provincial Secretariat for Justice, 1984).

Next, for certain offences the accused may choose a preliminary inquiry to determine whether there is sufficient evidence to send the matter to trial (Goff, 2004). In effect, this gives the accused "two kicks at the can" because, if there is not enough evidence, the matter is dropped.[4] Victims, as witnesses, are required to be present.

The victim's experience as a witness may be marred by encountering the accused and/or defence witnesses. Until the implementation of victims' services programs, these groups often shared a waiting room (Bard & Sangrey,

1986; Canadian Federal-Provincial Task Force, 1983). Victims and family members have often been excluded from proceedings (Karmen, 2001; Provincial Secretariat for Justice, 1984) or, if present, given little (if any) information on the disturbing evidence that may be presented (Amernic, 1984). In addition, witness fees are woefully inadequate to cover the costs of attending court (Canadian Federal-Provincial Task Force, 1983; Karmen, 2001).

Perhaps the single most upsetting thing for victims is that they may have to testify, in explicit detail, about the events of the crime. This can bring upsetting memories flooding back, often amounting to reliving the event (Karmen, 2001). For victims who are in counselling or on medication, this can exacerbate their condition. Indeed, in many cases giving testimony in a public courtroom, and being examined and cross-examined by lawyers, cannot be anything but a trying experience (Dickson, 1984). Ironically, "victims are often attacked by defence counsel as the opposite party" (Rubel 1986, pp. 233–234). For victims of violence and sexual assault, this may be experienced as re-victimization (Karmen, 2001; Waller, 1990).

Ultimately, the accused is either discharged or ordered to stand trial later (Goff, 2004). The former may upset victims. In the latter case, however, many of the above factors reoccur. The differences at trial are that there may be additional upsetting evidence, victims have endured a further period of uncertainty, and the issue is now whether guilt can be proven beyond a reasonable doubt. Thus, the victim may have to relive the crime twice and still face the possibility that the accused might face no legal sanction.

Finally, a conviction in a trial may be followed by appeals (*Criminal Code*, 1985, s. 675[1]). These can further extend the process, and victims face continued uncertainty. Indeed, they may fear for their safety in cases where the appellant is granted bail pending appeal (*Criminal Code*, 1985, s. 679).

Sentencing

If convicted, the court hears representations from the Crown and defence counsel before the offender is sentenced. Over time victims have objected to several aspects of this process: (1) lack of input (until the introduction of "victim impact statements" in 1988, victims were denied any input) (*Re Regina and Antler*, 1982); (2) an historical trend toward more lenient sentencing coupled with an increased emphasis on rehabilitation and community sentences (Amernic, 1984; Waller, 1990); (3) courts keeping public opinion at arms length, while ostensibly acting for public benefit (*R. v. Henein*, 1980); (4) continued lack of information (Dickson, 1984); (5) disparity and inconsistency in sentencing (Canadian Federal-Provincial Task Force, 1983; Goff, 2004); and (6) problems in obtaining restitution through sentencing (*Criminal Code*, 1985, s. 725; *R. v. Zelenski*, 1978).

Conditional Release

If imprisonment is ordered and sentencing appeals have been exhausted, the offender is incarcerated. However, victims express concern over a parole system that may release offenders after they have served a fraction of their sentence (Amernic 1984; Karmen, 2001).

Particularly upsetting had been mandatory supervision, under which offenders who were refused parole could automatically serve as much as the final third of their sentence in the community (Minister of Supply and Services, 1989; Provincial Secretariat for Justice, 1984). Until 1986, parole boards had no discretion to stop this process. However, studies showed that the incidence of violent crimes was far higher for these offenders than for those released on full parole (Ministry of the Solicitor General, 1981a,b), and victims lobbied for reform (Provincial Secretariat for Justice, 1984).

In addition, until relatively recently little information was available to victims (*Corrections and Conditional Release Act*, 1992; Walker, 1994). Correctional Services Canada or the National Parole Board may now release information that is already publicly available and victims may, but only upon request, receive additional information (Box 4.2).

Indeed, the *Corrections and Conditional Release Act* (1992) places the onus on the victim to request information, the rationale being that some victims prefer not to receive information about the offender.

Some object that: (1) by placing the onus on victims, those who do not request this information may be surprised by offenders who have been released and who seek revenge on the unsuspecting party (Stangret, 1991); (2) victims have no right to such information, and its release had, until the 1980s, been prohibited by the *Privacy Act* (Stangret, 1991); and (3) with the exception of personal addresses and phone numbers, representations by victims to the authorities have, as a matter of procedure, been shared with the offender (Correctional Services Canada, n.d.; Minister of Supply and Services, 1989; Stangret, 1991).

Conclusion

In the foregoing sections, I have considered the traditional legal position of Canadian victims of crime. Following the historical construction of crime as a matter between the state and the accused, I have detailed the practical effects of this root metaphor: a *de facto*, if not a *de jure*, lack of effective rights for victims. I have illustrated that once victims of crime make the decision to involve the authorities, they are the object of neglect, ignorance, and even abuse by the very institutions that they seek out for help. While few go through all of the steps above, it is clear that at each step victims face clear and wrenching problems.

BOX 4.2:
INFORMATION AVAILABLE FROM CORRECTIONAL AND PAROLE AUTHORITIES

Upon completing an information request form and filing it with the nearest office, victims of federal offenders may obtain the following information from Correctional Services Canada or the National Parole Board: (1) the offender's name; (2) the offence and court that convicted the offender; (3) the offender's sentence start date and length of sentence; and (4) the offender's eligibility/ review dates for temporary absences, day parole, and full parole.

If victims wish to obtain more details, they may also obtain (subject to an assessment to ensure compliance with laws governing information sharing): (5) the location of the penitentiary where the offender is being held; (6) information about an offender transferring from one institution to another; (7) the date on which the offender is to be released on unescorted or escorted temporary absence, work release, parole, or statutory release; (8) any conditions attached to the offender's unescorted temporary absence, work release, parole, or statutory release; (9) the offender's destination when released on any temporary absence, work release, parole, or statutory release, and whether the offender will be in the vicinity of the victim while traveling to that destination; (10) the date of any National Parole Board hearing; and (11) whether the offender is in custody and, if not, why not.

Source: Correctional Services Canada. (n.d.). *Victim Services at CSC*. Retrieved January 25, 2008, from http://www.csc-scc.gc.ca/victims-victimes

ENCOUNTERS WITH THE JUSTICE SYSTEM AND VICTIM CLAIMS

Building upon the discussion in Chapter 2 on the relationship between initial victim claims and victimization, in this section I note how such claims are modified by encounters with the criminal justice system. Drawing upon my victim services data, on a more diverse set of offences,[5] the effect of subjects' encounters in this context will be outlined, with an emphasis on differing responses and factors impacting victim claims.

By far the largest group of clients claimed that their initial victim identity was exacerbated by dealings with the justice system. Making up 60.9% of clients overall,[6] many claimed that they had been re-victimized:

> "We are victimized again and again. I was made to feel like more of a victim and nothing gets any better. You get so far

dealing with it and then they do something really dumb and it starts all over again. You relive that pain all over again. The justice system is the biggest factor in making me feel like a victim" (interview #2: female, age 48).

Clients in this group claimed that re-victimization resulted from institutional processes and the outcome of their cases. With respect to the former, they noted the general neglect of their rights in favour of those of the offender, lack of input on matters such as plea bargaining, opportunities for the offender to "play the system," lack of information, numerous delays, and cross-examination by defence counsel.[7] Indeed, several spoke of the offender continuing to abuse them through the system. Such encounters contributed a key ingredient of the victim claim: feeling powerless.

> "There is absolutely no mechanism in place for victim involvement, input, consultation, or even any kind of impartial third party that, if you're not happy with the way something is being done, you can appeal. It stinks. You're powerless and you're a victim all over again. Not only that, the accused has every break, gets all the benefit of the doubt, while the victim gets none. I was treated as an outsider, almost as less than human" (interview #12: male, age 43).

Some support workers echoed this view:

> "For many clients, the system itself becomes a burden as well as the crime. There's the management of getting through the crime itself, and then getting through the system and process on top of it. Victims often feel that they don't have a voice in the system—and that's a frustration that they vent to me. Many of their expectations come from TV, and they don't understand that the Crown isn't their lawyer. Victims are often frustrated and afraid. Going through the process affects their sense of self-power, their sense of coping, because no decisions are made by the victim once the case goes into the system. It becomes the state's case and therefore the victims feel that they have no voice and are powerless. The overall impact is very negative" (interview #30: female, age 47).

With regard to outcomes, expectations were a major factor, with many clients assuming the system would protect them and punish the offender in line

BOX 4.3:
INITIATION OF VICTIM CLAIMS IN THE
CRIMINAL JUSTICE PROCESS

"I dealt with a very confident, capable, articulate woman who said 'I'm not a victim' and insisted that she didn't want to be treated as one. She felt she would be able to manage just fine and was quite prepared to come to court, go through the process, and move on. The system certainly had a profound impact on her. The thing she was most surprised about was the process. She soon identified the accused as having all of the power and her as having none, and her fear of him grew. There were problems with delays and the offender breaching his undertaking, but at the trial the accused acted as his own lawyer. She was not only surprised, but this was absolutely devastating for her. He was found guilty and made quite a scene as he was being forcibly removed from the courtroom. Afterwards, as we were sitting there, another person [of the same ethnic background] came to the door. She thought it was him coming back and was absolutely paralyzed with fear. She said 'I don't know how I will get on from this day. I just don't know how it will be OK.' Her experience is not unusual" (interview #30: female, age 47).

Source: Kenney, J. S. (1999). *Unintended Consequences: The Interactional Dynamics of Victim Service and Support Programs.* Unpublished post-doctoral research, Dalhousie University, Halifax, NS.

with their ideas of justice. Many felt let down when this did not happen. For some, this occurred early, such as when offenders were released on restraining orders that were routinely breached. Others were upset when offenders were acquitted. Most, however, complained of "lenient sentences"[8] and how these are mitigated by the parole system:

> "When the system just gives him a slap on the hand I feel even more victimized because I don't believe the justice system has done what they should have been doing for me" (interview #28: female, age 24).

> "There is no truth in sentencing. I had to deal with reality, he had to deal with the law, and it is two totally different things. I was re-victimized as there was no justice for our family" (interview #4: female, age 52).

Again, clients in this group were at times echoed by support workers:

> "Many clients say 'Why did I even bother?' This is especially the case when the offender is acquitted or gets a minor sentence. Not only do victims wonder what their rights are when nothing happens, but [they] also discover that it's not always to their benefit to report a crime. They feel totally powerless and re-victimized. This can do more harm to them than the actual crime" (interview #24: female, age 42).

The next most common group of clients follows from Chapter 2. In Chapter 2, it was noted that victim claims do not necessarily follow victimization. This group, making up 17.4% of clients,[9] claimed that their experiences with the justice system *initiated* their sense of victim identity (Box 4.3)—often for the same reasons that those above claimed it exacerbated theirs. For example: "It was because of our dealings with the justice system that I realized that I am a victim" (interview #10: male, age 35).

Indeed, beyond feelings of victimization, in many of the above comments from the first two groups there was a sense of clients feeling somehow lowered, even shamed (Gilligan, 2003; Nathanson, 1994; Scheff and Retzinger, 2000) by going through such trauma without institutional redress.

The third group, making up 17.4% of clients,[10] commented that their encounters with the justice system had little or no impact on their sense of victim identity. Various reasons revolved around the fact that they had little involvement with the justice system, avoided involvement, limited their expectations, or focused their energies and attention elsewhere:

> "The perpetrator in our case was killed so we never had to go to court. The system had minimal impact in my case" (interview #14: male, age 38).

> "I figured that the less I got tied in it in terms of expecting a solution, the less disappointed I would be" (interview #3: male, age 29).

> "I wasn't worried about the criminal case. I really didn't pay much attention. I was thinking lawsuit" (interview #6: male, age 49).

Interestingly, support workers were well aware that "Some people decide to avoid the system and 'not let the offender take over any more of my life and time'" (interview #30: female, age 47).

BOX 4.4:
SUPPORT WORKERS ON THE MIXED IMPACTS OF THE JUSTICE SYSTEM

"If the system has worked for them such that the offender is charged and convicted, women feel stronger, that they have been heard—even though still sad. If not, she may view herself more as a victim and less as a survivor" (survey #1: female, age 37).

"Clients find it helpful when (a) they are believed, and (b) somebody in the system is able to do something. The problem is that they are often not listened to and the system is powerless in many ways to protect them. Some are re-victimized; others not so much if there is a conviction and a sentence they're happy with. Still, I could count on one hand the women who said that they had a voice in the system" (interview #8: female, age 27).

Source: Kenney, J. S. (1999). *Unintended Consequences: The Interactional Dynamics of Victim Service and Support Programs.* Unpublished post-doctoral research, Dalhousie University, Halifax, NS.

The last group, making up 4.3% of clients,[11] claimed that the impact of the justice system on their sense of victimization exhibited a tension between aggravating and mitigating factors:

> "It certainly was a learning experience. I had no idea of how they would try to tear you down—how the defence attorney can actually treat you. Yet, it was a part of the process of my dealing with my husband and all this huge fear that he represented and controlled over the years. So in one way it was a bad thing and in another it was good. When I heard the 'guilty' I was so pleased" (interview #19: female, age 46).

Significantly, support workers largely supported this viewpoint (Box 4.4), with all of the provincial victim services workers and 80% of women's shelter/outreach workers subscribing to the view that it was common, but not necessarily a given, for clients to develop a predominantly victim-centred identity through the justice system.[12]

It remains highly significant that no clients or support staff of any of the services unequivocally claimed that the justice system mitigates one's sense of victimhood.

Summing up: those clients who had extensive dealings with the criminal justice system overwhelmingly claimed that its procedures and outcomes either added to or initiated their sense of victimization. While some avoided this by limiting their involvement with, focus on, or expectations of the criminal justice system, and others pointed to various mitigating factors such as positive outcomes, these data suggest that much of subjects' sense of victimization derives from this source—and not from the crime alone.

HOMICIDE SURVIVORS' EXPERIENCES

Level of Involvement
The criminal justice system again emerged as a highly significant factor in survivors' experiences in my homicide data. Generally, those who claimed they fared worse were involved—as above—in drawn-out, disturbing encounters with legal institutions:

> "The legal process (pretrial, trial, verdict, and sentencing) only brings the pain of my daughter's death back to the first days after she was killed" (criminal injuries compensation board [CICB] #82: survivor's written response to board questionnaire: male, age 58).

> "When it's before the courts, you have to constantly relive it. The grief process is set back and prolonged by this stuff" (interview #29: female, age 37).

These sentiments were corroborated by both professional and lay observers. Consider a man's vehement response to another—who had complained that the offender in his case had committed suicide, so was never "brought to justice": "After spending 20 months in court, I don't wish that on a family of any victim. So just leave it alone! You can start to deal with your grief now" (interview #24: male, age 47).

Psychiatrists, both in my data (CICB #91: psychiatric report re: female, age 46), and other studies (Box 4.5) have corroborated such impacts of the criminal justice system.

Conversely, survivors who reportedly fared better were generally *not* involved in drawn-out interactions with legal institutions, often because the offender was dead:

> "When people say 'Oh, you're such a strong woman,' I say 'No. Not at all. I'm just a very ordinary housewife.' But [since the offender was dead] circumstances were such that I didn't have to watch that animal jerk my chain for three or four years. I

BOX 4.5:

PSYCHIATRIST'S OBSERVATIONS OF A HOMICIDE SUPPORT GROUP

If the losses of self claimed by victims can be seen, in part, as bereavement, then Klass (1988) has observed that—unlike with terminal illness or a sudden accidental death—grief in murder cases is prolonged by the criminal justice system, where families have few rights while the accused has many (p. 127). Until the trial is over (several years later), parents cannot begin to resolve their grief because the system keeps reopening their wounds—taking away the sense of power over their lives (pp. 127–128). This provides an opportunity for self-help organizations such as POMC (Parents of Murdered Children). Like other bereavement groups, POMC exhibits an experiential dimension where issues of living after loss are shared. It also shows an inter-psychic dimension where emotional attachments are transformed.

However, there is a political dimension rooted in the powerlessness and anger engendered by experiences in the justice system (p. 131). This is characterized by victims' anger being channelled into action: members help each other with their ongoing problems within the criminal justice system, and the group works toward reform (p. 131). Ultimately, this "is about the restoration of power in the face of ... overwhelming powerlessness" (p. 134).

Source: Klass, D. (1988). *Parental Grief: Solace and Resolution*. New York: Springer: pp. 131, 134.

didn't have to deal with these fools in parole who say 'Well we never predicted dangerousness.' I didn't have to deal with all that. It was over and done. So, it frees you. You can get on with it" (interview #17: female, age 50).

The one exception involved cases where survivors were unaware of legal proceedings or avoided them, only to discover the offender had been acquitted or received what they considered to be an "unjust" sentence.

In those cases where survivors did have dealings with legal institutions, those reportedly faring better often noted that their involvement was minimal:

"The only thing that we both discussed, and is probably very unusual, is that we didn't want to get involved with the court case at all. We put in a victim impact statement, and that was the extent to which we wanted to be involved—and I see in so many

cases, and with the [support] groups that, if you do get involved
in any of the court cases, you're emotionally involved, and you
can't get on with your grief. So, when I think back, I think that
that was a wise thing to do" (interview #5: male, age 50).

Indeed, in the few cases where survivors who claimed to fare relatively
well did have significant involvement with the criminal justice system, they
reported three moderating factors. First, they noted helpful officials:

"We had a lot of support. The sheriffs were good. We had a
fantastic Crown counsel that kept us really informed, and our
victims' service person, our Crown victims' service person was
really good" (interview #25: female, age 45).

Second, they felt that they had had an impact on the sentence, typically
through a victim impact statement:

"Apparently, given the sentence, my input was fairly effective.
It was very consistent with what we had asked for in this particular case. So I don't *think* that there was an injustice done. If
it was effective, you know, that's enough for me" (interview #7:
male, age 58; emphasis in original).

Finally, the offender had received a sentence that the survivors considered to be as just as possible under current law: "It [the sentence] was the
best that could be done for our daughter" (survey #11: female, age 60).

This is not to say these individuals did not suffer after receiving a "just"
verdict. They were, however, better off than others who had something further to be upset about.

Aggravating Factors

Survivors who reportedly fared worse generally noted aggravating factors
during their dealings with legal institutions. First, they reported poor treatment by officials:

"The Crown said to us, 'If you scream and cry, and make a great
big fuss in the paper or on TV that we've barred you from
attending this raise hearing, we will move the preliminary
hearing.' So they basically gagged us" (interview #27: female,
age 44).

"The defence were absolutely obnoxious! They did things that were very hurtful in the courtroom [sighs]. [The offender's second defence counsel] deliberately stood six to eight feet in front of us with pictures of [the deceased] that they took after they found her body. And they were facing us, not the witness, not the jury, not the judge. They were facing us. And we had never seen these pictures. We didn't want to see these pictures" (interview #32: female, age 46).

Next, there were problems with survivors being excluded from the courtroom:

"I got verbal instructions from the Crown that *I wasn't allowed past the door*. I wasn't allowed into the courtroom because I was a *witness*. So that's what they do. They've got a special way of keeping you out. They make you a witness. Even if they're not going to let you *appear*, they just say 'you are a witness,' and they *may* call you, so they can keep you out of any process they *want to by doing that*" (interview #32: male, age 47; emphasis in original).

Third, there were numerous delays between court hearings:

"I found that I was living from one court date to the next. That's how I was gauging time. Your life is sort of on hold until that day is there. It's always like that's the big day! But then, once you get to the big day, it's just as disappointing, and the next day too. The delays are the worst! You are all ready to go, and then you psych yourself up for days beforehand. And then, you get there, and it's a delay of some sort, and you've got to go home, and then you crash" (interview #25: female, age 45).

Fourth, survivors were greatly upset by matters pertaining to evidence. First, survivors complained about the exclusion of evidence: "I was disgusted. The jury did not hear half the story because they were out of the courtroom" (survey #3: female, age 58).

Next, survivors were very upset by evidence in favour of the offender:

"The system is brutal, because it makes the victim out like it was his fault, and they give all these stupid reasonings why the

BOX 4.6:
UPSETTING EVIDENCE

"[The offender] made a video re-enactment for the police the day he confessed. First we hear about it! Boom! There we are in the court, they put the video on, and we're watching as he goes through it. You could not imagine how horrible this tape was. He showed how he picked her up, and how he carried her nonchalant, you know, hands in the pocket, not nervous. He made this claim that he heard [the deceased's brother] calling her, and he was molesting her, and she screamed 'Mummy!' So he killed her! Just like that. She was dead when he assaulted her. She was on the ground, and he said that he kicked her in the head once, and then he stood on her chest. Then, he showed how he took this tremendous leap in the air and jumped on her. We're like ... we're sitting there going like ... [respondent gestures expressing shock and horror]. Then it showed how he went back to the apartment, went up to the bathroom and he said 'I had to take my shoe off, there was this thing in it. I think it was shit'—and he laughs! So we just freaked. You know how you know you're going to scream, and you're going to cry, and you're just completely out of control? And we'd never been warned" (interview #27: female, age 44).

Source: Kenney, J. S. (1998). *Coping with Grief: Survivors of Murder Victims.* Unpublished doctoral thesis, McMaster University, Hamilton, ON.

criminal did what he did. All the excuses, you know? And it just really ticked me off" (interview #25: female, age 45).

Also in this regard, survivors were disturbed by graphic, lurid evidence presented in court, often with no warning (Box 4.6).

Fifth, survivors complained about what they considered to be harmful procedures:

"To see that the scales are not balanced, that you are excluded from the entire process, that you are now viewed as the aggressor while the offender is depicted as the victim, is a total re-victimization and it cannot go on. To expect us to be the only people in that courtroom without representation, I think, is shocking" (interview #17: female, age 50).

Sixth, survivors complained about what they considered to be "unjust" rulings:

> "We had no idea what was going to happen. [The offender's] lawyer, the first time he ever lay eyes on us, stands up and he says to the judge 'Your Honour, I'd like to put forth a motion to the Court that we move the trial to [another city far away].' The guy from the Crown—we're waiting for him to get up and say 'We live here. This is where everybody lives. This is where the family is, this is where the murder happened ...' He stands up and he said 'We have no argument with that.' He sat down, and then the judge said 'Well I ... I have no choice here.' And we're going like 'Wait a minute here. Who ... who's in here for us?'" (interview #27: female, age 44).

Seventh, survivors were upset by verdicts that they considered unjust:

> "The verdict came in, and they said 'They find the defendant guilty of manslaughter,' and I don't remember too much that day, because I started crying. I couldn't stop. I guess a nervous breakdown, and they ended up bringing an ambulance. I mean, it was just like somebody had just stuck the knife in me. [The deceased] was stabbed 30 times in the face. Her face looked like hamburger, and [respondent makes noise of disgust] [the offender] got off on manslaughter! 'Accidental death!' How in the heck can it be? How? That's what bothers me. How can it be 'accidental death' when he had stabbed her that many times?" (interview #23: male, age 49).

Professional observers corroborated the negative effect of such verdicts:

> "My own clients [sighs], I try to prepare them that they're going to lose the case. I *always* prepare them. They're always disappointed. They still see [in sad voice] 'Ohhh! The person got off'; and, 'How come it's only that way?'; and 'I went through all this and they only got x number of years ...,' or whatever. Or probation. Or community service. They come out very angry. *Bitter*, very bitter" (interview #6: female therapist, age 46; emphasis in original).

Eighth, and closely related, was the upset survivors expressed regarding "unjust" sentencing:

"This guy [the offender] ... [respondent bangs fist on table] ... as far as I'm concerned he got nothing. He got nothing! The sentencing was a sham. We felt we were suckered and left in the sewers" (interview #20: male, age 37).

Observers corroborated survivors' accounts of the negative impact of such sentences:

"To refer back to this patient's persistent anger and hostility over the years since the incident in 1975, I believe the outcome of the legal aspects of the case, which, to him, was a gross injustice—and I can't see how anybody can think of the judgment made in any other terms then the patient—contributed significantly ... The perpetrator of this crime was given only a 90-day sentence to be served on weekends" (CICB #11, psychiatrist's letter re: male, age 35).

Finally, survivors' encounters with "the system" are not over once the trial, sentencing, and any appeals are concluded. The parole system may bring the whole matter up again. Compare the following two sharply contrasting extracts: the first from a woman who had dealings with the authorities, and the second from a man who did not have to because the offender was dead.

"[The offender] is coming back out. You've got to really decide whether or not you want to put your life on the line to say what you need to say. I mean, [my husband and I] we're making this fellow pretty mad! Oh my God! I mean that one phone call [from parole officials] where he was coming out at one year and four months: I was at work. I couldn't stop crying. I just had to leave, and, after two hours of non-stop, I went to the doctor. I had to go on drugs to get control of myself! That's how traumatized I was by it. There's no putting it behind us and getting on with our life. It just won't happen—until he's dead!" (interview #8: female, age 45).

"You can start to deal with your grief now, and one thing you've got to look at is [the offender] is never going to be paroled [laughs]. He's gone. He's toast" (interview #4: male, age 56).

Ultimately, survivors claimed the above factors aggravated the experience of victimization. Moreover, as with my victim services data, there was an implicit sense of clients feeling shamed (Gilligan, 2003; Nathanson, 1994; Scheff and Retzinger, 2000) by going through such trauma without institutional redress.

Gender and Coping

It is interesting that men and women, while both traumatized by extensive involvement with the system, experienced this trauma in different ways. For women, the main problem was fear; for men it was anger:

> "I think the worst part of this is fear—and the fear isn't going away, because he [the offender] is not going away. You can't let go" (interview #8: female, age 45).

> "At the trial, I was within maybe five minutes of killing him [the offender]. I took my shoelaces off and tied them in a knot— and my brother and I were sitting right behind him. And, my brother put his hand on my knee and said 'Don't'" (interview #12: male, age 61).

Survivors coped with the justice system in a wide variety of ways. While most chose to acquiesce as they were too upset to do more, among those who coped through involvement and activity there was a striking gender difference. Despite their fear, far more women than men pressured officials in legal institutions about their cases, sought information, and became politically involved in fighting for victims' rights. This greater involvement by women mirrors their vastly disproportional representation in self-help and "victims'" organizations: "I have found that it's the mothers that seem to fight. It's amazing!" (interview #16: female, age 56).

Many more women wrote letters, for example, to explain their situation or to get things off their chests. Other women became intensely involved with the police and other justice officials. Consider this woman's comments regarding her involvement relative to that of her husband:

> "I was doing all the fighting. I was fighting with the police. I was going to the press, I was doing it all—and it's not in my nature to do that. It's very much in his nature—and he's going behind trying to patch up the remarks I'm making, you know 'Get into your act here Crown prosecutor! You're representing my daughter. Get your act together!' And probation officers, he's going out apologizing for me being nasty to her, because she was nasty to me and didn't want to see me. Like, the whole thing was just

totally different from what I was expecting and counting on. It really surprised me" (interview #16: female, age 56).

Indeed, these new behaviours might be construed to reflect a changing self-concept among those who engaged in them: from passive "victims" to active "crusaders." One even claimed to "hate the word victim" (interview #17: female, age 50). For example, women more typically lobbied politicians (interview #23: female, age 46). Similarly, twice as many women sought legal help to help "get answers" (interview #22: female, age 46). Indeed, some women used the threat of litigation to great effect:

> "I said to [the prosecutor], 'Well, you know what, if he gets bail, I'm going to sue you.' I said 'If he comes one inch near me, I'm going to sue you, and I'm going to sue this damn city for allowing it.' He says 'You can't do that!' I said 'Oh yeah, watch me!'" (interview #22: female, age 46).

It is instructive to note that bail was later denied in this case.

Ultimately, it is clear that many more women than men focused their lives and even their identities around applying pressure to legal institutions. Men, on the other hand, seemed frequently less involved with such political activism, although they attended legal proceedings only slightly less frequently than women. Sometimes this reflected the male "provider" role: "You know, in our case I started probably doing most—but then it was a matter of dollars and cents and necessity" (interview #14: male, age 54).

Other times, men did not get involved in protests at the outset as they had faith in justice being done through the judicial system: "I think I probably coped better at that time than I did after the verdict. I mean, I still had this belief in law and order. I mean, I said 'Well, they got the guy. He's going away'" (interview #23: male, age 49).

In still other cases, however, non-involvement was due to fear of their own emotions. As noted in Chapter 3, those traditional men who fared worse, shamed by victimization and the failure to protect a loved one, often became overwhelmed with shameful feelings of guilt, which soon emerged as anger. Many such men reported being overwhelmed by anger upon encountering organized protest. Indeed, the same men tended to avoid court for the same reason:

> "The very first week [sniffs] of the trial stuff, I came. I couldn't come no more. I just couldn't. I didn't even go for the final sentencing and all that. I couldn't go. I couldn't face him any more.

I could not handle to see that guy's face in front of mine—in fear of what I would do without thinking. Because, I'll tell you, I just wanted to grab him, and rip his head off. You know?" (interview #20: male, age 37).

Such concerns were not unfounded. It was noted in the data that traditional men who did became extensively involved in police investigations, court cases, or political action coped by ruminating constantly about revenge: "I'm determined to get this guy. I'm so determined to get him that the hatred I have in me drives me to keep going" (interview #26: male, age 61).

Indeed, some men even planned ways of accomplishing this goal, corroborating the hypothesized link between shame and violence (Gilligan, 2003). Female observers corroborated this:

"You know what I'm frightened of? I'm frightened of what [my son] is thinking, what he might do eventually. Because he is a strong believer in 'an eye for an eye,' for a start, and he's a strong believer in 'You took my brother. You're not going to get away with this lightly'—and he has said it in so many words. He is very much like his dad. He is a quiet person, a quiet man. Oh my God!—He even went and got a tattoo on his chest with his brother's birth date on it, and the date of the murder, and then he's put underneath in brackets 'Yes, but you can't kill us both.' So, I'm wondering. He worries me. He really worries me. I said to him '[son's name], don't do anything that I'd be hurt about.' He says 'You leave it to me Mum. You leave it to me'" (interview #10: female, age 60).

There was thus good reason for such men to state they liked "to get away from it" (interview #30: male, age 64).

Finally, male and female survivors employed two strategies equally when coping with legal institutions. First, both relied on knowledgeable contacts to obtain information:

"They'd changed the courtrooms. But, [a local victims' organization] was on to that. Apparently, that's a trick they have. So thank heavens they were with us, because it was in a different place altogether" (interview #16: female, age 56).

"They've got a special way of keeping you out—they may make you a witness. But I was told how to get around that. A friend of mine told me what to say to the Crown attorney, and I *said it*, and, lo and behold, he took about five steps back, and ... a day or so later he came back and said 'Yeah, you are allowed to go in, but your testimony will be tainted, so you are going to have to make the choice.' And [laughing] I said, 'Well, as long as I've got the choice, I won't go in'" (interview #32: male, age 47).

Secondly, both men and women submitted victim impact statements:

"I put in a victim impact statement, and that was the extent to which I wanted to be involved" (interview #5: male, age 50).

"We had the chance to read our victims' impact statement—a wonderful new law given to the survivors of murdered victims" (survey #11: female, age 60).

Survivors sometimes found this helpful, usually when the sentence seemingly reflected their input (interview #5: male, age 50). Others who did not have this opportunity were upset by being "shut out" of the process. In the bitter words of one man: I wanted to make a victim impact statement, and the judge replied: 'I am not here to concern myself with those left behind to grieve. I must deal with the quality of the crime'" (survey #22: male, age 65).

Summing up, while most did not take an active stance with legal institutions, those who did coped differently by gender. Women more typically became involved in pressuring legal institutions through various means, living their lives around their case, and either using the victim role as a sword or recasting their identities as crusaders. Men were not as likely to become involved in these ways, nor to make these identity transformations, largely due to the provider role, faith in justice, or fear of losing control of their emotions. However, both found well-placed contacts in the system helpful, as did some who submitted victim impact statements.

CONCLUSION

In this chapter I have highlighted the significant impact of the criminal justice system in constructing victims' experiences. After reviewing the traditional legal position of the victim—as a witness rather than a party—I traced the powerless position of the victim during the sequence of a criminal trial, noting how at each stage of the process victims face clear and wrenching problems. All of this may be traced to the guiding principle of our justice system—the "legal fiction" that criminal law is a matter between the accused and the state. Ironically, such "fictions" relegate victims to a precarious reality.

I further corroborated this through two studies. First, data from my study of victim support groups revealed many difficulties in clients' dealings with legal institutions. Their encounters with the criminal justice system were perceived as overwhelmingly negative, with most claiming that court procedures and outcomes either exacerbated or initiated their sense of victim identity. Indeed, of those claiming that such encounters either had limited or mixed impact, many did not have extensive contact with the system either by choice or circumstance. Support workers agreed with such claims, asserting that clients frequently—but not inevitably—develop a predominantly victim-centred identity through the justice system. It is telling, however, that no clients or support staff in the sample unequivocally claimed that the criminal justice system mitigates one's sense of victimhood. While this is not really surprising given past literature and research in this regard (Kirchoff, Kosovski, & Schneider, 1994; Maguire & Corbett, 1987), it nonetheless calls for research on the development of better policies to redress this problem.

Secondly, in most cases homicide survivors who had few or no dealings with legal institutions claimed to fare better, and were reportedly able to move on with their grief. This was in contrast to those who had extensive involvement. Essentially, those without extensive dealings with legal institutions were freed to concentrate on grieving; those with much involvement claimed re-victimization in their interactions with the procedures, and particularly with the evidence graphically shown in hearings. Such interactions were seen as merely damaging their selves again and again, inhibiting their ability to grieve and, ultimately, to cope. Moreover, involvement or non-involvement with the legal system was not the sole dimension to consider. The data revealed that the various types of encounters experienced, plus survivors' sense of justice being done, also mediated their experiences and gendered coping abilities.

In the next chapter, I move on to consider one notable response to the issues discussed here: the emergence of the Canadian victims' movement.

ENDNOTES

1. Utilitarian reformers such as Cesare Beccaria and Jeremy Bentham strongly emphasized rational punishment and felt that active victim involvement would add an "irrational" element to the criminal justice process. Their ideas influenced the establishment of the first Director of Public Prosecutions in England, further restricting the victim's role.

2. This contrasts with the role of victims in countries with differing legal traditions. In France, for example, as well as in some other "civil law" countries,

the victim may, at his or her option, join a civil proceeding to a criminal proceeding. These proceedings are then conducted together in criminal court. Victims are given access to legal aid and legal representation, and are able to be a part of the process at bail and during the trial, sentencing, and, more recently, parole (Glendon, Gordon, & Osakwe, 1982; Joutsen, 1987).

3. The introduction of "victim impact statements" has modified this somewhat (see Chapter 6).

4. While a prosecution may be revived if new evidence appears, this is rare and is usually only done by direct indictment with the approval of senior provincial justice officials (Goff, 2004).

5. See the methodological discussion in Chapter 1 for details.

6. This breaks down further to include 15 of 24 clients of provincial victim services, seven of 12 clients from the impaired driving organization, and six of 10 clients from women's shelters/outreach services.

7. The more protracted a client's involvement with the justice system, the worse encounters were rated. While most found the police to be fairly helpful, opinions on prosecutors were split. It seemed that clients' experiences depended on their being assigned a prosecutor who would meet with them and keep them informed. Many were not. Finally, clients dealing with corrections and parole officials found these people to be extremely negative and focused on offenders' needs.

8. While victims in many jurisdictions have recently been allowed to submit "victim impact statements," the data show that these are not always suggested, that prosecutors do not always wish to submit one, that what can be said is narrowly constricted, that the defence counsel may cross-examine victims on these statements, and that their impact on the sentence is questionable.

9. This breaks down further to include four of 24 clients of provincial victim services, two of 12 clients from the impaired driving organization, and two of 10 clients from women's shelters/outreach services.

10. This breaks down further to include four of 24 clients of provincial victim services, two of 12 clients from the impaired driving organization, and two of 10 clients from women's shelters/outreach services.

11. This breaks down further to include one of 24 clients of provincial victim services, none from the impaired driving organization, and one of 10 clients from women's shelters/outreach services.

12. The impaired driving organization was the exception, with 72.7% suggesting that the justice system simply exacerbates clients' victim identity. This may be explained by the fact that support workers in this self-help organization are largely drawn from the ranks of victims, who, as noted above, overwhelmingly endorse the view that the justice system re-victimizes victims.

REFERENCES

Amernic, J. (1984). *Victims: The Orphans of Justice.* Toronto: McClelland & Stewart-Bantam Ltd.

Bard, M., & Sangrey, D. (1986). *The Crime Victim's Book.* New York: Brunner/Mazel.

Canadian Centre for Justice Statistics. (1999). *The Juristat Reader.* Toronto: Thompson.

Canadian Federal-Provincial Task Force. (1983). *Canadian Federal-Provincial Task Force Report: Justice for Victims of Crime.* Ottawa: Minister of Supply and Services.

Canadian Urban Victimization Survey. (1982). Ottawa: Minister of Supply and Services.

Clarke, P. (1986). Is there a place for the victim in the prosecution process? *Canadian Criminology Forum 8*(1), 31–44.

Correctional Services Canada. (n.d.). *Victim services at CSC.* Retrieved January 25, 2008, from http://www.csc-scc.gc.ca/victims-victimes

Corrections and Conditional Release Act, SC 1992, c. 20.

Criminal Code, RSC 1985, c. C-46.

Davis, R. C., Kunreuther, F., & Connick, E. (1984). Expanding the victim's role in the criminal court dispositional process: The results of an experiment. *The Journal of Criminal Law and Criminology 75*(2), 491–505.

Dickson, B. (1984). The forgotten party—the victim of crime. *UBC Law Review 18*, 319–334.

Gilligan, J. (2003). Shame, guilt, and violence. *Social Research 70*(4), 1149–1180.

Glendon, M. A., Gordon, M. W., & Osakwe, C. (1982). *Comparative Legal Traditions.* St. Paul, MN: West Publishing.

Goff, C. (2004). *Criminal Justice in Canada* (3rd ed.). Toronto: Thompson-Nelson.

Grossman, M., & Kane, C. (2004). Victims of crime and the Canadian justice system. In J. Roberts & M. Grossman (Eds.), *Criminal Justice in Canada* (pp. 106–119). Toronto: Thompson-Nelson.

Hagan, J. (1985). *Victims Before the Law: The Organizational Domination of Criminal Law.* Toronto: Butterworths.

Holstein, J. A., & Miller, G. (1990). Rethinking victimization: An interaction approach to victimology. *Symbolic Interaction 13*(1), 103–122.

Joutsen, M. (1987). Listening to the victim: The victim's role in European criminal justice systems. *Wayne Law Review 34*, 95–124.

Karmen, A. (2001). *Crime Victims: An Introduction to Victimology.* Belmont, CA: Wadsworth.

Kenney, J. S. (1995). Legal institutions and victims of crime in Canada: An historical and contemporary review. *Humanity and Society 19*(2), 53–67.

Kenney, J. S. (1998). *Coping with Grief: Survivors of Murder Victims*. Unpublished doctoral thesis, McMaster University, Hamilton, ON.

Kenney, J. S. (1999). *Unintended Consequences: The Interactional Dynamics of Victim Service and Support Programs*. Unpublished post-doctoral research, Dalhousie University, Halifax, N. S.

Kirchoff, G. F., Kosovski, E., & Schneider, H. J. (Eds.). (1994). *International Debates of Victimology*. Moenchengladbach, Germany: WSVN.

Klass, D. (1988). *Parental Grief: Solace and Resolution*. New York: Springer.

Loseke, D. R. (1993). Constructing conditions, people, morality, and emotion: Expanding the agenda of constructionism. In G. Miller & J. A. Holstein (Eds.), *Constructionist Controversies: Issues in Social Problems Theory* (pp. 207–216). New York: Aldine.

Maguire, M., & Corbett, C. (1987). *The Effects of Crime and the Work of Victim Support Services*. Gower: Aldershot.

Ministry of the Solicitor General. (1981a). *Mandatory Supervision—A Discussion Paper*. Ottawa: Minister of Supply and Services.

Ministry of the Solicitor General. (1981b). *Solicitor General's Study of Conditional Release*. Ottawa: Minister of Supply and Services.

Nathanson, D. (1994). *Shame and Pride: Affect, Sex, and the Birth of the Self*. New York: W. W. Norton.

Provincial Secretariat for Justice. (1984). *Ontario Government Consultation on Victims of Violent Crime Report*. Toronto: Provincial Secretariat for Justice.

R. v. Henein. (1980). 53 CCC (2d) 257 (Ont. CA).

R. v. Zelenski. (1978). 86 DLR (3d) 179 (SCC).

Re Regina and Antler. (1982). 69 CCC (2d) 480 [29 CR (3d) 283] (BCCA).

Rubel, H. C. (1986). Victim participation in sentencing proceedings. *Criminal Law Quarterly 28*, 226–250.

Sacco, V. F., & Johnson, H. (1990). *Patterns of Criminal Victimization in Canada*. Ottawa: Minister of Supply and Services.

Scheff, T., & Retzinger, S. (2000). Shame as the master emotion of everyday life. *Journal of Mundane Behaviour 1*(3), 303–324.

Schneider, J. (1985). Social problems theory: The constructionist view. *Annual Review of Sociology 11*, 209–229.

Sebba, L. (1992). The victim's role in the penal process: A theoretical orientation. In E. A. Fattah (Ed.), *Towards a Critical Victimology* (pp. 195–221). New York: St. Martin's.

Smith, D. A., & Klein, J. R. (1984). Police control of interpersonal disputes. *Social Problems 31*(4), 468–481.

Stangret, L. (1991). The rights of victims. *Policy Options Politiques 12*(2), 19–23.

Victims: Questions and Answers on Parole. (1989). Ottawa: Minister of Supply and Services.

Walker, W. (1994, April 14). Victims of crime ignored: Report. *Toronto Star*, p. A1.

Waller, I. (1985). Victims v. Regina v. Wrongdoer: Justice? *Canadian Community Law Journal* 8:1–20.

Waller, I. (1990). Victims, safer communities, and sentencing. *Canadian Journal of Criminology 32*, 461–469.

CHAPTER 5

Emotion and the Rise of the Victims' Rights Movement

(with Karen Stanbridge)

INTRODUCTION

Between 1979 and 1984, 28 victim-advocate groups, consisting of 150 branches, were formed across Canada, claiming 250,000–400,000 members (English 1984). Like their American counterparts, organizations such as Victims of Violence and Citizens United for Safety and Justice were largely composed of white, middle-class, middle-aged, well-educated individuals who had experienced the loss of a loved one to violent crime (Kenney, 1998; Weed, 1995). They shared the broad goals of mutual social support, the need to change public attitudes toward the role of victims in the criminal justice system, the desire to obtain services or resources from different levels of government, and (among the most politic) the urgent sense that the justice system needed to be changed to better reflect the interests of crime victims (Kenney, 1998). During this period their representatives began to appear in the media, at court, and at political proceedings to rally public support and lobby government for system change.

As the public visibility and legitimacy of these groups increased, limited procedural and substantive changes were introduced to the *Criminal Code*, parole, and other criminal procedures. The Canadian Federal-Provincial Task Force on Justice for Victims of Crime (1983; hereinafter, the Task Force) made recommendations that partially met victims' concerns. Demands for the abolition of mandatory supervision (automatic release of offenders at the two-thirds point of their sentence) increased in parliament, and the National Parole Board instituted its controversial procedure of "gating"—re-arresting suspected dangerous offenders who were about to be so released. While gating was declared illegal in 1983, it was formalized in a rewriting of the *Parole Act* three years later. In 1987, a motion to introduce capital punishment was seriously debated in parliament, culminating in a free vote. While the motion was defeated 148–127, it received considerable support. In 1989, parliament passed Bill C-89, amending the *Criminal Code* in line with many of the Task Force recommendations. This allowed victim impact statements, *in camera* hearings, improved restitution and return of property, a ban on the identity of witnesses, and a "victim fine surcharge" on fines to help pay for victim services. Also debated were escapes from halfway houses, the Montreal massacre (culminating in proposed changes to gun laws), and bail reform.

"Victims' rights" emerged as a potent issue in 1980s Canada, thanks in part to the efforts of crime victims to raise public awareness of their grievances and cast solutions in terms of policy and system change. Existing explanations of the rise of the Canadian victims' rights movement are, however, at best incomplete. This chapter addresses this via recent work on emotions in social movements theory. First, we critically review existing explanations and find that, although studies that locate the impetus for the movement in contemporary organizational, political, and cultural conditions are superior to the popular view of the movement as a spontaneous response by frustrated victims, they downplay the strong, embodied emotions—grief, anger, and injustice—that accompany victimization. We then draw upon recent theorizing on the place of emotions in social movements to "bring emotions back in" and to explore how the strong feelings associated with victimization and the victims' movement intersected with social conditions in 1980s Canada to contribute to the movement's emergence and success.

To this end, we have assessed original interviews with members and leaders of some Canadian victims' rights and victim support groups (Kenney, 1998) and contemporary media accounts of the movement. We show that the movement's dual aims—therapy and activism—required that it filter communication of "oppositional emotions" (Whittier, 2001) to maintain its organizational integrity, on one hand, and public legitimacy on the other. It had to preserve space for its (victim) members to display their embodied emotions in an unrestricted manner, while carrying the burden of screening what it thought was emotionally viable behaviour to exhibit to the press and public in light of then current, situated "feeling rules."

Emotions were also central to the movement's efforts to transform hitherto passive responses to victimization into anger and active demands for system change, serving as more than merely a strategy, but the very ground upon which activism was constructed and contested. While true that contemporary organizational, political, and cultural conditions facilitated these efforts (as context-specific explanations have confirmed), they were also linked to emotions in ways that personalized the emotional experience of victims of crime for non-victims, enhancing public sympathies. The media played a crucial if unintended role, providing a ready channel through which the anguish, impotence, and injustice felt by victims could be expressed and displayed by groups' members and leaders and communicated to a wider audience.

This chapter thus explores some of the "emotion work" (Hochschild, 1983) performed by the Canadian victims' rights movement in concert with mobilizing resources, seizing and creating political opportunities, and framing grievances. It supplements context-specific explanations of the emergence of the movement by highlighting the role that the representational articulation and construction of emotional mutuality played in its success. Our findings underscore the complexity of this role, and the importance of continuing to explore the place of emotions in social movements generally.

NEGLECTED VICTIMS

What was behind the rise of activism among Canadian victims of crime in the early 1980s? Contemporary media reports suggest that activism developed in response to the neglect of victims' needs and concerns in the Canadian *Criminal Code*. An article in the *Globe and Mail* in April 1984 is typical. Reporter Victor Malarek highlighted the impotence of victims and linked it to the emergence of the movement. He described victims as "[standing] in the shadows of the justice system—bitter, disillusioned, frustrated, angry and confused." Victims, he said, are "shunted to the sidelines" and treated "as an embarrassment or nuisance." In contrast, he said, the justice system "caters to the criminal." Victims of crime "watch as the offender—the accused who broke into their home, raped, murdered—[becomes] the focus of attention ... while they [are] simply sent home." However, he continued, victims and their families are "not about to let the system defeat [them]." They have decided "to fight back" by forming victims' advocacy groups (Malarek, 1984a).

Malarek's account portrays the movement as a natural outcome of the frustrations of "neglected victims" of crime. While a media report, it is consistent with traditional "relative deprivation" approaches that portray activism as the rational expression of participants' frustration or hostility toward an "enemy" identified as the source of their deprivation (Gusfield, 1963; Searles & Williams, 1962). Despite intuitive appeal, as with relative deprivation theory the neglected victims approach says nothing about what Goodwin, Jasper, and Polletta (2000) called "the actual stuff of contentious politics" (p. 69) needed to initiate, build, and sustain an effective social movement, such as the creation and maintenance of social networks, processes of mobilization, and the resources required for collective action. Nor does it explain the timing of this movement's appearance or its public and political appeal.

POLITICAL OPPORTUNITIES, MOBILIZING RESOURCES, AND RESONANT FRAMES

Others have sought to address these issues. The Task Force (1983) claimed that the Canadian victims' movement was fostered by four factors: advances made by women's groups to change perceptions and institutions surrounding victims of violence; a public belief that crime was increasing and "something should be done"; the promotion of the issue by individuals holding a financial and emotional stake in the delivery of victim/witness assistance programs; and the opinions of some criminal justice officials that the system would benefit from the inclusion of victims' voices. Such factors are consistent with Clarke's (1986) observations on the rise of the movement. Clarke added that the "law and order" program[1] of that period contributed to the appeal of the victims' rights message, framing the criminal justice system as "soft on criminals."

It is true that, by 1980, Canadians had witnessed a gradual but marked reduction in the severity of sentencing, reflecting a move from the retributive, punitive aspect of sentences to a more rehabilitative stance. There was also a trend toward more liberal laws governing conditional release. In addition, traditional legal alternatives for victims, such as private lawsuits in the civil courts, were effectively failing.[2] Criminal injuries compensation tribunals exhibited problems including lengthy bureaucratic delays, lack of public awareness, and at times vigorous investigation of claimants (Dickson, 1984; Elias, 1983; Fattah, 2000; Task Force, 1983; Weed, 1995). All these issues fostered a widespread belief that "authorities cannot be trusted," another factor that Clarke (1986) noted as contributing to the victims' rights movement. Clarke located the origins of distrust in the 1960s, but these and more recent developments heightened public uncertainty surrounding the ability and desire of traditional authorities to safeguard the interests of (law-abiding) citizens.[3]

Finally, Rock (1988) considered organizational factors, arguing that the movement was conceived not by victims but by staff who were originally hired by the federal government to create a survey measuring the effects of crime-prevention programs. As the staff members learned more about victims' assistance programs in other countries, they "began to consider themselves experts on victims ... and ... turned more and more toward promoting their own initiative" (p. 130).

These rationales are broadly consistent with leading approaches in social movements theory, including resource mobilization and mobilizing structures theories (McCarthy & Zald, 1973, 1977; Tilly, 1978; Tilly, Tilly, & Tilly,

1975), political opportunity structure or political process theory (PPT) models (McAdam, 1982; Tarrow, 1994; Tilly, 1978), and approaches that stress the influence of cultural factors on social movement emergence and activities, especially framing theory (Snow & Benford, 1988, 1992; Snow et al., 1986). The Task Force (1983) noted that the support of "insiders" facilitated the movement's success, consistent with the resource mobilization approach; inroads forged by the women's movement advocating on behalf of abused women provided structural opportunities for these victims of crime to seek redress, opening up the political "space" that concerns proponents of PPT. Rock's (1988) depiction of the victims' rights movement as an unintended consequence of a state action is also consistent with the PPT model. Furthermore, like the literature on framing, these explanations look to the ideas, meanings, and symbols "out there" in the cultural milieu to help account for the rise of the movement. The movement's message achieved "cultural resonance" by drawing upon the prevailing perception that crime was increasing and the public's general distrust of traditional authorities, which helped to "bring home" the message to potential recruits and outsiders.

Just as the resource mobilization, PPT, and cultural/framing approaches arose to address deficiencies in relative deprivation theory, these explanations correct some of the difficulties of the "neglected victims" explanation and help to address the question "why now?" By encouraging exploration of the political and cultural contexts within which the movement emerged, these explanations are better able to account for the *timed* appearance of the movement. They highlight that the early 1980s saw the coming together of a number of social experiences in Canada, which helped to galvanize and politicize victims of crime who had until then suffered injustice as a largely personal experience. They also suggest how and why the group's message may have struck a chord with the public at the time.

WHAT HAPPENED TO EMOTIONS?
Given the passions inherent in victims' rights, these explanations seem strangely unaffected. In seeking to refine accounts of the movement as the direct outcome of victims' frustration with the justice system, they downplay the role of strong feelings in the constitution and development of the movement and the public's response. The bitterness, neglect, and injustice felt by the victims portrayed in Malarek's story have largely disappeared, replaced by detached descriptions of structural precedent, opportunity, and rational calculations of equity. We need to address the place of emotions in the Canadian victims' rights movement, its emergence, and limited successes. How to do this without running into the problems of traditional approaches that focus on feelings, however, is a challenge faced by students of social movements.

EMOTIONS AND SOCIAL MOVEMENTS

The emotions that once served as the foundation for analyses of collective behaviour experienced a decline in importance in social movements theorizing in the 1960s. In the last decade, however, growing dissatisfaction with the "detached" nature of the theories dominating the field since has led to a resurgence of interest in the role of emotions in collective action. Wary of the pitfalls of privileging feelings over other factors as catalysts for collective behaviour, however, theorists have sought to bridge the gap between relative deprivation theory's *inflation* of feelings as the sole basis for collective action and more recent approaches' *devaluation* of feelings as incidental outcomes of other cultural and structural factors. To do this, theorists have explored how emotions mediate communications and interpretations of social movement activities and claims.

Social movement researchers have drawn upon the sociology of emotion, a field that rejects traditional notions of emotions as essential or fixed, instead approaching them as socially constructed and mediated by historical and cultural conditions. Hochschild (1983, 1990) disputed emotion theories that assume that emotions are the same across cultural contexts, or that broadly similar social factors "trigger" the same sorts of biological reactions. She also challenged perspectives in which feeling is constituted entirely by social influences. Superior, she said, are interactionist perspectives that assign significance to cultural factors but still include biological factors as socially shaped "ingredients" in the emotion process. Of particular relevance is her idea of the "signal function"—that emotion operates like a sense, communicating information to the self about "what is out there from where I stand" (Hochschild, 1990, p. 119).

Among social movements researchers, such an approach has helped to bridge the gap between relative deprivation theory's inflation of feelings as the sole basis of collective action and more recent approaches' devaluation of feelings as incidental outcomes of other cultural and structural factors by regarding emotion and culture as concurrent. Thus, Aminzade and McAdam (2001) included emotions in the cultural "repertoires" of symbols that movement leaders use to frame their claims to members and the public. Just as movement leaders manipulate symbols and meanings to generate *cultural* resonance around their cause, they also exploit the norms surrounding emotions to generate *emotional* resonance.

This approach to emotions as "one more" of many cultural variables that leaders must manage and mobilize on a movement's behalf—the coexistence of emotion and culture—has been supplemented by studies that have elaborated upon the intersection of emotion and culture (Goodwin et al., 2000, 2001). Thus, Robnett (2004) noted that emotional resonance is specific to social location, varying with gender, class, and ethnicity. Schrock, Holden, and Reid (2004) demonstrated that it varies with the extent to which the frames of movement of the collective action align or disagree with the emotional location, or emotional lives, of the intended recipients. Such studies suggest that, in order for their frames to resonate culturally *and* emotionally in the desired direction, movement leaders must consider how specific cultural repertoires interact with the varied emotions that their claims may evoke among their different audiences, members and outsiders alike.

Of special importance is work surrounding the role of emotions in victims' groups. In her study of adult victims of child abuse, Whittier (2001) showed how difficulties can arise because of the dual aims of many victims' organizations: therapy and action. Conflicts can arise in victims' movements because these often generate "oppositional emotions." Thus, attempts by groups to politically empower victims by encouraging them to shed their feelings of guilt and hopelessness can be undermined by media presentations of victims as "damaged" and pitiful. The latter may generate more public awareness of abuse victims, but succeed only in generating pity and convincing outsiders of victims' incompetence. Similarly, Dunn (2004) showed how movements must frame victims carefully to sustain membership and public feelings of sympathy. To evoke outsiders' compassion, victims must appear blameless. The need to establish victims' non-responsibility and weakness, however, conflicts with wider Western cultural norms that uphold personal responsibility and strength. Movements must find a way to bridge conflicting expectations or risk public rejection of their grievances. Trickier still is to inspire outsiders to not only pity or sympathize, but also to back members' calls for political redress. Such a task requires fostering feelings of injustice, that "hot cognition" that Gamson (1992, p. 91) said is essential to mobilization. Leaders and supporters must communicate the victim experience and arouse this righteous anger among outsiders to convince them to support systemic change.

Clearly, victims' groups must filter the embodied emotions communicated, carefully constructing the emotional field to achieve their aims. To explore how this was accomplished in the Canadian victims' rights movement, we follow Whittier and Dunn and distinguish between the emotional and cultural expectations inside the group and the expectations of outsiders or the public, examining the extent to which these coincide or diverge. Like Whittier, we explore the logistics associated in dealing with the "oppositional emotions" that are characteristic of victims' groups. Consistent with Dunn, we identify the features of the victim role that require careful communication to secure public identification and construction of sympathy. Dunn focused on blamelessness, but here we highlight the victim's *grieved response* to the tragedy as a crucial determinant of public sympathy. As Dunn's victims must negotiate the passivity implied by blamelessness with a strong cultural belief in personal responsibility, leaders of the victims' movement must navigate victims' suffering through current cultural norms surrounding grief.[4] Finally, we discuss how movement leaders and supporters succeeded in fostering feelings of injustice among the Canadian public regarding their cause.

Here we draw upon Flam (2005), who identified several key ways in which social movements use emotions to "re-socialize their (potential) members and the larger public" (p. 24): undermining passive responses to their claims and establishing "new, assertive emotions" in their stead; cultivating anger and suspicion toward the authorities that we have been socialized to obey to counter fears of retribution; and "shaming" elites into moral conduct. Success depends on the political and social context, including the presence or absence of beliefs that may "immunize against new ideologies." Thus, social movements must pick up and recast the feeling rules surrounding their issue, and so redefine the appropriate emotional response to the matters that concern them.[5] Thus, our study explores how the Canadian victims' rights movement succeeded in recasting the appropriate emotional response to victimization from private grief to public anger, and from pity to indignation and demands for political redress.

Emotions and the Inward Face of the Movement

The existing literature on victims' groups and self-help associations, together with the results of original research conducted by Kenney (1998), helps us to approach the role of emotion within the Canadian victims' rights movement of the 1980s. Research shows that personal grief is a key reason for victims of crime to join and maintain membership in victim "self-help" groups, whether focusing primarily on victim support or political activism (Kenney, 1998; Weed, 1995). Certainly the opportunity to share their grief with others who have lost a loved one to violence plays a part. As one member reported, "I found it easier to talk about [the deceased] and my experience at meetings because I was among people of similar situations and feelings" (survey #14: male, age 35). Many described the close connection that forms with other victims (Box 5.1).

Associated with this is the victim's perception that no one else is willing to listen to expressions of their grief. The victim has reached or surpassed the limit of their friends', family members', or others' sympathy and no longer feels comfortable talking (or is no longer permitted to talk) about their loss (Box 5.2).

If we consider these statements in the context of the sociology of emotion and Hochschild's work, victims' groups—self-help or activist—are composed

BOX 5.1:
CLOSE CONNECTIONS FORMING AMONG VICTIMS IN VICTIM SUPPORT GROUPS

"When you put your arms around a woman and she breaks down in tears and says 'My daughter's been murdered,' and we tell her that our son had been murdered, there's a bond there that nobody else can understand ... I've found that they felt my pain—so you cling to those people" (interview #15: female, age 49).

Source: Kenney, J. S. (1998). *Coping with Grief: Survivors of Murder Victims.* Unpublished doctoral thesis, McMaster University, Hamilton, ON.

BOX 5.2:
THE SOCIAL ISOLATION OF VICTIMS

"Close friends [don't] want to talk to you. They are afraid to mention [the deceased's] name because they think it may trigger off a big setback. Things just fester inside. There's a deep sense of aloneness, frustration, and nobody to help you" (Malarek, 1984b).

"I found my own friends wanted me to get over this" (interview #16: female, age 56).

"[Our] families won't let us talk about it 'cause they're dealing with guilt or something of their own, and won't allow us to really express ourselves" (interview #19: female, 53).

Source: Kenney, J. S. (1998). *Coping with Grief: Survivors of Murder Victims.* Unpublished doctoral thesis, McMaster University, Hamilton, ON.
Don Sullivan, quoted in Malarek, V. (1984b, April 10). Programs help crime victims deal with solitude. *The Globe and Mail,* p. M2.

of individuals who, by virtue of their having transgressed "feeling rules" surrounding grief, assume they are compelled to seek emotional support elsewhere. In their historical and spatial contexts they are "emotional deviants" (Thoits, 1990) who have gone beyond what others deem an appropriate emotional response to their situation. Indeed, such rules have been noted by researchers who are interested in social responses to people who have experienced undesirable life events. Silver and Wortman (1980) acknowledged that, in the early 1980s, North Americans who were experiencing a life crisis were often "prevented from free expression of their feelings" by people encouraging them to "be strong" (p. 314). This happened for several reasons,

BOX 5.3:
THE ABILITY TO EXPRESS ONESELF IN VICTIM GROUPS

"Victims of crime really know what you're feeling ... There's none of this pussyfooting around. You can say it as it is" (interview #16: female, age 56).

"In our group, for the first time we could cry freely, holding no tears back ... We could question, get angry, and we could wonder aloud if we could ever find meaning in life again ... There I found a place to unload my anger, fears and frustrations ... I can come here, and we can dump on each other without criticism" (CICB #87: female, age 65).

Source: Kenney, J. S. (1998). *Coping with Grief: Survivors of Murder Victims.* Unpublished doctoral thesis, McMaster University, Hamilton, ON.

including a discomfort born of observers' lack of experience with such situations. It was also affected by wider beliefs surrounding how much and how long trauma should be exhibited (Wortman & Lehman, 1983). Crime victims were especially vulnerable because of the long-term depression that often accompanies victimization (Coates & Winston, 1983). By continually revisiting their grief, victims broke current constructions of "sympathy etiquette" that mandated claiming some sympathy in appropriate circumstances, but not claiming too much (Clark, 1987). They were then either shamed into silence or spurred to find an outlet (Gilligan, 2003; Nathanson, 1994; Scheff & Retzinger, 2000).

Victims' groups provide a place where individuals can express their grief more extensively than permitted in their former social contexts (Box 5.3).

Despite this, not all victims feel that they benefit from participating in groups that place few or no bounds on how much or how long victims can grieve. This can itself trigger upset (Box 5.4).

For most activist members of victims' groups, however, the space and time to express their deep, embodied, ongoing grief and bitterness without previous restrictions is as important a component of the experience as it is to those who seek support only.

What might this mean to our understanding of the Canadian victims' rights movement? There is evidence that communication of grief was as important a factor influencing recruitment and retention of group members 25 years ago as it was 10 years ago. Victims of Violence (VoV) is a Canadian victims' rights group that was founded in Ontario in 1982 by Don Sullivan and Shirley and John Harrison, individuals who lost their daughters to

BOX 5.4:
POTENTIALLY UPSETTING ASPECTS OF VICTIM GROUPS

"It's hurtful in the fact that it makes you continue to relive, and to re-experience the feelings each time you talk to somebody who's living proof of the trauma they are dealing with. It's very debilitating, for someone who has suffered a loss, for that to be your life—you know, to be in a victims' group" (interview #13: male, age 46).

Source: Kenney, J. S. (1998). *Coping with Grief: Survivors of Murder Victims.* Unpublished doctoral thesis, McMaster University, Hamilton, ON.

murder. The first, the largest, and then most public victims' rights group in Canada, VoV garnered great media attention with their leaders' frank criticisms of government officials and demands that the Canadian legal process be changed to acknowledge the rights of victims (Amernic, 1984). However, even an activist organization such as this placed the delivery of emotional support to victims ahead of system change. At their inaugural meeting, VoV listed their primary identity as being "a self-help group to comfort, console, counsel, and cope with our personal tragedies"; their targets for change came later (Amernic, 1984, p. 106; see also pp. 173, 176–177).

In his description of a VoV meeting, Amernic wrote: "VoV's primary objective of consoling the bereaved begins at the first introduction. No matter how horrible the circumstances of the death, those who come to test the waters for the first time are immediately engulfed in a sea of empathy" (p. 173). Beyond providing support to victims over the telephone and through correspondence, leaders organized more formal counselling sessions. These were private sessions during which victims "[poured] out all the innermost feelings of hate, frustration, disgust bitterness, bewilderment, and guilt that haunt the loved ones of murder victims, the survivors," surrounded by others who had had the same experience (pp. 176–177).

The movement's focus on policy change might have served as a "new" reason for individuals to join who would otherwise not have participated in a self-help group; their public emphasis on activism over therapy may have attracted victims who were inspired by this new message or were repelled by the constant re-telling of painful memories. Even so, given the priority assigned to emotional support by VoV's leaders, and judging how important emotional freedom continued to be to the members of victims' organizations in the 1990s, freedom from then-current feeling rules restricting the expression of grief in other social contexts was an important incentive for victims to seek out and stay with the movement in the 1980s. Despite the focus of the movement and its leaders on policy change, the construction of a safe space of emotional freedom had to be maintained to attract and retain group members.

Emotions and the Outward Face of the Movement

Grief is a key emotion expressed by members of the victims' rights movement. While this may serve to bond members together, it can also disconcert and even repel outsiders in some historic, structural, and spatial contexts. This has implications for a victims' movement that seeks the support of outsiders. Clearly, according to the historic feeling rules surrounding grief noted above, it would be detrimental to the movement's aims for leaders to always publicly exhibit the intense, personal feelings of grief that are expected within the movement, at least in the longer term. Although anyone who has experienced a tragedy has the "right" to a short-term expression of such intensity of emotion, extended expression could breach the "sympathy margins" of many and risk public aversion (Clark, 1987). Thus, movement leaders have to filter the expression of "oppositional emotions" (Whittier, 2001) to effectively construct a mutual emotional ground upon which their activism can be played out and the public's response engaged.

Simultaneously, victims' rights leaders wish to mobilize public support for their cause. Under Flam's (2005) model, leaders have sought to recast existing feeling rules surrounding victimization ("suffer in silence" or, in the case of outsiders, offer comfort, sympathy, and pity) and foster an active response to the issue. This may entail cultivating anger and suspicion toward authorities among members and the public, and shaming officials into correcting a criminal justice system that the leaders perceive as unjust. This involves contextualizing their demands in the existing social and cultural milieu, anticipating and overcoming any existing ideologies to ensure their claims resonate emotionally with outsiders, and evoking in outsiders some of the injustice that victims feel at the hands of the system (Flam, 2005).

How did the Canadian victims' movement of the 1980s satisfy these complex and conflicting emotional demands to successfully manage its outward face? Here we examine two means: effective (public) leadership and a sympathetic national press. While overlapping, the former framed victimization and victims' rights to sustain the oppositional emotions needed to maintain and promote the victims' movement, while the latter helped to locate victims' rights in the social and political context of the time to ensure that their message resonated emotionally with the public.

Public Leadership[6]

The oppositional emotions needed to sustain the Canadian victims' rights movement of the 1980s—the intense and unrestrained feelings expressed inside and the more filtered expression of emotions for public display—were evident in the public actions and statements of spokespersons. Commonalities can be found in the communications of individuals such as Don Sullivan, a former police officer who co-founded VoV after his daughter Pamela was murdered in 1980; David Nairn, a Canadian Forces officer whose daughter was stabbed to death in 1983; Donna Edwards, whose son was paralyzed in a shooting at a variety store in the early 1980s; and Leslie Crisp, whose daughter's fiancé was murdered. In media reports, they presented and recounted their own and other victims' grief in ways that retained the emotional intensity characterizing the experience—and hence appealed to group members and other victims—yet in a manner gauged to be more palatable for the consumption of a diverse public. By expressing their emotions in a restrained and rational manner, rather than in an abandoned one, and by emphasizing that their purpose is to fight for justice for all victims, not to seek vengeance for personal wrongs, these public representatives of the victims' movement enabled the mutual construction of an engaging view of the emotional turmoil experienced by victims of crime for various outsiders, without making them feel too uncomfortable.

Sullivan's emotionality is clear in his public statements and in media accounts. Thus in his foreword to Jerry Amernic's book, *Victims: Orphans of Justice* (1984), he wrote of the "painful memories" he worried would be stirred up if he and his wife agreed to cooperate with Amernic on the book (Sullivan, 1984, p. x). His emotionality is also present when he describes how his wife "gave him strength when [he] faltered" (p. xii) during the arduous criminal proceedings against his daughter's murderer. Sullivan's anguish and anger are evident throughout, from the moment the reality of his daughter's murder hit him and he "broke down and wept" (Amernic, 1984, p. 11), through the nights when he would sit in his daughter's room and cry while he rocked in her rocking chair. We see him running from the courtroom in tears after catching a glimpse of photographs taken of his daughter at the murder scene, and how he went home and cried after the first day of the trial.

In a feature on victims' rights in the *Globe and Mail*, Sullivan described the days following his daughter's death when "just coping with day-to-day life at times seemed unbearable" (Malarek, 1984b). Other articles described how David Nairn, too, "broke down" relating his experiences in front of the assembly of police chiefs he was addressing ("Victims of crime face injustices," 1985), and how Donna Edwards "fought back tears" when describing her ordeal to a Toronto conference for victims of crime (Fagan, 1984). In all cases, however, the victim's anguish was understated and controlled, displayed openly for only short periods to facilitate the construction of an emotional ground of engagement. Thus Amernic (1984) quoted family members describing

> ## BOX 5.5:
> ## PUBLICLY DEFINED MOTIVATIONS OF VICTIM ACTIVISTS
>
> Public accounts present advocates as inspired not by vengeance or personal gain, but for system change to help ensure that others would not have to endure the same experiences. Thus, David Nairn's motivation "is not revenge but stems from a more practical concern": improving the administration of sentencing to prevent criminals from being released too early and risking further victimization ("Victims of crime face injustices," 1985).
>
> Similarly, Don Sullivan (1984) wrote: "If one victim can draw strength from this nightmarish experience that I and mine have gone through, then I will have been vindicated in agreeing to this book."
>
> In another interview (Malarek, 1984a), Sullivan said: "I ... never want to take one single right away from anyone, even someone who committed ... [a] heinous crime. All I would like is that every victim have the same rights in law."
>
> **Sources:** Malarek, V. (1984a, April 9). Crime victims' search for justice: From arrest to parole, accused benefits from safeguards. *The Globe and Mail*, p. M3.
> Sullivan, D. (1984). Foreword. In J. Amernic, *Victims: The Orphans of Justice* (pp. ix–xiii). Toronto: McClelland & Stewart-Bantam Ltd.: pp. xi, ix–x.
> Victims of crime face injustices, police chiefs told. (1985, July 4). *The Globe and Mail*, p. 10.

Sullivan as the "strong one" in the weeks following his daughter's murder, a sensitive man compelled by love and responsibility to swallow his grief for the sake of those close to him. Tears over his loss were checked, anger toward the murderer suppressed, and his embodied anguish directed toward "working with the system": writing letters, seeking help from sympathetic politicians and media people, and building a grassroots movement to press for change (*passim*). Similarly, Nairn and Edwards composed themselves and continued speaking to their respective audiences and the press. We thus catch glimpses of their intense emotional response to their experiences—enough for other victims to identify with them and to arouse the compassion of outsiders—but expressed appropriately, constructed in a restrained manner and through the proper channels, following their sense of outsider sympathy etiquette.

In these same accounts, spokespersons' activism is presented as inspired not by vengeance or the promise of personal gain, but as an opportunity to lobby for system change to help ensure that others would not have to endure the same experiences (Box 5.5).

Indeed, Sullivan reportedly turned down an invitation to run for political office, feeling he could better accomplish his aims from a position of political neutrality (Amernic, 1984).

Sullivan and Nairn's legitimacy was bolstered by their status as "public servants" committed to the general good. Sullivan was a former police officer,

Nairn a Canadian Forces officer, positions that command prestige and respect. Accounts of Sullivan repeatedly referenced his former profession, in addition to his time in the Navy and as a fire fighter (Amernic, 1984; Malarek, 1984a); Nairn was consistently referred to as "Lieutenant-Commander Nairn" or "Cmdr. Nairn" ("Victims of crime face injustices," 1985). Furthermore, Nairn and Sullivan are both male, an anomaly in the world of victims' and self-help groups, which are dominated by white, middle-class women. Amernic's portrayal of Sullivan as the "rock" supporting the devastated women in his family (and later in VoV) evokes the cultured construction of the traditional strong and dispassionate male protector of more fragile females. This, in 1980s Canada, represented the gendered embodiment of a viable, indeed engaging form of emotional expression rendering this leader's claims both more dramatic, yet more reasonable. Indeed, Amernic draws this contrast several times. Compared to another founding member of VoV, Shirley Harrison, Sullivan was clearly more controlled: "While she was very emotional and obvious with her grief, in public and in private, he showed a public face that was somewhat more calm and collected" (Amernic, 1984, p. 91).[7]

It is hard to determine the extent to which the embodied emotion displayed by Sullivan and other spokespeople was unconscious or orchestrated, although Amernic (1984) admitted that Sullivan was "anything but naïve": "He knew about giving the media enough hard facts and human emotion to further dramatize his story and play it up for all it was worth" (p. 127). Regardless, he and his counterparts succeeded in publicly articulating the strong emotions associated with the victim role in ways compatible with historic, situational feeling rules to maintain the oppositional emotions required of the victims' movement. Their grief was clearly profound, but unobtrusive; it did not embarrass or repulse, but engaged many in a oneness, constructing a common emotional arena. Their anger was intense, but was directed toward appropriate ends—the mutuality of the greater good. Revealing some of the depth of their anguish, while contributing to and respecting the bounds of situational and societal norms surrounding such emotions, movement leaders "walked the line" between grief-stricken victim and courageous (and hence emotionally discreet) survivor of violence. This fostered public sympathy toward victims of violent crime and reduced the likelihood of audiences rejecting their claims.

A Sympathetic Media

Movement leaders were adept at framing victims' claims in ways that generated emotional resonance among fellow victims and the public. But the media provided them a ready platform from which to communicate their grievances, and presented those grievances in the context of related events and discourses.

This result was by no means inevitable. The media is central to modern mobilization efforts, but because those in the industry have their own agendas, they cannot be relied upon to frame issues in the way a movement may wish (Gamson, 1992; Walgrave & Manssens, 2005). In the case of the early Canadian victims' rights movement, however, victims' claims coincided with several factors that rendered support of victims' rights in the media's interest. Indeed, circumstances satisfied many of the conditions that Walgrave and Manssens (2005, pp. 135–136) identified as favourable to media mobilization: "victims' rights" was a fairly simple issue, making it easy to report in full detail; it was an issue presenting the forces of "good and evil" clearly, encouraging emotional consensus; it pitted "the people" against elites (and hence allowed the media to "cash in" on public discontent); it allowed the media to present itself as a sensitive defender of a consensus issue; and it coincided with a "disturbed time" in Canadian society (characterized, as Clarke [1986] and the Task Force [1983] noted, by a general distrust of the authorities and the perception that crime was increasing).

Considering these conditions, and using Flam's (2005) model as a guide, we can observe how the media helped those in the victims' rights movement to communicate their efforts to recast historic feeling rules surrounding victimization to outsiders, and to locate their messages in wider social and political conditions to foster the feelings of injustice needed to mobilize the public. To "re-socialize" an audience emotionally, Flam (2005) said that social movements must (1) establish an assertive (rather than a passive) emotional response to their cause, and (2) cultivate anger and suspicion toward authorities to shame them into acting. A movement's success depends on contextualizing the re-socialization process in the prevailing social and political climates. These practices are woven together in media accounts surrounding the Canadian victims' rights movement.

The media was especially adept at placing and keeping the victims' rights message in the context of the more widespread public fear of crime that Clarke and the Task Force noted in 1980s Canada, and the public's distrust of authorities. Media reports of the movement commonly underscored the "ordinariness" of victims of violent crime, thereby enhancing identification, a sense of oneness, and the notion among readers that anyone could become a victim. David Nairn's daughter was described as a typical Grade 12 honours student, murdered not by an unknown assailant, but by the son of a former neighbour ("Victims of crime face injustices," 1985). Donna Edwards's son just happened to find himself in a variety store robbery when he was shot (Fagan, 1984). And of Sullivan, Amernic (1984) wrote: "There will surely be more Don and Pat Sullivans in Canada, more men and women who blink for a moment and open their eyes to find a child murdered. It could happen on the way to the grocery store. It could happen on a holiday. It could happen walking home from work" (p. 265).

Such looming tragedy was invariably linked to system deficiencies and uncaring or incompetent officials who were more concerned with protecting themselves and criminals than the victim. "Justice is just a money-making academic exercise," David Nairn was quoted as saying in the *Globe and Mail* ("Victims of crime face injustices," 1985). "Our prison system is like a sieve," he added, contrasting the attention paid to his daughter's murderer—"There were no legal aid lawyers flitting around us"—with the disregard paid to his family by officials who failed to inform Nairn of the offender's release. Donna Edwards described how the two men who shot her son, "laughed as [he] was wheeled into court," but could "be walking the streets next year due to a loose parole system" (Fagan, 1984). And in the series of articles by Malarek, the neglect experienced by victims is that of the Everyman relative to criminals. "I can't find anything in the *Charter of Rights* that guarantees any rights to the victim," Sullivan is quoted as saying. "Yet I can find all kinds of rights guaranteed to anyone that's accused of anything under the sun" (Malarek, 1984a). Throughout the series runs the theme of officials inhibiting changes from occurring: the police fail to instruct victims about possible compensation (Malarek, 1984b); defence lawyers protest attempts at introducing victim impact statements (Malarek, 1984c). They react in this way, Sullivan commented, because, in contrast to victims' fear and grief associated with their real loss, lawyers fear losing power over the process. "What defense lawyers are afraid of is that during the trial process, for every mother of a murderer who gets up and cries about Johnny, the mother of a murdered girl will get up and cry about her daughter. This is what they're scared of" (Malarek, 1984c).

These themes are elaborated in *Victims: The Orphans of Justice*, in which Amernic (1984) details the discourtesies and disregard that Sullivan and his family suffered at the hands of the police, criminal justice officials, and politicians after his daughter's murder. Sullivan's experiences revealed to him a defective process and "shattered" his trust in the justice system. "At first I was under the impression that we had elected people and appointed officials in Ottawa who were looking out for our rights, our well-being, and our safety. Well, how bloody naïve I was" (quoted in Amernic, 1984, pp. 47–48). Innocent people are doubly victimized, Sullivan said, "not just by criminals, but by the criminal justice system ... those very people whom we elected to look out for our rights, safety, and well-being" (Sullivan, 1984, pp. x–xi). Sullivan emerges in *Victims* as the principled voice of "the people" against injustices that are prolonged by officials concerned with maintaining a process from which they benefit: "He was no speech maker" and poorly educated compared to "senior civil servants and elected politicians, never mind silver-tongued lawyers and other professionals who had a stake in the system, and who weren't about to let the ordinary father of a murder victim upset their lives. But at least he felt that right was on his side" (Amernic, 1984, p. 56).

A sympathetic media focused on cultivating fear of victimization and anger toward officials, helped "re-socialize" Canadians toward a more active response to victims' claims, and spurred officials to act in the face of reported humiliations and perceived outrages. The media focus helped to frame victims' rights in the context of the prevailing fear of crime and suspicions surrounding authorities, while the ordinariness and emotional resonance fostered by movement leaders greased the wheels.

DISCUSSION

The Canadian victims' rights movement of the early 1980s owes its emergence partly to conditions surrounding contemporary institutions (such as the degree of "openness" of the political and criminal justice systems to victims' claims) and broader cultural beliefs (such as "something should be done about crime" and "authorities cannot be trusted"). As shown, the capacity of the movement to effectively articulate the strong emotions associated with victimization was also a crucial factor shaping the movement's constitution and development.

To preserve the support function of the group that attracted most of its members, the movement had to provide a space for relatively unrestricted displays of personal grief. Movement leaders who were seeking public sympathy to the plight of victims, however, had to filter their expressions of emotion so as to not surpass the historic, situated "sympathy margins" of outsiders. Furthermore, the movement sought to mobilize the public in support of their claims; it wished to transform typically passive responses to victimization to more active ones. Leaders, with the crucial assistance of the media, did this by fostering some of the emotions associated with the victim experience in outsiders: the fear associated with being victimized, the grief that accompanies losing a loved one to criminal violence, the humiliation stemming from their mistreatment by the system, and the anger derived from being dealt with unjustly. Simultaneously, leaders partially extended their embodied emotions into a mutually constructed emotional field with the audience, fostering a sense of oneness and engagement and further extending the margins of sympathy. Clearly, much emotion work was required to sustain the movement's organizational and political goals.

Although the leaders were able to maintain this "emotional balancing act," success was by no means automatic. The "dual goals" of victims' groups—therapy and action—could lead to tensions and unintended outcomes.

BOX 5.6:
POTENTIAL TENSIONS BETWEEN VICTIMS' NEEDS AND A GROUP'S FOCUS

"Until [another survivor arrived] I was disappointed with [the victims' group], because [the leader] is there, but she's above all this. She's up there, doing what she needs to do to change at the government level. That's great, but she's not there to give moral support. The only contact we had was [the office administrator], a little bit of support, but nothing solid. With [the leader] it was just letters, but nothing more" (interview #8: female, 45).

Source: Kenney, J. S. (1998). *Coping with Grief: Survivors of Murder Victims.* Unpublished doctoral thesis, McMaster University, Hamilton, ON.

BOX 5.7:
TENSIONS BETWEEN RAISING AWARENESS AND POLITICAL INVOLVEMENT

"My wife and I went to one memorial service, and, when I saw the Liberal Members of Parliament standing up there speaking, [we] walked out ... When we saw people who we knew, from personal experience, had fought against victims' rights, it's bad enough they're taking credit, and being introduced by the lady in [the victims' organization], we walked out and we had no contact with any of them again" (interview #12: male, age 61).

Source: Kenney, J. S. (1998). *Coping with Grief: Survivors of Murder Victims.* Unpublished doctoral thesis, McMaster University, Hamilton, ON.

Beyond internal disagreements concerning the most effective way to frame an issue, members could experience a disjuncture over the predominant focus of the group, potentially impacting the group's capacity to attract and retain members (Box 5.6).

Indeed, the demands on leaders to raise awareness of victims' issues, and the inevitable compromises that accompanied this task, could clash with the emotional honesty that must characterize the movement at its core (Box 5.7).

In each case, members felt disillusioned by the lack of emotion and political strategizing exhibited by leaders. In the first, the member stayed in the group only because she found another victim to provide her with the kind of support that was not forthcoming from the leader; in the second, the

> BOX 5.8:
> ## A SUCCESSFUL COMBINATION OF APPARENTLY CONTRARY GOALS BY LEADERS
>
> "After the trial, our [group] coordinator, she gave me jobs to do. She kept me busy. She asked me to do an interview on the radio. She said 'I think you're ready.' I said 'I've never done an interview in my life!' [laughs]. She says [in a suggestive, cute tone of voice] 'This will make you stronger.' It did" (interview #19; female, age 53).
>
> **Source:** Kenney, J. S. (1998). *Coping with Grief: Survivors of Murder Victims.* Unpublished doctoral thesis, McMaster University, Hamilton, ON.

members quit. Clearly, social movements must be aware of the difficulties that oppositional emotions can create and take steps to diffuse potential conflicts and limit member dissatisfaction.

Conversely, there may be times when varying emotional contexts interact positively, such as when a movement leader is able to bridge the emotional needs of a victim with the needs of the organization by combining the dual and seemingly contrary goals of the group—therapy and action—in a way that satisfies a member (Box 5.8).

But this is possible only with careful monitoring of members and their emotional needs in relation to the political requirements of the group. Again, organizations that are aware of such possibilities (and pitfalls) will fare better than those that are not.

Researchers have sought to "bring emotions back in" to social movement analysis. Our study of the Canadian victims' rights movement supports the utility of this pursuit. Emotions must be understood not only as "one more" of the many cultural and other factors available to movement leaders to manage and manipulate, but also as factors that operate *in concert* with the organizational and political activities of the movement. Cultural resonance and emotional resonance are not necessarily concurrent; in framing movement goals to achieve the former among the public and potential members, leaders must be aware of how those frames resonate emotionally—positively and negatively—with various audiences. Movement leaders ignore these interactions at their peril.

CONCLUSION

By pointing to the strategic management of emotion, to the careful emotional balancing act between organizational and public contexts, we contribute to an understanding of the emergence of the Canadian victims' rights movement specifically, and to social movement theory generally. Attention should now shift to the characteristics, successes, failures, and organizational trajectories of other victims' groups. Various Canadian victims' groups have emerged, flourished, and then folded (e.g., CAVEAT in the 1990s). It would be interesting for researchers to study whether a breakdown of this emotional balancing between organizational and public contexts, along with victim politics, plays a part in what appears to be a limited lifespan for such groups. Furthermore, what role does government—and government funding—play in more enduring organizations, and how much does this compromise group goals? Finally, given questions about the relative influence of the victims' movement on emerging programs and services (Elias, 1983; Rock, 1988), research should address the degree to which the movement has impacted the development of such initiatives.

ENDNOTES

1. The diffuse "law and order" program accompanied the rise of the new right in the USA, Britain, and other countries. It included themes that the current criminal justice policies were lenient, ineffective, and provided an insufficient deterrent to crime (Davis, 1981; Weed, 1995).

2. A pioneering study by Linden (1968) showed that, in 1966 Toronto, only 1.8% of victims surveyed collected anything by filing a civil suit. He also noted that only 14.9% of respondents considered suing, 5.4% consulted a lawyer, and 4.8% tried to collect from their attackers. A later study had similar results (Dickson, 1984). The 1988 General Social Survey found that in only 1% of reported victimizations were attempts made to seek redress through the court system (Sacco & Johnson, 1990).

3. In Canada, this was highlighted by notorious cases such as that of serial killer Clifford Olson who, between 1980 and 1981, killed 11 children in British Columbia. Olson was arrested in August 1981, and the police agreed to pay $100,000 to Olson's family in exchange for information concerning the whereabouts of the bodies of the victims. Later convicted and imprisoned, Olson sent letters to some victims' families describing his crimes in graphic detail.

4. The interactionist literature has long recognized the cultural specificity of grief. Over 20 years ago, Lofland (1985) observed that the experience of grief—"its symptoms or texture, its shapes or phasing, as well as its onset and duration"—were "highly particularized" across time and space (p. 175). Earlier still, Charmaz (1980) noted that the expectations surrounding grief, even the subjective experience of bereavement as grief inducing, were culturally variable.

5. There are (acknowledged) shades here of Gamson's (1992) work on how social movements evoke political consciousness by framing their causes to

create a "system of beliefs" around their issue to include components pertaining to injustice, agency, and identity. Although Gamson recognized that feelings underlie these frames, he located his analysis squarely in the framing literature, whereas Flam's (2005) formulation places emotions at the centre of her typology.

6. Our focus on the leaders and spokespeople representing the Canadian victims' rights movement reflects academic observations surrounding the important role of leaders in collective action. Recent scholarship on movement leaders highlights how the "leadership capital" and "symbolic capital" wielded by leaders affects mobilization, activation of third parties crucial to movement development, and the extent to which movements may be repressed by states and other opponents (Nepstad & Bob, 2006).

7. Nairn and Sullivan's (publicly) restrained responses to their grief resembles that of other male victims. Researchers have noted that male victims of crime tend to be less visibly "emotional," less willing to talk about their anguish, and less likely to join support groups than female victims (Kenney, 1998; Staudacher, 1991). Nairn and Sullivan's "masculine" representations of their suffering were interpreted more positively by the public than the less-controlled displays of grief forthcoming from the women around them, demonstrating the gendered nature of grief management and reception.

REFERENCES

Amernic, J. (1984). *Victims: The Orphans of Justice*. Toronto: McClelland & Stewart-Bantam Ltd.

Aminzade, R., & McAdam, D. (2001). Emotions and contentious politics. In R. Aminzade, J. Goldstone, D. McAdam, E. Perry, W. Sewell, S. Tarrow, et al. (Eds.), *Silence and Voice in the Study of Contentious Politics* (pp. 14–50). Cambridge: Cambridge University Press.

Canadian Federal-Provincial Task Force. (1983). *Canadian Federal-Provincial Task Force Report: Justice for Victims of Crime*. Ottawa: Minister of Supply and Services.

Charmaz, K. (1980). *The Social Reality of Death: Death in Contemporary America*. Reading, MA: Addison-Wesley.

Clark, C. (1987). Sympathy biography and sympathy margin. *American Journal of Sociology 9*(2), 290–321.

Clarke, P. (1986). Is there a place for the victim in the prosecution process? *Canadian Criminology Forum 8*(1), 31–44.

Coates, D., & Winston, T. (1983). Counteracting the deviance of depression: Peer support groups for victims. *Journal of Social Issues 39*(2), 169–194.

Davis, M. (1981). The new right's road to power. *New Left Review 128*, 28–49.

Dickson, B. (1984). The forgotten party—the victim of crime. *UBC Law Review* *18*, 319–334.

Dunn, J. L. (2004). The politics of empathy: Social movements and victim repertoires. *Sociological Focus 37*(3), 235–250.

Elias, R. (1983). Symbolic politics of victim compensation. *Victimology 8*(1–2), 213–224.

English, K. (1984, November 11). Victims of violence: Too many to ignore. *Toronto Star*, p. A-1.

Fagan, D. (1984, June 2). McMurtry and Kaplan enter fray; get tough with criminals, victims say. *The Globe and Mail*, p. 18.

Fattah, E. A. (2000). Victimology: Past, present, and future. *Criminologie 33*(1), 17–46.

Flam, H. (2005). Emotions' map: A research agenda. In H. Flam & D. King (Eds.), *Emotions and Social Movements* (pp. 19–40). London: Routledge.

Gamson, W. (1992). *Talking Politics*. Cambridge: Cambridge University Press.

Gilligan, J. (2003). Shame, guilt, and violence. *Social Research 70*(4), 1149–1180.

Goodwin, J., Jasper, J., & Polletta, F. (2000). The return of the repressed: The fall and rise of emotions in social movement theory. *Mobilization 5*(1), 65–83.

Goodwin, J., Jasper, J., & Polletta, F. (2001). Introduction: Why emotions matter. In J. Goodwin, J. Jasper, & Polletta, F. (Eds.), *Passionate Politics* (pp. 1–24). Chicago: University of Chicago Press.

Gusfield, J. (1963). *Symbolic Crusade: Status Politics and the American Temperance Movement*. Urbana, IL: University of Illinois Press.

Hochschild, A. R. (1983). *The Managed Heart: Commercialization of Human Feeling*. Berkeley: University of California Press.

Hochschild, A. R. (1990). Ideology and emotion management: A perspective and path for future research. In T. D. Kemper (Ed.), *Research Agendas in the Sociology of Emotions* (pp. 117–142). New York: State University of New York Press.

Kenney, J. S. (1998). *Coping with Grief: Survivors of Murder Victims*. Unpublished doctoral thesis, McMaster University, Hamilton, ON.

Linden, A. (1968). Victims of crime and tort law. *Canadian Bar Journal 12*, 17–33.

Lofland, L. (1985). The social shaping of emotion: The case of grief. *Symbolic Interaction 8*(2), 171–190.

Malarek, V. (1984a, April 9). Crime victims' search for justice: From arrest to parole, accused benefits from safeguards. *The Globe and Mail*, p. M3.

Malarek, V. (1984b, April 10). Programs help crime victims deal with solitude. *The Globe and Mail*, p. M2.

Malarek, V. (1984c, April 11). Effect of emotionalism feared: Voice-for-victim trend disturbs lawyers. *The Globe and Mail*, p. M2.

McAdam, D. (1982). *Political Process and the Development of Black Insurgency, 1930–1970*. Chicago: University of Chicago Press.

McCarthy, J. D., & Zald, M. N. (1973). *The Trend of Social Movements in America: Professionalization and Resource Mobilization*. Morristown, NJ: General Learning Press.

McCarthy, J. D., & Zald, M. N. (1977). Resource mobilization and social movements: A partial theory. *American Journal of Sociology 82*(6), 1212–1241.

Nathanson, D. (1994). *Shame and Pride: Affect, Sex, and the Birth of the Self*. New York: W. W. Norton.

Nepstad, S. E., & Bob, C. (2006). When do leaders matter? Hypotheses on leadership dynamics in social movements. *Mobilization: An International Journal 11*(1), 1–22.

Robnett, B. (2004). Emotional resonance, social location, and strategic framing. *Sociological Focus 37*(3), 195–212.

Rock, P. (1988). On the birth of organizations. *LSE Quarterly 2*(2), 123–153.

Sacco, V. F., & Johnson, H. (1990). *Patterns of Criminal Victimization in Canada*. Ottawa: Minister of Supply and Services.

Scheff, T., & Retzinger, S. (2000). Shame as the master emotion of everyday life. *Journal of Mundane Behaviour 1*(3), 303–324.

Schrock, D., Holden, D., & Reid, L. (2004). Creating emotional resonance: Interpersonal emotion work and motivational framing in a transgender community. *Social Problems 51*(1), 61–81.

Searles, R., & Williams, J. A., Jr. (1962). Negro college students' participation in sit-ins. *Social Forces 40*(3), 215–220.

Silver, R. L., & Wortman, C. B. (1980). Coping with undesirable life events. In J. Garber & M. E. P. Seligman (Eds.), *Human Helplessness: Theory and Applications* (pp. 279–340). New York: Academic.

Snow, D., & Benford, R. (1988). Ideology, frame resonance, and participant mobilization. In B. Klandermans, H. Kriesi, & S. Tarrow (Eds.), *From Structure to Action: Social Movement Participation across Cultures* (pp. 197–217). Greenwich, CT: JAI Press.

Snow, D., & Benford, R. (1992). Master frames and cycles of protest. In A. Morris & C. M. Mueller (Eds.), *Frontiers in Social Movement Theory* (pp. 133–155). New Haven, CT: Yale University Press.

Snow, D., Rochford, E. B., Jr., Worden, S. K., & Benford, R. D. (1986). Frame alignment processes, micromobilization, and movement participation. *American Sociological Review 51*, 464–481.

Staudacher, C. (1991). *Men and Grief*. Oakland, CA: New Harbinger.

Sullivan, D. (1984). Foreword. In J. Amernic, *Victims: The Orphans of Justice* (pp. ix–xiii). Toronto: McClelland & Stewart-Bantam Ltd.

Tarrow, S. (1994). *Power in Movement: Social Movements, Collective Action, and Mass Politics in the Modern State*. Cambridge: Cambridge University Press.

Thoits, P. A. (1990). Emotional deviance: Research agendas. In T. D. Kemper (Ed.), *Research Agendas in the Sociology of Emotions* (pp. 180–203). New York: State University of New York Press.

Tilly, C. (1978). *From Mobilization to Revolution*. Reading, MA: Addison-Wesley.

Tilly, C., Tilly, L., & Tilly, R. (1975). *The Rebellious Century 1830–1930*. Cambridge, MA: Harvard University Press.

Victims of crime face injustices, police chiefs told. (1985, July 4). *The Globe and Mail*, p. 10.

Walgrave, S., & Manssens, J. (2005). Mobilizing the white march: Media frames as alternatives to movement organizations. In H. Johnston & J. A. Noakes (Eds.), *Frames of Protest: Social Movements and the Framing Perspective* (pp. 113–140). Lanham, MD: Rowman & Littlefield.

Weed, F. (1995). *Certainty of Justice: Reform in the Crime Victim Movement*. New York: Aldine de Gruyter.

Whittier, N. (2001). Emotional strategies: The collective reconstruction and display of oppositional emotions in the movement against child sexual abuse. In J. Goodwin, J. M. Jasper, & F. Polletta (Eds.), *Passionate Politics: Emotions and Social Movements* (pp. 233–250). Chicago: University of Chicago Press.

Wortman, C. B., & Lehman, D. R. (1983). Reactions to victims of life crises: Support attempts that fail. In I. G. Sarason & B. R. Sarason (Eds.), *Social Support: Theory, Research, and Applications* (pp. 463–489). Boston: Martinus Nijhof.

CHAPTER 6

Policy Responses

INTRODUCTION

Despite the victims' movement, policy responses to victim concerns remain limited. In this chapter I critically consider broad policy responses to victimization. I begin by looking at traditional alternatives to criminal justice, namely the civil courts and criminal injuries compensation board (CICB) programs. Next I discuss more recent initiatives, including victims' bills of rights and victim impact statements. Finally, given the growth of public and community-based programs, I provide qualitative analyses of provincial victims' services programs, private victim support/advocacy organizations, and women's shelters and community outreach services. Chapter 7 covers restorative justice.[1]

I elaborate three general themes. First, since the term "victim" is open to diverse interpretations (Weed, 1995) and victims' goals are not the primary motivating force behind legislation, compensation, and victims' services programs (Rock, 1990), their policies often reflect prior institutional and organizational contexts. Second, given programs' often limited responses to victims' substantive interests, there is Elias's (1983) theme of "symbolic politics" (i.e., token responses rendering the appearance that something has been done, while largely serving official needs). Finally, some programs have counter-intuitive effects (e.g., despite formal attempts to avoid the victim role, it may be facilitated otherwise).

THE CIVIL COURTS

Canadian courts have traditionally held that victims have no legal status in criminal matters because they can pursue a civil lawsuit. They may succeed in a civil lawsuit if their allegations are proven on a "balance of probabilities," a lower standard than in criminal cases. Indeed, if the defendant does not respond, then a "default judgment" may be granted.

Yet victims face practical difficulties:

- Identification: If unable to identify or locate the offender, then they cannot serve court documents—effectively precluding a lawsuit (Canadian Federal-Provincial Task Force, 1983; Linden, 1969).

- Timing: If suit is brought with criminal charges pending, the defence counsel will seek to undermine victims' credibility, claiming the charges are motivated by financial gain (Karmen, 2001). Conversely, limitation periods may expire before the victim has made enough of an emotional recovery to file suit (Karmen, 2001; Van Ginkel, 1990).

- Costs: Where the victim wins, the damages may be offset by their legal costs (Canadian Federal-Provincial Task Force, 1983).

- Collection: While there are costly, time-consuming mechanisms to execute on judgments, none are effective against defendants who have no assets, are facing prior judgments, have property encumbered by secured or preferred debts, or are bankrupt (Canadian Federal-Provincial Task Force, 1983).

- Defence and countersuing: Lawsuits may be defended and relatively poor offenders may counter-sue, at little initial cost, on a contingency fee (Karmen, 2001), while financially comfortable victims pay their own legal costs.[2]

Such factors have traditionally inhibited victims' use of the civil courts as "not worth the costs" (Karmen, 2001, p. 283). In 1966 in Toronto, only 1.8% of respondents collected anything by filing suit, despite economic losses suffered by 74.2%. Only 14.9% considered suing, a mere 5.4% consulted a lawyer, and 4.8% tried to collect (Linden, 1969). A 1974 Vancouver study found similar results: "only 4% ... succeeded in recovering anything" (Dickson, 1984). The 1988 General Social Survey found that only 1% of reported victimizations involved attempts to seek civil redress in court (Sacco & Johnson, 1990).

However, activists have recently highlighted this option (Karmen, 2001), with some victim programs advising lawsuits to recoup financial losses from the offender (Schmalleger, MacAlister, & McKenna, 2004). While significant damages have been awarded, particularly involving sexual assault or domestic violence, lawsuits are carefully targeted—they are effective only where defendants have "deep pockets" (McAlister, 2003). Lawyers will generally not take cases without good odds of recovery, and parties' financial positions are key. Add that legal aid is increasingly limited to the criminal accused who are facing jail (Goff, 2004) and it becomes clear that victims of impecunious offenders—most cases—cannot pursue litigation.

CRIMINAL INJURIES COMPENSATION BOARD PROGRAMS
State-funded victim compensation schemes emerged throughout the Western world in the 1960s. They were rooted in dissatisfaction with the civil courts, and it was felt that administrative tribunals would provide quicker, more efficient compensation (Canadian Federal-Provincial Task Force, 1983). Until 1992, Canadian CICB programs were cost-shared between the federal and provincial governments, although boards were constituted and administered provincially. While all programs were not identical, they did share common features:

> "All the Canadian compensation schemes are designed to aid the victims of violent crime. This includes surviving dependants of victims of homicide, and usually persons responsible for the maintenance of the victim. All programs also compensate 'Good Samaritans' who are injured in the course of attempting to enforce or assist in the enforcement of the law. Finally, all jurisdictions consider the possible contributory behaviour of the victim in assessing eligibility and size of an award.

> "The compensation schemes are all designed to alleviate the pecuniary loss of the victim. Compensation may be obtained for losses incurred as a result of the injury, death or disability of the victim. In addition, compensation can also cover the losses to dependants as a result of a victim's death, to pay for the maintenance of a child born as a result of rape, or for other expenses deemed reasonable by the jurisdiction in question. Some programmes also compensate for pain and suffering" (Canadian Federal-Provincial Task Force, 1983, p. 33).

Practical Problems of CICB Programs
While sounding helpful compared to the courts, there were many practical problems. For example, notoriously underfunded board budgets resulted in low awards (Fattah, 2000) and compensation was far less than civil courts would order (Dickson, 1984; Provincial Secretariat for Justice, 1984), and, if victims sued, they could recover only an amount above the compensation paid, because tribunals were entitled to their share back (Dickson, 1984). In addition, collecting criminal fines held priority over compensation orders (Fattah, 2000), there were maximum limits on awards,[3] and collateral benefits (e.g., employment insurance or welfare) were deducted (Canadian Federal-

BOX 6.1:
THE EXPLOITATION OF CICB PROGRAMS BY THIRD PARTIES

"Crime victims may be seen as a client group with new-found assets. In 1991 the Texas Attorney General filed suit against a chain of psychiatric hospitals for exploiting crime victims to get third-party payments ... [accusing] the psychiatric hospitals of soliciting crime victims through "bounty hunters," i.e., a patient referral service, and subjecting them to unnecessary treatment ... until the state's $25,000 maximum payment was used up. Medical hospitals also saw the victim compensation funds as a mechanism for cost recovery for treating injured crime victims. This raises the issue of who benefits from a victim compensation fund—the crime victims or ... mental health counsellors, ... hospitals along with police and prosecutors who can purchase cooperation from the victim."

Source: Weed, F. (1995). *Certainty of Justice: Reform in the Crime Victim Movement.* New York: Aldine de Gruyter: p. 137.

Provincial Task Force, 1983). Property damage or loss was rarely covered—despite many victims not having or being unable to afford insurance (Fattah, 2000)— and not all boards compensated pain and suffering, or recognized that it spread beyond the primary victim (Canadian Federal-Provincial Task Force, 1983). Eligibility or compensation was denied for numerous reasons.[4]

There were lengthy bureaucratic procedures and investigative processes (Walker, 1994), including means tests (Fattah, 2000), which were often difficult when there were bills to pay following victimization (e.g., for medical equipment) and exacerbated when injury or post-traumatic stress made it hard to work (Provincial Secretariat for Justice, 1984). In addition, applicants reported being "grilled" at hearings over their role in the incident, their financial position, and/or the extent of their injuries (Provincial Secretariat for Justice, 1984, p. 82). Victim compensation was not well known or well advertised[5] (Fattah, 2000; Provincial Secretariat for Justice, 1984; Walker, 1994), and many missed the periods for application[6] (e.g., one year post-offence). Finally, victims and these programs were sometimes used by others to further their pecuniary interests (Box 6.1).

Many provinces reorganized their programs once federal–provincial cost-sharing ended in 1992 (e.g., amalgamating with either victims' services or workers' compensation programs), instituting severe cutbacks in eligibility and coverage (e.g., eliminating or harshly curtailing awards for pain and suffering, restricting awards to brief counselling only). While these programs were limited and problematic before, the options they give to victims are

> ## BOX 6.2:
> ## SYMBOLIC POLITICS
>
> Programs characterized by symbolic politics provide "symbolic, political or psychological gestures instead of programs with real substance, particularly in the form of concrete ... assistance for significant numbers of crime victims. A political event may be considered as symbolic when it uses language or gestures or policies in a way that detracts attention from tangible issues of resource allocation. Emphasis is put. on quieting public demands or concerns with a policy pronouncement that either fails to materialize, or if so, nevertheless fails to produce any substantial, tangible results" (Elias 1983: 214). These enable politicians to rhetorically claim that something has been put in place, while failing to provide most applicants with substantial assistance.
>
> **Source:** Elias, R. (1983). Symbolic politics of victim compensation. *Victimology 8*, 214.

now further reduced. The upshot is that few victims apply to CICBs and even fewer are minimally compensated. What can be made of this?

Symbolic Politics

Robert Elias (1983) argued that such schemes have very little to do with compensating victims, but rather are examples of "symbolic politics" (Box 6.2). Other academics have highlighted disjunctions between the "symbolic" political value of such "token" programs versus their substantive poverty (Fattah, 2000; Maguire & Shapland, 1997; Miers, 1990; Weed, 1995).

Elias (1993) noted that in many states of the USA, unprecedented numbers of legislators co-sponsored CICB programs. They loudly trumpeted their support for programs, and the public greeted this with great favour. Ironically, many of the same parties later voted against funding appropriations, or for meagre funding with restrictive eligibility requirements. "Even from the beginning therefore, the actual commitment to creating substantive programs was low, but the political advantages of supporting the plans were nevertheless realized" (Elias, 1983, p. 214).

Then there is the lack of substance in practice. Elias surveyed CICB officials and 342 victims of two programs in New York and New Jersey. The victims were broken down into four separate samples: Brooklyn applicants and non-applicants and Newark applicants and non-applicants. Less than 35% of applicants received compensation (and many of these considered the compensation insufficient). Less than 1% of all violent crime victims even applied. Most of those who dealt with the tribunals exhibited a worse attitude toward future cooperation with the authorities because of their treatment, and this was particularly salient among uncompensated or "inadequately" compensated claimants. The few who were satisfied with their compensation (or who never applied) were more inclined to support the programs, government, and justice institutions. This group was apparently impressed that policymakers had been considerate enough to provide compensation programs. Elias stated:

> "A perfect example of symbolic politics: the public is thankful for the program and hopes it will never need it, when in fact, should the program ever be needed, for the vast majority of people, it will not actually be there!" (Elias, 1983, p. 219).

Elias concluded that victim compensation has serious problems that are unlikely to be fixed. This is because the real commitment to victims is unclear, with governments preferring to stick "band-aids" on after the fact rather than effectively dealing with substantive issues (Elias, 1983, pp. 221–222).

VICTIMS' BILLS OF RIGHTS

Many provinces have passed "victims' bills of rights." For example, s. 3(1) of the Nova Scotia *Victims' Rights and Services Act* (1989) sets out that victims have "rights" to be treated with "courtesy, compassion and dignity"; to have their "privacy" respected; to access social, legal, medical, and mental health services "responsive" to their needs; and to have property returned "as soon as possible." After setting out qualifications of available resources and what is "reasonable" in the "circumstances," additional rights are specified. These "may" include rights to be informed of the accused's name, the offence charged, the scope, nature, timing, and progress of the prosecution, the legal role of the victim, and court procedures and crime prevention measures; to be kept apart "where necessary" from the accused and defence witnesses; the opportunity to make a victim impact statement; and to be informed of services and mechanisms to obtain "remedies," which presumably include criminal injuries compensation (the subject of much of the act), but could also refer to civil lawsuits and restitution orders.

These provisions largely mirror those of Bill C-89: *An Act to Amend the Criminal Code (Victims of Crime)* S.C. 1988, c.30., passed in May of 1988 by the federal government (Goff, 2004). Several important things must be noted about this and other similar provincial legislation[7]: (1) these "rights" are extremely vague; (2) many are limited by "availability of resources" and what is "reasonable" in the circumstances; (3) most involve the provision of information, not an active role in the process; (4) even when more specific (e.g., separate waiting rooms "where necessary"), they are still subject

to limitations; (5) such legislation typically contains sections that specifically deny victims legally enforceable remedies (Beloof, 1999) should they
feel these "rights" have been violated (e.g., s. 12 and s. 13 in the Nova Scotia *Victims' Rights and Services Act*); and (6) even if enforceable rights are
listed, provincial legislation can easily be struck down if it conflicts with the
accused's constitutional rights under the *Charter of Rights and Freedoms*.

Ultimately, calling such limited provisions "rights"—without any means
of redress—does violence to the concept of a "right," rather than provide
any substantive means for victims to address their concerns. This is another
example of symbolic politics (Elias, 1983; Weed, 1995).

Federally, victim "rights" have become slightly—but *only* slightly—more
substantive. The 1999 *Criminal Code* amendments[8] attempted to ensure that
victims are informed of their opportunity to prepare an impact statement
before sentencing and have the choice to read it aloud, required statements be
considered following verdicts of not criminally responsible due to mental disorder, extended protections restricting cross-examinations of victims of sexual
or violent crime of up to 18 years of age by self-represented accused, required
consideration of victims' safety in bail decisions, allowed victims with mental
or physical disabilities a support person when giving testimony, and permitted judges to ban publication of victim or witness identities where necessary
for the administration of justice (Goff, 2004). These amendments removed
judicial discretion such that victims now have a "right" to make impact statements, provided increased (but limited) opportunities for victim input in bail
and parole hearings, and facilitated testimony by the most vulnerable victims.

Nevertheless, these changes have largely been built *around* the existing
procedural structure. Indeed, if these "rights" come into conflict with the
over-determining constitutional rights of the accused then, as mere legislation, they can be struck down. Thus, while they are slightly more substantive
than provincial legislation, they do little to alter the victim's traditional power
position. At best, they may serve official needs (Elias, 1983; Rock, 1990) as a
public relations exercise and, possibly, provide more cooperative witnesses.
Such "rights" are but a pale reflection of those wielded by the accused.

VICTIM IMPACT STATEMENTS

Until relatively recently, victims were denied input on the sentence of convicted offenders (*Re Regina and Antler*, 1982). That changed in 1988 with Bill
C-89 (Goff, 2004). Since then, "victim impact statements" have, under certain
circumstances, been allowed into evidence, enabling victims to inform the
court—after conviction, but before sentencing—how the crime affected them.

Several procedural problems have emerged with victim impact statements. Until recently, statements were allowed only at the discretion of the

BOX 6.3:
LOW PARTICIPATION IN VICTIM IMPACT STATEMENT PROGRAMS

"In one South Carolina study a review of 945 case files found victim impact statements in only 8.8% of the cases. A separate sample of 206 felony cases found that only 50 victims (24%) were notified that they could submit victim impact statements at an upcoming sentencing hearing and in 31 cases (62%) they did ... In California, a year after the passage of Proposition 8, only 14 victims had appeared before the Board of Prison Term (at probation or release hearings), or about 2% of the 818 cases considered by the Board."

Source: Weed, F. (1995). *Certainty of Justice: Reform in the Crime Victim Movement.* New York: Aldine de Gruyter: p. 136.

sentencing judge (i.e., they were often disallowed) and had to be filed two days before sentencing (problematic when sentencing occurred immediately). In addition, there are administrative/evidentiary restrictions on victims' comments (e.g., victims cannot "speak to sentence") and impact statements provide an opportunity for victim cross-examination. Furthermore, statements have not always been forwarded to correctional and parole authorities.[9] The 1999 amendments to the *Criminal Code*, noted above, dealt with several of these issues, but did not address the content restrictions[10] and potential victim cross-examination, or ensure that statements are forwarded.

Beyond procedure, Erez and Laster (1999) reported that impact statements have little or no influence. Judges, prosecutors, and defence counsels routinely objectify and downplay the injuries experienced, imposing an implicit "reasonable victim" test to evaluate statements. Studying 500 felony cases in Ohio between 1985 and 1988, Erez and Tontodonato (1990) found that statements have a minimal impact on outcomes, because the offender and offence characteristics remain of primary importance. At best, the evidence for the impact of victim impact statements is inconclusive (Erez, 1994).

Next, rates of victim participation have generally been low (Box 6.3). In Canada, participation rates varied after the introduction of this option in 1988 (Goff 2008, p. 273). Since that time, studies have revealed low rates of participation (Roach, 1999).

Some have surmised this may reflect the fact that, until recently, impact statements have been curtailed by prosecutorial discretion (Roberts, 1992); others infer victims' reluctance to expose themselves to adversarial challenge (Roach, 1999).

Fourth, despite individual instances of victim support, researchers have challenged the assumption that impact statements increase victim satisfaction. In a study of six Canadian cities, researchers discovered no significant difference in victim satisfaction with justice when impact statements were used compared to when they were not. While some found statements a useful opportunity to express their feelings and exchange information, satisfaction was unaffected. Indeed, most held negative attitudes toward sentencing both before and after their cases were heard (Giliberti, 1990). Similarly, a study of 293 New York victims of assault, robbery, or burglary found no evidence that statements facilitated greater feelings of involvement with the trial, satisfaction with the justice process, or satisfaction with sentences (Davis & Smith, 1994). Indeed, in a study of 397 South Australian felony victims Erez, Roeger, & Morgan (1997) found that impact statements negatively impacted satisfaction with the criminal justice system via unfulfilled expectations.

Lastly, even if impact statements have value beyond the above, they remain without the over-determining force of offenders' constitutional rights. If push comes to shove, victims lose.

Ultimately, the victim impact statement initiative remains more rhetoric than reality. While it is an option that did not exist until recently, and improvements have been made in the process, impact statements have an inconclusive impact on sentences and low participation rates, and entail low victim satisfaction. One is left wondering about the rationale behind them. Perhaps, again, they present an option that has no significant value for victims, but that can be enlisted symbolically to show that "something is being done" (Elias, 1983).

PROVINCIAL VICTIMS' SERVICES PROGRAMS

The last several decades have witnessed an unprecedented development in victim services in the USA, Britain, Canada, and many other countries (Davis, Lurigio, & Skogan, 1999; Fattah, 2000). The Canadian Resource Centre for Victims of Crime (1998) provided a useful framework for classifying the range of services available in Canadian provinces and territories: four basic program models emerge (Box 6.4).[11]

Funding comes from a variety of government sources, departments of justice, and the Victims' Assistance Fund.[12] The latter is funded through "victim fine surcharges" that are added to offenders' fines at the time of sentencing. These are authorized under the *Criminal Code* and provincial legislation (Marriott-Thorne, 1998).

Among the most comprehensive criminal justice initiatives for victims are provincial victims' services programs.[13] These incorporate—and run—many of the programs discussed above (e.g., CICB, victim impact statements), and

BOX 6.4:
FOUR BROAD TYPES OF VICTIMS' SERVICES PROGRAMS

"(1) Police-based services: usually located in police detachments/ departments. These deal with victims as soon as possible after contact with the justice system begins. Help may include: death notification, information about the justice system and investigation, assistance with impact statements and compensation applications, referrals, etc;

"(2) Crown/court-based victim/witness services: usually located in courthouses, [working] very closely with the Crown's office. The emphasis is on court preparation, including: information about the court process, tours of the courthouse, emotional support, facilitating meetings with the Crown, working with child victims/ witnesses, etc;

"(3) Community-based victim services: these ... are usually not government operated, but may benefit from government funding. They usually specialize in the types of victims they deal with, e.g., sexual assault centres, domestic violence transition homes;

"(4) System-based services: the victim only has to go to one place to get the types of services they can access from both police- and crown-based programs ..."

Source: Canadian Resources Centre for Victims of Crime (CRCVC). (1998). *Balancing the Scales: The State of Victims' Rights in Canada.* Ottawa: CRCVC: p. 64.

also provide specialized support/referral services for victims in the justice system (e.g., victim witness programs, court support). In this section I emphasize their dealings with victims during the court process.

I use the Nova Scotia Victims' Services Division as illustrative example. Set up in the Department of Justice in 1989 under the *Victims Rights and Services Act* (1989), and restructured following a study on victims' needs and services (Murphy, 1991), this agency contacts and provides support services to victims involved in the court process, typically after charges have been laid. Operating largely as an information and referral service, it provides voluntary programs and services, including court preparation sessions, the child victim witness program, funding for counselling through criminal injuries compensation, and assistance with impact statements (Marriott-Thorne, 1998). "Victim services officers" talk to clients—either by telephone or in person—in an attempt to explain the court process. They provide emotional support, keep clients informed about their case, pass on relevant forms and documentation, and liaise with prosecutors, other justice officials, counsellors, and community organizations.

From its inception, the caseload of the Victims' Services Division increased steadily. Between 1993 and 1999 its caseload jumped from 432 to 3,790 clients annually (Victims' Services Division, 1999).[14] When I studied the program in 1999–2000, the most common types of help required, besides emotional support, were information, assistance with applications or court processes, and liaison with the justice system (Victims' Services Division, 1999). Most clients (77.5%) were women aged between 20 and 40 years, which was not surprising because the program prioritizes victims of violence and highly traumatized individuals. Most referrals involved various forms of assault, uttering threats, peace bonds, and (to a lesser extent) sexual assault. Client referrals were often made before court proceedings began, with most made by the Crown, closely followed by self-referrals and those by the police.

My qualitative study critically considered the encouragement versus discouragement of victim identity by this service and two private support organizations. Aside from observing officers in their dealings with clients, clients and support staff were interviewed.[15] Respondents[16] asserted that encounters with provincial victim services had a mixed impact. Many clients simply pointed to things that they liked and disliked about the service, while support staff responded with factors that they considered to be helpful and unhelpful to clients. However, such surface issues masked a larger tension. Officers were aware of and attempted to deal with the potential for increasing a client's sense of victimization through support practices. These attempts were not exhaustive, and clients' claims of victimization were encouraged or increased despite them.

Officers were sensitized to the possibility that their dealings with clients might engender a further sense of victimhood:

> "I don't identify them as victims. The only way that term comes up is self-identification. If a person identifies to me that they've been a victim of an assault, then I certainly understand that and I affirm that back to them. If the person identifies themselves as having had an incident, or something unpleasant has happened, I certainly give them information, give them options from that perspective as well. I think there are a whole lot of issues around the term 'victim.' If people feel they've been victimized and they're overwhelmed by that victimization, then there's certainly a set of options to respond to that. If people feel that they have suffered an unpleasant situation and want to

know the consequences—they're looking for information and they're looking to continue to take control of their life, I provide the information option—and I give them a whole range of options to choose from" (interview #30: female, age 47).

Indeed, the same interviewee suggested that "knowledge is power" and that her job was to "normalize" clients' situations as "short-term problems," after which they would get their "balance back." Other officers suggested that their job with clients was to "build them up" (interview #24: female, age 42). In some cases, clients appreciated this approach; other times not:

> "If I need anything I can call and they listen. They believe me and understand. Every time that I called them they gave me the information that I need. I have control with them, and they aren't going to keep going unless I want them to. They aren't treating me as helpless, but are trying to build me up more" (interview #31: female, age 28).

> "I was confused and shattered, but found that they didn't help me in my confusion. They just treated me like I was a normal person who had walked off the street looking for some information, like I had total control of all my faculties. I was in need of answers and they couldn't tell me anything. They don't even make you feel they could help. I was made to feel that I was not important, like I was shunned" (interview #11[b]: female, age 43).

Beyond differing client responses, a separate sense of victimization may develop out of inconsistent implementation of this philosophy. For example, the officer above was observed to ask a client "Have you been a victim of crime?" She then immediately softened her voice and added, "It's not easy, is it?" Another, after outlining the institutional narrative, stated: "We're not really into labelling people, other than identifying them as a victim." She said that she tell clients: "This is not your fault, this is about the offender taking responsibility" (implicitly altercasting clients as victims). She also said that she gives clients information on the "cycle of abuse" so they can understand their situation: "You can't move on unless you identify where you are" (interview #16: female, age 43).

While inconsistency was important, something else was critical: victim services' location in the Department of Justice—and its close ties to the justice system, the negative impact of which has been noted on victims. Staff, clients, and workers in other support organizations commented on this. Officers themselves noted:

> "I have to walk a fine line and avoid criticizing the system. I can't commiserate with clients in that regard" (interview #16: female, age 43).

> "One of the most difficult areas is if a victim believes that the victim services officer can somehow change the process. I understand that, but certainly don't have any more power than the victim" (interview #30: female, age 47).

While able to provide information, make referrals, and help access procedural adjustments such as victim impact statements, the role of the victim services officer does not change clients' traditional lack of rights vis-à-vis the offender and the state. Officers face restrictions *built around* the traditional criminal process. Thus, they must explain the legal restrictions on what victims can write, that impact statements not meeting these criteria can be rejected, and that they cannot prevent defence cross-examination on these statements.

Such restrictions have prompted criticism from workers in community organizations:

> "Victim services is part of the system. While some workers are willing to go the extra mile, they take a lot of flak for it from the Department of Justice. They are constantly being pulled and defending what they're doing" (interview #25: female, age 42).

> "Some of them may care, but there is only so much they can do. Their hands are tied" (interview #11[a]: male, age 47).

One client criticized how these restrictions inhibited his officer's role, claiming that they impacted on the powerlessness he associated with the victim identity (Box 6.5).

Other clients were less generous. A common complaint was that "it's all about what happens in court, and they don't want to talk about anything but court and how you felt there" (interview #20: female, age 17). Others complained that content restrictions on impact statements inhibited them from expressing their experiences: "There is a lot of 'you can't say this' and 'you can't say that'" (interview #21: female, age 35). While policies protect officers from being subpoenaed, cross-examined by the defence counsel, and

BOX 6.5:
POWERLESSNESS FOSTERS POWERLESSNESS

"Victims services is the only bright spot in the whole system. While they're caring, there's got to be some kind of legislative change put in place so they have some teeth, so if the victim doesn't agree with the way things are going they have some avenue of appeal instead of feeling so bloody powerless. I feel so sorry for the victims services officer. She may be there to provide a service, but the bottom line is she is bloody near as powerless as the victim. There is nothing in place to allow her to have any kind of real clout. It's like she's both inside and outside some conversations we have. It's like she's supposed to be an advocate of the victim, but when she deals with the Crown it's like 'Why the hell are you sticking your nose in?' The way things are, she is little more than a feel-good option—better than nothing, but almost a figurehead" (interview #12: male, age 43).

Source: Kenney, J. S. (2001). *Unintended Consequences: The Impact of Victim Support Organizations on Victim Identity.* Unpublished post-doctoral research, Dalhousie University, Halifax, NS.

potentially damaging their clients' case, officers must also ensure that victims' input is not excluded. Clients find this hard:

"Victim services told me not to talk about my case. It's in your face all the time to be quiet or you'll hurt the case. That's the biggest problem 'cause you can't talk about your experience, even though you're there because you need help. It re-victimizes by shutting you up. It's very limiting and adds to the feeling of the horrible secret in the first place. It triggers those feelings, and is not empowering, but inhibiting" (interview #21: female, age 35).

Ultimately, while many clients found the information provided helpful to some degree, both clients and support staff from other organizations were critical of these institutional restrictions, particularly when they sensed that some officers were just doing a job:

"It's a token response. They were good listeners, but I almost felt at times when talking with them that they had a list in front of them. That's the feeling I got. Very quickly I realized who signed their paycheques. It's a conflict of interest. They know if they want their jobs they can't go outside of political policy. The system is the key—they are in so let's protect ourselves. I felt they thought I would go so far, realize I couldn't fight the system, and learn to accept it. It definitely made me feel more like a victim, more reliant on the system" (interview #23: female, age 48).

"Victim services staff get a salary, go to the office and do their job. It is a more structured approach than ours and they don't want to cross professional boundaries" (interview #7: female, age 53).

Officers responded in three ways. Some noted that legislation limited their actions, wished they could do more, and blamed the system: "I often take the heat for the system's failures" (interview #24: female, age 42). Others asserted that their contributions to client claims of victimhood were, at best, limited, because they dealt with clients only for a short time (interview #30: female, age 47). Still others claimed that clients already saw themselves as victims, minimizing accentuation of victimhood during encounters (interview #30: female, age 47). Yet, these do not entirely negate their impact or clients' claims to victimhood.

Ultimately, there was a tension between attempts to avoid encouraging further claims to victimhood and the presence of factors that did just that. Victims' services programs illustrate the curious paradox of attempting to encourage empowerment in an institutional context where staff have little or no power themselves—like trying to give someone a hand-up with both hands tied behind your back.

Several comments are in order. First, organizations that design such programs tend to conceive of victims in a manner that fits their pre-existing goals and functions (Weed, 1995). Thus, in the Department of Justice, as in studies of US victim witness programs, the "purpose is to gain the victim's cooperation in proceeding against the accused" (pp. 106–107). Support outside of the witness goal is largely disregarded or the client is referred elsewhere.

Second, this suggests unmet needs. In a study of US victims' services programs, Davis et al. (1999) found failure to meet important, short-term victims' needs (e.g., safety, crime prevention, property replacement). Less than 5% of respondents reported being helped by such programs beyond counselling and advice. Similar problems may exist here.

Finally, there is the issue of symbolism versus substance. Many programs aimed at victims have been created without regard to or investigation into their expressed needs (Shapland, Willmore, & Duff, 1985). Indeed, victims' interests have never been the force behind such programs (Rock, 1990). Some have claimed that victims were being used to further the "law and order" agenda (Mawby & Gill, 1987); others that victims' services programs serve official needs, not victims' needs (Elias, 1983). Given the above, such claims are not far fetched.

PRIVATE VICTIM SUPPORT/ADVOCACY ORGANIZATIONS

While support workers ostensibly assist victims, thereby helping to improve their psychological condition (Winkel & Renssen, 1998), "even the best responses to victimization may be aversive to the victim" (Taylor, Wood, & Lichtman, 1983, p. 25). Research has highlighted several potential problems with the relationship between support workers and their clients: (1) misperceptions are problematic, particularly support workers potentially overstating—and perpetuating—the seriousness of clients' psychological problem (Denkers, 1996; Dineen, 1996; Winkel & Renssen, 1998); (2) support workers may make unwarranted attributions (Batson, O'Quin, & Pych, 1982), inferring that the problem lies with the client instead of with their situation (Conrad & Schneider, 1980; Dineen, 1996); and (3) support workers may exhibit an "upward bias" in their expectations of clients' social comparison processes: while victims can enhance well-being by comparing themselves with less fortunate others (Wills, 1991; Wood, 1996), there is evidence that support workers may expect victims to feel similar or cope similarly to other victims, thereby threatening therapeutic success (Winkel & Renssen, 1998). Despite this, little has been done to examine the impact of support workers on clients. Thus, study of both parties, and their interactions, is warranted.

Through interviews and observations of an organization for the victims of impaired driving,[17] in this section I consider the interrelation of such dynamics and victims' experiences. Central is the therapeutic issue of encouragement versus discouragement of victim claims.[18]

This organization was privately run, focused on specific offences, combined support and advocacy functions, and operated largely through victim volunteers rather than professional employees, suggesting dynamics that might not be found in other groups.

Support Practices and Coping

Most clients indicated that encounters with this organization had both aggravating and mitigating aspects, often simply noting things they liked and disliked. Support volunteers responded with factors that they considered to be helpful and unhelpful to clients. Such surface issues masked a larger tension. As with the victim support officers discussed earlier in this chapter, trained support workers in this organization were aware of and attempted to deal with the potential for increasing a client's sense of victimhood through support practices. These strategies were not exhaustive, with victim claims perpetuated regardless.

Clients encountered both other victims and non-victim volunteers, some of whom (both from the victim and non-victim groups) had taken a national training program on dealing with victims. When contacted by clients, trained individuals generally provided emotional support and information on common problems and services, and were sensitized to the issue of encouraging victimhood. The organization did not approach potential clients and encouraged "boundaries" so that supporters did not assert "this was my experience and you are going to experience this too" (interview #17, female, age 52). Rather than taking over clients' responsibilities, the organization encouraged "listening," "normalization," and "helping people to help themselves" (interview #4, female, age 53), so as "not to make them more of a victim" (interview #29, female, age 44). A volunteer described the following:

> "I've taken the training, so I've been taught how to talk to victims, what to say and what not to say ... Basically, you're taught to be a good listener. Let the victim talk and talk ... and cry if they want to cry—and there is nothing wrong with crying with them. We're also taught not really to make suggestions to them. All suggestions and thoughts have to come from them and we listen. If they had a suggestion, I would say 'Would you like to do that? Do you think that would make you feel better?' If yes, I would say 'If you feel you would like to give that a try, then do it. Do you need any help with doing that?'" (interview #17, female, age 52).

Clients often appreciated such practices. Some claimed to find an "outlet" where they could repeat their story to people who listened and "understood" (interview #29, female, age 44); others said they found "talents I didn't know existed before" (interview #11(a) male, age 47). Indeed, one man commented: "I have never felt treated in a condescending way as a helpless victim. They respect your space if you want, will listen if you want to talk. Nothing is pushed on you" (interview #6, male, age 49).

Others, however, were perplexed and frustrated:

> "[The organization] doesn't encourage people to see themselves as victims. It's like they don't want the work or something. I feel [this organization's] hands-off approach is too limited.

> They should treat people more as victims than they do—they
> can't hurt you any more than you've already been anyways. I'd
> like to see more initiating of personal contact, more laying out
> of what is going to happen, or what could happen than is done
> right now" (interview #11(b), female, age 43).

Outside of the differing reactions, problems arose in applying this philosophy. There was an expressed need to "screen out" of training those "that feed off others' tragedy, making them dependent." There was also controversy over applicants who "push their ideas on people," which "really upsets the other victims" (interview #17, female, age 52).

Despite this, the main problem involved the consistent practice of this philosophy. Some admitted asking "leading questions," making suggestions, and using personal experiences in their conversations with new clients (interview #29, female, age 44). In addition, there were implicit characterizations of clients as victims in the organization's literature. Consider contrasting quotes from a support volunteer and a client, respectively:

> "During the course we are given all these pamphlets about cop-
> ing with grief, different stages of grief, [post-traumatic stress
> disorder], etc. But they don't want you to push that on people—
> more to understand it. Then they give you pamphlets on vic-
> tims hoping you are going several times to see the victim. Dur-
> ing one of those times you bring these pamphlets, read them
> together, and have a little discussion" (interview #17, female,
> age 52).

> "The opinionated pamphlets National makes available on
> grieving, the justice system, etc., bring you down more, and
> can dash your hopes" (interview #14, male, age 38).

This also illustrates the problem of providing information without encouraging further upset. Trained volunteers provided information on grieving, the justice system, things that might trigger upset, and upcoming issues and events, risking creating self-fulfilling prophecies:

> "I told a mother 12 months to the day, not exactly, but 12 months
> would be the very worst time for her, because of all the courses
> I have taken and all the grieving courses I have taken. Twelve
> months from the day would be the worst crash of all ... And a
> year later she called me one day and said 'I think you better

come over. It has happened. Right back to day one'" (field
notes, male, age 45).

Thus, despite training, clients' sense of victimization may be encouraged.
While some supporters claimed clients already saw themselves as victims
(interview #17, female, age 52), clients often disagreed:

> "They told me I was a victim. I didn't know what to classify
> myself as before that" (interview #1, female, age 65).

> "Initially I wouldn't say I saw myself as a victim until I realized
> what victim meant to many other people. [The organization]
> has a very broad definition of victim, which I found through
> meeting others, as well as looking in the national office man-
> ual" (interview #10, male, age 35).

Such issues were exacerbated among untrained members. Since this
organization operated in part as a support group, participants risked passing off their experiences on others. There were two sides to the issue. On
one hand, the organization could provide far more "personal" contact than
government victim services, where others "understood," enabled downward
comparisons, provided purpose, and taught about coping:

> "It gave me a purpose. It helped me a lot with my grieving. It
> made me see I'm not the only victim in the world. It helped me
> in seeing a lot of different aspects of different victims, what
> they went through and will go through, some better off and
> some worse off than me" (interview #1, female, age 65).

> "It has been a good learning experience. It has been a way to
> see how others deal with their problems ... That is one of the
> things that helped me early on" (interview #10, male, age 35).

On the other hand, encounters could also increase clients' upset: "Many
victims focus on the perpetrator and the negative aspects. All this negativity
brings people down" (interview #6, male, age 49). Indeed, encountering others' upset and experiences could trigger a volunteer's own negative feelings:

> "Sometimes it is really depressing when you are working with
> other victims. I do find that depressing because there are so
> many victims with their sad stories, and I do know how they

feel and what they have facing them. I find that frightening for them. It sets me off sometimes and gets me down" (interview #4, female, age 52).

Also, untrained individuals may give inappropriate advice: "Others try to help when they haven't sorted out their own problems ... If I base my recovery on an organization, then there are all kinds of things that other people can do that can damage that recovery" (interview #3, male, age 29).

Finally, such encounters can prolong a sense of victimization: "The sad part is we are still constantly having to be victims all the time" (interview #4, female, age 52). Indeed, while some felt that "for the first year or two [the organization] will help them cope, help them hold their own" (interview #4, female, age 17), several victim volunteers found it necessary to pull back:

> "At some point it's healthy to make a break or it just keeps the wound open. I have seen people who are ready to move on-who are survivors—and I'd rather they did for their own mental well-being 'cause it's not good for them to be around that environment. Because, unfortunately, we're always adding new membership. Some people benefit from the support of the organization, piece their lives back together as best they can, and are OK now. That's a healthy decision on their part. Involvement isn't good for everybody. There are others who are dependent on [the organization] to keep their own wound alive, and that becomes an emotional crutch to them. They constantly have this grief in their lives" (interview #29, female, age 44).

"Professional Victims"

Beyond these matters, organizational issues became significant. "Victims" and "non-victims" comprised this organization—often in overlapping roles. The inclusion of both parties was seen as both a leveller and balancer:

> "[The organization] is very inclusive of both injured victims, bereaved victims, and non-victims. The victim role is a great leveller of boundaries [at National level especially]" (interview #6, male, age 49).

> "Non-victim membership helps balance the constant focus on 'poor me.' Instead of being non-functional and unfocused, you need somebody who hasn't had that kind of pain to be there. Whether it's in court or at the funeral home or whatever.

BOX 6.6:
THE HIERARCHY OF VICTIMS AND VICTIM CLAIMS

"In [the organization], there is a hierarchy of victims, with those who have lost a child at the top, lost siblings next, injured third, and non-victims—or victims by association—at the bottom. I feel without a non-victim balance people feel obligated to see themselves as victims and victimized by each case that comes along. Otherwise they will be looked at differently, lose status and attention. Even non-victims feel this pressure. All contributes to a further feeling of victimization. In this chapter, without the efforts of non-victims, all the victims would become professional victims. Many don't see that" (Interview #14, male, age 38).

Source: Kenney, J. S. (2001). *Unintended Consequences: The Impact of Victim Support Organizations on Victim Identity.* Unpublished post-doctoral research, Dalhousie University, Halifax, NS.

Somebody who cares, but is not hampered by that" (interview #7, female, age 53).

However, problems occurred making this balance work. These were related to perceived hierarchical differentiation on victim status (Box 6.6).

This was partly rooted in the differential treatment of victims externally, such as when the media would ask spokespersons "Are you a victim?"— changing tone accordingly (interview #7, female, age 53). Indeed, advocacy may partly require such a differentiation (e.g., anticipating criticism over a controversial public display, one was observed to say "If we get a hard time, we'll just put a mother up front"). It was also seen in differential—and deferential—treatment of victims in the group (interview #17, female, age 52). Indeed the first question often asked of newcomers was "Are you a victim?" (field notes). All of this culminated in the emergence of what some termed "professional victims" (Box 6.7).

This characterization was controversial. Some "victims" agreed, distancing themselves from such individuals to gain balance in their lives (interview #14, male, age 38). Others felt it unfair:

"I don't see anything wrong with being a professional victim. It's a good motivator, and if you're focused enough or rational enough, it's OK. I'm not sure about the amount of time people stay involved, but I feel that I'm going to be a victim until the day I die. I have been victimized and nothing is going to change that.

> BOX 6.7:
> ## THE LABEL OF "PROFESSIONAL VICTIM"
>
> "There is a difference between victims who fight for change, but have outside activities and interests, and professional victims. All they have is [the organization]. That's all they live for is to say 'My child was killed by a drunk driver.' They don't have anything else. They don't have a life. After they get up in the morning, that's all they do all day long—suffer. Everything that is in their life they relate back to their loss—or their injury in some cases. This is distinguished from a victim doing professional things (e.g., getting legislation changed). These people do not go to psychiatrists or counsellors. They don't want to be healed or re-channelled because they wallow in that. It's their claim to fame. That's the danger in these organizations. They will not heal because they don't want to lose that—distinguished from finding a cause where you still have a life outside. You have to grow in other ways too, not just in that particular area. Being a professional victim is a health danger—mental health which goes to physical health. You need some kind of balance—to be multi-dimensional rather than uni-dimensional" (Interview #7, female, age 53).
>
> **Source:** Kenney, J. S. (2001). *Unintended Consequences: The Impact of Victim Support Organizations on Victim Identity.* Unpublished post-doctoral research, Dalhousie University, Halifax, NS.

Why not be a professional one? I have learned a lot about myself the last three years ... I found being a victim was a learning experience and I keep on learning all the time about myself, the system, other victims ... I've found a purpose in my life that I didn't have before. Before the tragedy I was one of the crowd. Now that I'm a victim, I'm sort of plucked out of that crowd. Now, all of a sudden, I'm somebody" (interview #11(a), male, age 47).

This manifested in disagreements and problems: "There is a real victim/non-victim separation in our chapter" (interview #7, female, age 53). This led to further claims of victimization:

"Office politics re-victimizes. One woman was pushed out of the chapter, which precipitated a victim/non-victim split. One member in particular seems to wear the word 'victim' on her forehead, and is causing problems. She is a professional victim. Others feel used and abused, and are divided by gossip. This re-victimizes as well. As a manager she is pathologically inept—and some of us want to fire her—but we can't easily do so" (interview #7, female, age 53).

"I have some problems with internal politics in the local chapter. There was a non-victim troublemaker I got rid of, and some people in the chapter are still mad. The back-stabbing is getting on my nerves, and my skin is even breaking out. Before that I was fine. Now I feel victimized, and may step down [from my position]. I'm thinking about getting counselling" (interview #1, female, age 65).

But conflict was not limited to "victims" and "non-victims"—internecine difficulties emerged between "victims" as well:

"I initially felt that I was going to be taken care of here, as we all have the same mission. However, I experienced conflict with both victims and non-victims over my forceful ways, and was told to 'keep a rein on it.' There are various tensions within the group over style, sharing, awarding of programs, tasks, and compensation, which left me feeling that I was being victimized by my own—being pulled in and pushed away at the same time. For example, being promised, but then not being given a place in a training program, not being able to tell my story since another victim is always telling hers, plus ongoing politics and undercurrents. I have to do the dirty work without any compensation, but perks are awarded to others. In fact, I feel used in that my case was an opportunity to get attention for [the organization], but I wasn't treated with the respect due a victim in the long run. I felt victimized, and almost left" (interview #2, female, age 48).

"If you are going to do this, do it for the right reasons, don't do it for a spotlight. Do it because you want to help somebody" (interview #14, male, age 38).

Indeed, a "non-victim" staff member stated: "Right now, politics is hurting our chapter, and we're losing members. Poor management results in playing favourites, gossip, and pitting victims against non-victims and each other. This is re-victimization" (interview #7, female, age 53).

Much inter-victim conflict appeared to be linked to competing claims of victimization relative to the perks and attention associated with the hierarchy above. Similar to "victim contests" (Holstein & Miller, 1990), individuals appeared to be claiming, implicitly, that "I'm a bigger victim than you are," each upping the ante by finding other reasons to feel victimized and undermining others' claims by casting blame. Indeed, some "non-victims" joined in, referring to themselves as "victims by association." This vicious cycle continually reinforces victimhood among all concerned. Needless to say, newcomers encountering—and being drawn into—such a dynamic have great difficulty finding support that enables them to avoid the victim identity.

These results corroborate questions about therapeutic gain. While some found encounters supportive and helpful, others viewed themselves as increasingly disempowered, upset, or victimized. Furthermore, comparative research should consider how the former may be increased and the latter problems minimized to help avoid internal conflict and fostering victimhood in such groups.

WOMEN'S SHELTERS AND COMMUNITY OUTREACH SERVICES

I now examine clients' encounters with women's shelters and outreach services,[19] focusing on encouragement versus discouragement of victim claims.[20]

Privately run, although often receiving some public funding, women's shelters provide a safe haven for victims of domestic violence. In addition to shelter, food, clothing, and child care, they offer emotional support, court support, referrals (e.g., for Legal Aid, social assistance, housing), counselling, and support groups. Outreach services provide support for non-residents or former residents (e.g., referrals, security signalling devices), particularly education, counselling, and support groups.

As with the other two groups discussed in this chapter, most clients indicated that their encounters with these groups had both aggravating and mitigating aspects, often simply noting things they liked and disliked. Support staff responded with factors that they considered to be helpful and unhelpful to clients. Again, these surface issues masked a larger tension. Workers were aware of and attempted to deal with clients' potential for increasing victimhood through support practices. These strategies were not exhaustive, with victim claims perpetuated regardless.

Thus, support workers claimed they attempt to avoid having expectations of clients, letting clients direct what support role they play:

> "I let whatever they tell me they need me for determine more
> specifically what my role will be. I feel personal boundaries

are important. I try not to judge or to urge clients to make specific choices. I try not to have expectations of clients" (interview #8, female, age 27).

"Our approach is based on the client's choices. If she is unsure on an issue, staff point out the options and the possible consequences. We have a real hands-off policy around advice. We don't give advice, we give options. In five years of collecting departure stats no one has indicated that staff was telling them what to do" (interview #9, female, age 39).

However, this approach was not consistently followed:

"I might make a suggestion, such as discussing their situation with the police, but I won't push them. I try not to have expectations of clients, but it's hard sometimes. In one case I told a client who kept complaining of telephone harassment 'Don't talk to him'" (interview #25, female, age 42).

"I hope that the expectation of all the staff is that the women will go through their own process—and I think it is unrealistic. I mean, my expectation is that a woman will learn to take care of herself and won't put herself in the situation where she is being abused ... Sometimes we want more for our clients than they want for themselves. I think I'm aware of that—most staff are—but it is very difficult to see a woman come back seven times" (interview #9, female, age 39).

Clients largely corroborated that they had choices, but were more vocal about staff expectations:

"I had control. I had the choices somewhat. Sometimes they tried to steer you in the right directions—in a direction you might not think is right—but they never made your choice for you. They would suggest" (interview #22, female, age 32).

"They basically gave me support and some sensible advice that I just didn't have before. I was the one that would call the shots; they just listened. I didn't do everything they thought I should" (interview #18, female, age 28).

"When I decided to go back to my husband I felt they looked down on the fact I was even considering it. I felt they were trying to persuade me not to" (interview #26, female, age 33).

This tidy situation described in which clients "call the shots" while staff make suggestions is not entirely accurate, particularly when staff commented:

"Many victims are looking for someone to tell them what to do. They're used to that" (interview #9, female, age 39).

"In counselling, I believe in 'windows of opportunity' when a person is really vulnerable and really wanting to do the work. It is just amazing what you can do" (interview #9, female, age 39).

Could it be that subtle suggestions by staff, coupled with clients' needs, provide a fertile ground for personal transformation? It was certainly clear many clients experienced radical changes in perspective. Thus, shelter staff noted how clients are suddenly "able to understand that abuse happens to others too. On some level they feel less isolated" (interview #9, female, age 39), while clients commented that learning from others, they "didn't feel so alone" (interview #27, female, age 29).

Indeed, there were opportunities for clients to make downward comparisons. Thus, one support worker commented, "It's a real eye-opener that they're not the worst off, that they're all in this together" (interview #9, female, age 39). Clients agreed:

"Most helpful were the women—listening to all the women. All talking together and telling each other stories. It is almost like a healing process ... there are also women that have worse-case scenarios and you look at them and you say 'Wow, I thought I had it bad. This poor woman has been thrown down basement stairs ...' It's unreal some of the things you hear" (interview #28, female, age 24).

There were also opportunities to redefine personal responsibility.

"Since my involvement with outreach I feel better about myself. Before I felt things were my fault. After I dealt with them and I learned about other people having the same kind of problems,

you realize it is not you. You're not alone and it's not your fault"
(interview #22, female, age 32).

Finally, there were changes in clients' sense of strength, ability, and self-image. Staff commented: "I have seen some dramatic changes in the confidence of clients over time: making eye contact, becoming involved in activities, and showing care for their personal appearance ... They're back in control and taking stock of the situation" (interview #25, female, age 42).

Clients corroborated that staff listen, boost, and involve them. For example, being repeatedly told "how much of a dynamite woman you are" (interview #28, female, age 24); being given "little projects to do" and "[invited] into the Women's Collective where my voice actually meant something" (interview #21, female, age 35). The most dramatic instance involved a client who was given self-defence training:

"The self-defence course made me feel like I was bulletproof ...
I had a confrontation with the offender three weeks later. He
was breaching his undertaking and I threw him off my property. It felt really, really, really good. You lose that intimidation.
It made me feel strong. I think just the look on his face when I
threw him across the room was enough. I loved it, loved every
second of it" (interview #27, female, age 29).

Much of this suggests an implicit—but unnamed—utilization of clients' initial powerlessness in a context enabling them to actively define them-selves in terms of traits uncharacteristic of the victim role.

But is there another side to clients' encounters? Certainly shelters do not always provide a "healthy living environment," and various rules and required chores could pose difficulties:

"Clients don't like chores and our structured environment,
with a curfew and rules against alcohol and drugs—especially
younger girls. They often feel their choices are inhibited. This
can be upsetting, particularly in a strange environment with
lots of others and personality conflicts. Some also find it upsetting that supportive males can't visit. The shelter is not an easy
place to live, and can exacerbate mental health issues. Problems sometimes arise in 'caretakers' trying to take care of other
women instead of dealing with their own issues. Issues around
the safety of kids are problematic as well, women going down
for a smoke without their child. Things are the most difficult

when they are planning to return to their relationship, and Children's Aid is suggested. They feel betrayed, and that we've broken their confidence" (interview #9, female, age 39).

There was a third issue that was particularly upsetting to some clients: the sometimes intensive focus on what happened to them. Counsellors freely admitted this—with institutional narratives as explanation:

> "Many are still in denial, and find the education groups difficult because it requires them to look at themselves and their experience" (interview #9, female, age 39).

> "In counselling, some women find it upsetting when not at the stage where she wants memories dredged up" (interview #25, female, age 42).

Clients, however, had their own viewpoint (Box 6.8).

This illustrates a tension between providing information and suggestions that enable clients to make choices, and providing a rigid environment where choices are limited and suggestions are pursued until they may re-victimize. Naturally, support workers had answers to implications of re-victimization such as "denial" and their time-limited involvement ("a six-week shelter"), and stressed a client's responsibility to ultimately make changes herself (interview #25, female, age 42). Still others claimed that clients were already victims, or blamed the justice system:

> "I feel that those clients whose sense of victim identity increases over time are those that present as such at the outset, then get screwed by the system. While some may be reflected back in interactions with me, this is a small part of the time. More has to do with the system itself" (interview #8, female, age 27).

There was a dynamic central to both these replies and the organization's philosophy. Despite disclaimers that support was determined by clients, practices were premised on a strategy of "empowerment." This did not negate sympathy, but rather than sympathizing to the point of encouraging a sense of weakness, clients were encouraged to recognize their strengths, take charge, and cast aside the helplessness and lack of power in their lives. Downplaying the victim role loomed large in this strategy: "We're not into labelling, but empowerment" (interview #25, female, age 42). Indeed, when asked about the victim role in clients' encounters, one staffer replied: "This

BOX 6.8:
"FACING IT HARD"

"Their approach was more or less to face what happened and face it hard, because it is easier to get over it once you face what happened. They focus so much on looking at what happened that it really made me think of it more. They were always pushing me: 'We are going to get a deep sense of your thoughts and get you over it faster.' They kept pushing me to pursue the case. That's not understanding at all. They would pressure and pressure it, saying 'Next time we are going to do this,' gradually working towards the incident. I don't like it when they ask me personal questions, going deeper and deeper and telling you that they want to hypnotize you and do all these scary things to your mind. Every time my counsellor would ask a question I would answer it and she would just sit there and stare at me for five minutes and not say a word—just making me more uncomfortable. They kept pushing it, going deeper and deeper into it where you got so uncomfortable that you started picturing it again. I found it really hard because you got so deep into it that I would doze off and have nightmares while I was daydreaming. They never wanted to talk about anything but the scariest part. One time she even said I might have enjoyed the feeling [of the sexual assault] and now feel guilty. I was disgusted. I got too scared, fed up and quit. While they told me I had choices to do things I felt I had no control over what I wanted. They kept pushing their own agenda, saying they want to spend more time with me doing more counselling. They had expectations of me despite what they said. I don't think I would be where I am today if I kept going" (interview #20, female, age 17).

Source: Kenney, J. S. (2001). *Unintended Consequences: The Impact of Victim Support Organizations on Victim Identity.* Unpublished post-doctoral research, Dalhousie University, Halifax, NS.

isn't really relevant to the women who use our service" (interview #9, female, age 39). Another elaborated:

"I don't use the word victim. Most women dislike it and it adds to their feelings of powerlessness. I use the word survivor. In fact, if they're saying 'victim, victim, victim, here I am with a big X on my forehead, look at me' I start talking about survivor. I stress how much strength it takes to stay in a situation like that, that it takes definite survivor skills to be able to maintain a household, raise children, etc., in that kind of atmosphere. I draw that out and let them see that in individual counselling and support groups ... We emphasize that clients have the strength to move beyond the abuse because of the strength it took to get here in the first place. They have the control and choices, but we help them reclaim their selves" (interview #25, female, age 42).

Such efforts to downplay victimhood raises the question of whether this unintentionally results in its encouragement in another way. Why do clients need to be empowered? Is a strategy of empowerment implicitly premised on helplessness? Is this not a component of the victim identity? Indeed, despite disclaimers about labelling, it may be that this strategy implicitly altercasts new clients as victims, even when they may have not thought of themselves in this way before.

However, such questions were overwhelmed by two support practices: support groups and counselling. In each, despite earlier disclaimers, support workers exposed clients to materials that clearly defined and helped them to "realize" that they were victims of abuse. Thus, a counsellor noted she goes "out on a limb" to provide unsolicited information (Box 6.9).

Many clients also learned about the "cycle of violence" and "signs of abuse" in groups:

"When we go to group it teaches us what is abuse. Actually the first day they gave us a scribbler and all these things on what is sexual abuse ... the list is five inches long. You tick off what applies to you, and that is how I figured out, 'Yeah, I had to do that. Yeah, I had to do that ...' That is how you find out, because a lot of women didn't realize just the extent of how it was—and you don't while you are still at home. Group therapy helped me realize that I was abused. People don't realize what is classified as abuse. Something can be happening to you, but you don't realize that. You know that it is wrong, but you don't really see it as abuse or put a name to it. There was economical abuse, sexual abuse, physical, emotional—that was the biggest one: a lot of head games. They helped me see I was a victim so I could make sure that it wouldn't happen again" (interview #27, female, age 29).

Indeed, on occasion staff did not leave clients to their own conclusions:

BOX 6.9:
UNSOLICITED MATERIAL DEFINING CLIENTS AS VICTIMS

"I provide the information clients ask for, plus the profile of an abusive man. That can be helpful for women, who go 'My God, that's him!' This is especially helpful if women are not sure whether or not they are being abused. It helps break their denial and uncertainty as to whether they were abused, and redefines their situation. Support groups continue this redefinition. We run two support groups, each of which runs 10 sessions over 10 weeks. In the first group we initially give very basic information on what the cycle of violence looks like, what abuse looks like, and different kinds of abuse. Then it evolves into issues of self-esteem, self-esteem building, making choices, etc. In the second group we pretty well carry on from there. It recognizes that they have been abused, that abuse did happen to them, but that they were not responsible for that abuse" (interview #25, female, age 42).

Source: Kenney, J. S. (2001). *Unintended Consequences: The Impact of Victim Support Organizations on Victim Identity.* Unpublished post-doctoral research, Dalhousie University, Halifax, NS.

"They do let you know that you have been victimized and that being victimized is not an easy thing" (interview #28, female, age 24).

"They believed I was a very high-risk victim. It brought home the sad truth—the reality of it more" (interview #18, female, age 28).

Overall, aside from the limited circumstances in which clients felt re-victimized, it would appear that support practices largely resulted in a temporal pattern. This involved: (1) clients coming to claim that they were abused in the past; and (2) being encouraged to gain strength, power, and self-esteem to avoid victimization—and seeing themselves as such—from that time forward. In other words, shelters may initiate—but simultaneously operate to truncate—clients' claims to victimhood, largely in the past tense:

"They do let you know that you are a victim, that you were victimized, but at the same time they try to build your self-esteem so good that you don't feel way down bottom. They try to get away from that" (interview #28, female, age 24).

Ultimately, despite disclaimers about being client-directed, the empowerment support philosophy underlying these organizations was premised on an implicit view of clients as victims. While attempting to downplay the victim role in one way, it simply entered the picture in another. Ironically, these organizations used the victim role—and encouraged claims to victimization—as a foundation upon which to build its precise opposite.

CONCLUSION

This chapter is central to this book, corroborating, in a Canadian context, that since the term "victim" is open to diverse interpretations (Weed, 1995), victim policies may primarily reflect prior institutional and organizational contexts. More research, on a more diverse group of victim programs, should be done to determine how much this pattern holds or varies—with an emphasis on the context of newly emerging programs.

Next, given public programs' often limited response to victims' substantive interests, the theme of "symbolic politics" (Elias, 1983) was found to be more widely applicable than originally formulated in relation to criminal injuries compensation. Thus, one may legitimately question whether "rights" without redress deserve the name, whether ineffectiveness renders the term "victim impact statement" an oxymoron, or whether, in a criminal justice system where victims do not have the procedural rights of a party, empowering victims is mere ideology in a service where victim service officers have little to no power themselves. This is not a welcome situation for victims of crime. Two clinical psychologists have made the following comment:

> "Providing rights without remedies would result in the worst of
> consequences, such as feelings of helplessness, lack of control,
> and further victimization ... Ultimately, with the crime victims'
> best interests in mind, it is better to confer no rights at all than
> 'rights' without remedies" (Kilpatrick & Otto, 1987).

Criminal justice reforms have a long history of initially grandiose claims deflated by subsequent research (Goff, 2004). Further research, on a broader group of victim programs, should be done to determine the impacts of such programs on victims; indeed, whether it is possible that anything can be done within our current system—or can be found in others—to effectively improve the lot of victims. Perhaps these must become more political issues than legal ones.

Finally, counter-intuitive, interactional impacts exist in various programs that potentially encourage a further sense of victimization, broadening victim claims beyond those rooted in the crime and the justice system—corroborating questions about potential risk to therapeutic gain (Winkel & Renssen, 1998). While staff in three organizations exhibited an awareness of this danger, and outlined policy approaches to avoid it, each nevertheless had difficulties. Institutional tensions between policy and practice—in differing services with varying clienteles, organizational structures, and funding arrangements—demonstrably impacted some clients, indicating that initiation, renewal, or broadening of claims to victimhood can occur in different ways. While some found their encounters with support workers helpful, others claimed to be increasingly disempowered, upset, or victimized. The goal of future researchers should be to consider how the former may be increased and the latter problems minimized. The research goal should be practical: better victim services for all. In the words of Fattah (2000):

> "One has to wonder why it is that when the field of victim services is flourishing, research on the effects of victimization and on the impact of victim assistance is hard to come by. And yet it seems obvious that individualized care, individualized assistance, and personalized treatment or counselling require a profound knowledge of the differential impact of victimization and the differential needs of crime victims. Clearly, this is an area that offers golden opportunities for original empirical qualitative research" (p. 40).

ENDNOTES

1. Additional, specialized legislative initiatives are discussed in Chapter 9.
2. A related problem arises with common assault. As this is the lowest assault offence, the Crown sometimes declines to prosecute. Victims who wish charges to proceed must hire a lawyer, while impecunious accused may get legal aid. This is exacerbated if busy prosecutors prioritize caseloads by labelling more serious violence "common assault."
3. Ontario had a maximum lump-sum award for injury or death of $25,000 or $1,000/month (periodic). It also restricted awards to $150,000 (lump sum) and $250,000 (periodic) as the total compensation payable to all applicants regarding one occurrence (*Compensation for Victims of Crime Act*, RSO 1990, c. 24, s. 19[1] and [2]).
4. Eligibility often depended on reporting the offence and willingness to cooperate with the authorities. Most excluded (or reduced) awards to victims who contributed to their victimization. There was often a high minimum dollar limit for requested compensation, below which victims did not qualify.

Applicants bore the burden of proof, often difficult when offenders have dis-appeared with no witnesses. Thus, many did not qualify. In the 1999 Nova Scotia Victims' Services Division *Activity Report*, the most common reasons for denying claims included insufficient evidence of an eligible offence (79 cases), the behaviour of the applicant (14 cases), the case was brought outside of the limitation period (14 cases), the applicant had not cooperated with law enforcement (eight cases), and "other" (six cases). Denials and dismissals made up 34.5% of decisions.

5. This partially flowed from underfunding: "It is easy to understand why it is in some countries there is a deliberate attempt not to publicize these state compensation schemes" (Fattah, 2000, p. 35). Many victims never learn that such programs are open to them. A 1987 Gallup Poll reported that 73% of Canadians were unaware of these programs (Gallup Report: May 4, 1987 *Most Unaware of Compensation for Victims of Violence* (Toronto: Gallup Canada, Inc.). Earlier, only one in 55 eligible Ontario victims were reported to have sought compensation (Malarek, V. (1984b, April 10). Programs help crime victims deal with solitude (*The Globe and Mail*, 10 April 1984, p. M2).

6. Victims were out of luck unless they could persuade officials to extend the deadline (e.g., Compensation for Victims of Crime Act, RSNS 1989, c. 83, s. 8).

7. All of the provinces have built legislation around the ideas of providing infor-mation, support, and referrals because the victim still lacks party status in criminal proceedings.

8. Chapter 25 (Bill C-79). Criminal Code (victims of crime), An Act to amend the *Criminal Code*. SC 1999, c. 25, s. 17.

9. Dawna Speers, Correctional Service of Canada Liaison for CAVEAT, per-sonal communication, 1994.

10. Content restrictions exist to avoid unfairly biasing the sentencing court against the offender. However, many victims don't realize or accept this rationale, and consider restrictions disempowering.

11. The Victim Services Survey (Brzozowski 2007, 3–4), run for the second time in 2005–2006, largely confirms the categorization of services in this 1997 report. It divides Canadian victims' services programs into police-based, court-based, community-based, and system-based agencies. The main difference is that it counts sexual assault centres separately from community-based agencies and sets out a separate category for Ontario's Victim Crisis Assistance and Refer-ral Services, which could be subsumed under one of the other categories.

12. Some private organizations also conduct their own fundraising to avoid becoming "co-opted" by government.

13. Community-based services are dealt with in the following sections.

14. Given that Nova Scotia has over 900,000 people and a 1999 crime rate of approximately 7,733 per 100,000 population, this is probably much lower than the "dark figure" of victims who had no contact with the program (Tremblay, 2000). In the USA, Davis et al. (1999) found that less than a third of the victims in their sample had contact with victims' services programs.

15. See Chapter 1 for a discussion of the methodology used in studying these groups.

16. The data involve adults, so conclusions do not cover the child victim witness program.

17. See Chapter 1 for a discussion of the methodology used in studying this group.

18. The relative impacts of the crime and of the justice system are discussed in Chapters 2 and 4, respectively.

19. See Chapter 1 for a discussion of the methodology used in studying this group.

20. The relative impact of the crime and of the justice system are discussed in Chapters 2 and 4, respectively.

REFERENCES

Batson, C. D., O'Quin, K., & Pych, V. (1982). An attribution theory analysis of trained helpers' inferences about clients' needs. In T. A. Wills (Ed.), *Basic Processes in Helping Relationships* (pp. 59–79). New York: Academic Press.

Beloof, D. (1999). The third model of criminal process: The victim participation model. *Utah Law Review 2*, 289–330.

Brzozowski, Jodi-Anne. (2007). *Victim Services in Canada, 2005/2006*. Statistics Canada–Catalogue no. 85-002-XIE, Vol. 27, no. 7.

Canadian Federal-Provincial Task Force. (1983). *Canadian Federal-Provincial Task Force Report: Justice for Victims of Crime*. Ottawa: Minister of Supply and Services.

Canadian Resources Centre for Victims of Crime (CRCVC). *Balancing the Scales: The State of Victims' Rights in Canada*. (1998). Ottawa: CRCVC.

Compensation for Victims of Crime Act, RSO 1990, c. 24, s. 19[1] and [2].

Conrad, P., & Schneider, J. (1980). *Deviance and Medicalization: From Badness to Sickness*. Columbus, OH: Merrill.

Criminal Code (victims of crime), An Act to amend the *Criminal Code*. Chapter 25 (Bill C-79). SC 1999, c. 25, s. 17.

Davis, R., Lurigio, A., & Skogan, W. (1999). Services for victims: A market research study. *International Review of Victimology 6*, 101–115.

Davis, R., & Smith, B. (1994). Victim impact statements and victim satisfaction: An unfulfilled promise? *Journal of Criminal Justice 22*, 1–12.

Denkers, A. J. M. (1996). *Psychological Reactions of Victims of Crime: The Influence of Pre-crime, Crime, and Post-crime Factors.* Amsterdam: Vrije Universiteit.

Dickson, B. (1984). The forgotten party—the victim of crime. *U.B.C. Law Review 18*, 319–334.

Dineen, T. (1996). *Manufacturing Victims: What the Psychology Industry Is Doing to People.* Toronto: Robert Davies Publishing.

Elias, R. (1983). Symbolic politics of victim compensation. *Victimology 8*(1–2), 213–224.

Erez, E. (1994). Victim participation in sentencing: And the debate goes on ... *International Review of Victimology 3*(1–2), 17–32.

Erez, E., & Laster, K. (1999). Neutralizing victim reform: Legal professionals' perspectives on victims and impact statements. *Crime and Delinquency 45*(4), 530–553.

Erez, E., Roeger, L., & Morgan, F. (1997). Victim harm, impact statements, and victim satisfaction with justice: An Australian experience. *International Review of Victimology 5*(1), 37–60.

Erez, E., & Tontodonato, P. (1990). The effect of victim participation on sentence. Outcome. *Criminology 28*(3), 451–474.

Fattah, E. A. (2000). Victimology: Past, present, and future. *Criminologie 33*(1), 17–46.

Giliberti, C. (1990). Study probes effectiveness of victim impact statements. *Justice Research Notes 1*, 1–8.

Goff, C. (2004). *Criminal Justice in Canada* (3rd ed.). Toronto: Thompson-Nelson.

Goff, C. (2008). *Criminal Justice in Canada* (4th ed.). Toronto: Thompson-Nelson.

Holstein, J., & Miller, G. (1990). Rethinking victimization: An interaction approach to victimology. *Symbolic Interaction 13*(1), 103–122.

Karmen, A. (2001). *Crime Victims: An Introduction to Victimology* (4th ed.). Belmont, CA: Wadsworth.

Kenney, J. S. (2001). *Unintended Consequences: The Impact of Victim Support Organizations on Victim Identity.* Unpublished post-doctoral research, Dalhousie University, Halifax, NS.

Kilpatrick, D., & Otto, R. (1987). Constitutionally guaranteed participation in clinical proceedings for victims: Potential effects on psychological functioning. *The Wayne Review 34*, 17.

Linden, A. (1969). Victims of crime and tort law. *Canadian Bar Journal 12*, 17–33.

Maguire, M., & Shapland, J. (1997). Victim participation in the criminal justice system. In R. C. Davis, A. J. Lurigio, & W. J. Skogan (Eds.), *Victims of Crime* (pp. 231–244). Thousand Oaks, CA: Sage.

Malarek, Victor. (1984b). "Programs Help Crime Victims Deal with Solitude." *The Globe and Mail*, 10 April 1984, p. M2.

Marriott-Thorne, J. (1998). *Presentation to the Parliamentary Committee of Justice and Human Rights*. Halifax, NS: Nova Scotia Victims' Services Division, Department of Justice.

Mawby, R. I., & Gill, M. L. (1987). *Crime Victims: Needs, Services, and the Voluntary Sector*. London: Tavistock.

McAlister, D. (2003). *Financial Compensation for Victims of Crime: Tort Damages as Restorative Justice?* Unpublished MA (criminology) thesis. Simon Fraser University, Burnaby, BC.

Miers, D. (1990). *Compensation for Criminal Injuries*. London: Butterworths.

Murphy, C. (1991). *Victims' Needs and Services in Nova Scotia Research Project*. Halifax: Dalhousie University.

Provincial Secretariat for Justice. (1984). *Ontario Government Consultation on Victims of Violent Crime Report*. Toronto: Provincial Secretariat for Justice.

Re Regina and Antler, (1982), 69 CCC (2d) 480 [29 CR (3d) 283] (BCCA).

Roach, K. (1999). *Due Process and Victims' Rights: The New Law and Politics of Criminal Justice*. Toronto: University of Toronto.

Roberts, T. (1992). *Assessment of the Victim Impact Statement Program in British Columbia*. Ottawa: Department of Justice, Research, and Sentencing Directorate.

Rock, P. (1990). *Helping Crime Victims: The Home Office and the Rise of Victim Support in England and Wales*. Oxford: Clarendon Press.

Sacco, V. F., & Johnson, H. (1990). *Patterns of Criminal Victimization in Canada*. Ottawa: Minister of Supply and Services.

Schmalleger, F., MacAlister, D., & McKenna, P. (2004). *Canadian Criminal Justice Today*. Toronto: Pearson/Prentice-Hall.

Shapland, J., Willmore, J., & Duff, P. (1985). *Victims in the Criminal Justice System*. London: Gower.

Taylor, S., Wood, J., & Lichtman, R. (1983). It could be worse: Selective evaluation as a response to victimization. *Journal of Social Issues 39*(2), 19–40.

Tremblay, S. (2000). *Canadian Crime Statistics, 1999*. Ottawa: Statistics Canada, Cat. No. 85-002-XPE.

Van Ginkel, D. (1990). Finally compensating the victim: Harder v. Brown. *Canadian Journal of Family Law 8*, 388–394.

Victims' Rights and Services Act, SNS 1989, c. 14.

Victims' Services Division. (1999). *Activity Report: April 1, 1998–March 31, 1999*. Halifax: Nova Scotia Department of Justice.

Walker, W. (1994, April 14). Victims of crime ignored: Report. *Toronto Star*, p. A.1.

Weed, F. (1995). *Certainty of Justice: Reform in the Crime Victim Movement*. New York: Aldine de Gruyter.

Wills, T. A. (1991). Similarity and self-esteem in downward comparison. In J. Suls & T. A. Wills (Eds.), *Social Comparison: Contemporary Theory and Research* (pp. 51–78). Hilsdale, NJ: Lawrence Erlbaum.

Winkel, F. W., & Renssen, M. R. (1998). A pessimistic outlook on victims and an "upward bias" in social comparison expectations of victim support workers regarding their clients. *International Review of Victimology 5*, 203–220.

Wood, J. V. (1996). What is social comparison and how should we study it? *Personality and Social Psychology Bulletin 22*(5), 520–538.

CHAPTER 7

Restorative Justice

(with Donald Clairmont)

INTRODUCTION

Chapter 6 highlighted many of the difficulties posed by amendments, programs, and victim services that have been built around existing criminal justice institutions. Criminal justice professionals in search of an alternative have long advocated models of restorative justice (RJ). These draw upon peace-making, mediation, negotiation, alternative dispute resolution, conflict management, and constructive engagement, particularly between victims and offenders (Braithwaite, 1999; Umbreit, 2001). Such ideas have spurred initiatives worldwide. However, little is known about the interpersonal dynamics in RJ (Latimer, Dowden, & Muise, 2001). This is ironic because it has been argued that process is the heart of RJ, the focus should be on means, not outcomes, and that RJ should be defined by practice (Presser, 2004a). Academics have stressed the need for research on the actual processes involved, particularly "how it works" (Cormier, 2002).

While descriptions exist of the general sequence of events in RJ sessions (Karmen, 2001) and of theoretical constructs such as "re-integrative shaming" (Braithwaite, 1999), the underlying mechanisms of RJ must be empirically fleshed out. While shaming coupled with acceptance may help to bring resolution, the hypothesized impact on recidivism has been qualified (Harris, 2006). Sessions involve greater re-integration than the court system, but are not seen as less stigmatizing by participants (Harris, 2006). How disapproval is expressed triggers the emotions of participants: "shame-guilt" is correlated with empathy, while "unresolved shame" and "embarrassment-exposure" are correlated with anger and hostility—each holding different implications for future behaviour (Harris, 2006, p. 342). Our observations of youth victim–offender sessions, involving various offences, shed light on the pragmatic roles of emotion, institutional narratives, rhetorical claims, and strategic action, showing how sessions work and raising issues for researchers, practitioners, and policy makers.[1]

RESTORATIVE JUSTICE AND ITS DISCONTENTS

While research has found participants' views of RJ to be largely positive (Clairmont, 2005; Karmen, 2001; Masters, 2002; Strang, 2000; Zedner, 2002), concerns have been raised about relative victim satisfaction compared to offenders (Acorn, 2004), the "minority" who report negative experiences (Strang et al., 2006), and that victims who do not participate hold less restorative views (Hill, 2002). In turn, it has been questioned whether offenders' views are adequately represented (Toews & Katounas, 2004). Victims do not neatly hold retributive or restorative attitudes (Herman, 2005) and reported satisfaction may reflect status quo conceptions of justice (Presser, 2004a). In addition, attrition of satisfaction in follow-up interviews raises questions about what is missed by exit surveys with fixed-response questions, at times administered by authoritative institutions (Clairmont, 2005).

Since "the victim is called upon to elaborate the collateral ways in which she has suffered as a result of the crime" (Acorn, 2004, p. 145), especially where the offender is a young person,[2] RJ may involve, in part, the narrative construction of identities that encourage labelling as "victim" as opposed to "deviant" (Presser, 2004b), thereby permitting diverse definitions of the situation.[3] Based on our observations, we believe that an examination of how *all* parties employ the victim role is warranted. Victimization claims serve as interpretive instructions advising actors how they should understand persons, circumstances, and behaviours (Holstein & Miller, 1990). Kenney (2002, p. 259) added that both victims and offenders may use the victim role as a "sword" (to achieve goals) and as a "shield" (to deflect criticism), and may alternate strategies as needed. Linking victim status to one party is tied to the assignment of victimizer status to another (Holstein & Miller, 1990), and may mobilize sympathy and alter social distance. As both sides in RJ may use narrative resources to present themselves favourably—in relation to what happened, what was behind it, and in the current session—it is prudent to consider if, ironically, sessions turn into adversarial "victim contests" (Holstein & Miller, 1990, pp. 113–115) where belief in victim claims rests on "credibility, influence, and warrant for honouring one set of claims over another" (p. 114).

Emotion plays a key mediating role (Harris, 2006). Clark (1990) asserted that actors can use emotions in a variety of "micro-political strategies" to enhance "place." Hochschild (1983) considered how individuals manage emotions in line with emotional norms and Thoits (1990) argued that, when emotions are incongruent, one may be seen as "emotionally deviant." If parties are manipulated to foster an image of one as a victim and another as a victimizer—that is, deserving of sympathy or not—then they may use emotions to define the situation and buttress negotiating positions.

While resolving such emotions is key to meaningful outcomes, and the RJ process requires an appearance of understanding, critics doubt that empathy will emerge (Acorn, 2004). Despite the best of intentions, shame may undermine potential empathetic responses and encourage further anti-social orientations and behaviours (Harris, 2006). Indeed, going through a traumatic experience without institutional redress, then adding shame, may be provocative (Gilligan, 2003; Nathanson, 1994; Scheff & Retzinger, 2000). As such, developing empathy may be hard, but building narratives based on shared interests may underlie formally acceptable conclusions.

Related issues involve whether dispute resolution occurs in a relatively hierarchical or egalitarian context (Hoffman, 2001); the roles of ideology, organizational imperatives, power differentials, caseworker practices, and conference dynamics (Tjaden, 1994); "transformative" as opposed to "managed" processes (Dukes, 1993); professionalization, use of voice, and non-verbal signals (Anderson & Snow, 2001; Holstein & Gubrium, 2000; Loseke, 2001); mediator styles of problem-solving versus settlement orientation (Kressel et al., 1994); facilitator competency (Boyack, Bowen, & Marshall, 2004; Gustafson, 2004; Raye, 2004; Wonshé, 2004); and the role of participants such as supporters of the parties (Karp et al., 2004). Finally, links to the criminal justice system may result in programs that narrowly emphasize the responsibilization—rather than restoration and re-integration—of young offenders (Gray, 2005). When organizational factors prevail, questions arise about how "restorative" processes are. If escape and reform are blocked, parties may adopt a blame strategy to absolve themselves of fault (Nespor, 1986), re-embodying the adversarial process.

Our ethnographic study of possible underlying dynamics in 28 youth RJ sessions in a mid-sized Canadian city thus cuts to the core of what RJ is all about.[4]

THE RESTORATIVE JUSTICE PROCESS

Upon the proposal of a police officer or prosecutor, an "offender" who has "accepted responsibility" can "choose" to enter this RJ program to avoid court. "Victims" are then contacted to see if they wish to participate. The RJ agency's paid staff handle case management, arrange meeting dates and the venue (e.g., a school, church hall, or community centre), and assign facilitators (usually trained volunteers). Before each session, two facilitators arrive, review the case notes, and plan who is to do what (e.g., formally begin the session, lay out the ground rules). Once the parties have arrived, the lead facilitator, sometimes referring to cue cards, emphasizes that the session is voluntary and confidential. Procedure is discussed: designated victims, offenders, and supporters will have a say, describe what happened, outline the impact of the offence, discuss issues that emerge, and work toward an acceptable solution that will be written up as a contract. Rules are noted: only one person may speak at a time, what is said is confidential, and others must be treated with respect. Facilitators conclude that their role is to speak little, but to help parties work through the incident, establish common ground, and "keep things on track." This pre-emptively conveys institutional talk and directs clients to specific narratives, providing symbolic resources for the encounter to follow.

Sessions have two phases: (1) parties discuss the incident and its impact; and (2) a resolution contract is worked out. Either the victim or offender is asked to begin by describing the incident and its impact from that particular point of view. After each has spoken, facilitators prompt them to move on to the "contract phase." Phases vary in length, although each often takes up about half of the approximately two-hour session. Throughout, facilitators occasionally intervene to identify and summarize issues and possible solutions, move things along if the discussion is wandering, or step in if a particularly difficult issue threatens the outcome. If an agreement is reached, facilitators write up a contract, have it signed, and send it back to "the agency," which monitors offenders' compliance. If not completed, the matter is referred back to the justice system.

RESTORATIVE JUSTICE AS IT HAPPENS

Victims' Assertive Claims

Victims, picking up on institutional narratives, often underscored their given status by assertive references to just "how serious" the young offender's actions were, and how things could have been "much worse." We call this the "You got lucky so you better give me what I want" strategy (Box 7.1).

Other common claims referred to costs incurred, inconveniences suffered (e.g., insurance claims), shock at offenders' identities and the breach of trust involved, disrespect shown by the offender, how offenders' actions related to a previous trauma, special occasion or items of sentimental value ruined, and the broader social impact (e.g., on co-workers, customers). Some added medical conditions rendering them vulnerable, their profound feelings of shock and terror (e.g., recurring violent images, inability to sleep in a burgled bedroom), and problems working and with getting on with life. All attempted to enhance the victim position and overcome offender claims.

Victim supporters elaborated victims' suffering or emotionally emphasized "what could have happened." A police officer who arrested a youth who was beating another on the ground exclaimed: "Try going to the rehab centre and seeing young people who now need to have their diapers changed!" (case #15). A woman whose son was assaulted and robbed, emotionally proclaimed:

BOX 7.1:
USING THE VICTIM ROLE AS A SWORD (CASE #19)

Facilitator: Why were you throwing rocks from the overpass?

Offender: I had nothing else to do. I was bored.

Facilitator: So, how do you feel about what happened to [the victim and her mother]?

Offender: I'm sorry I ruined your afternoon.

Victim: [Suddenly pulls out a photo of her shattered window, points to it and exclaims] This is my *Mom's head!* It could have caused serious damage. I had glass all down my back. It could have been much, much worse. [Offender], you need to know how serious this could have been. I could have had a baby in the car.

Facilitator: She could have swerved into traffic and killed someone—just because you were bored. What if a child had been in the seat?

Offender: I could have been in worse trouble.

Facilitator: [Shaking his head] Don't think about your trouble. Think about the people. It's six months later. You're in the best-case scenario—no one was hurt.

Source: Kenney, J. S., & Clairmont, D. (2009). Using the victim role as both sword and shield: The interactional dynamics of restorative justice sessions. *Journal of Contemporary Ethnography* (in press).

"[Sternly] I want to get it through your head and consider what if he *died?* How would your Mom feel if that happened to you? Even if it wasn't intended? If you know someone doing something, just get away from it. Don't do something that could hurt someone and not be able to take it back! Think about your future. Does it help to hang with someone that will bring you down? The only reason I'm here is that I'm hearing positive things about you, and I want you and my son to both have a future. I hope things work out. Second chances are good, but not third" (case #2).

Such dramatic enhancement strategies raise the shame level substantially, putting the offender's camp on the defensive. However, the pointed nature of such claims highlights whether embarrassment-exposure or unresolved shame, rather than the guilt-shame associated with empathy, will result (Harris, 2006). Indeed, they lead us to consider the strategic potential of constructed empathy.

BOX 7.2:
USING THE VICTIM ROLE AS A SHIELD (CASE #3)

Offender: From then 'til now I've totally changed into a different person. I don't hang with bad kids anymore. I'm more respectful for my age. I have more feelings for others. I was overwhelmed at the feelings of these people losing things attached to their relatives. Our place was broken into afterwards, now I can't understand why I did it. I felt so bad I thought of suicide. I got beat up by one of the guys 'cause they thought I told on them.

Offender's mother: He got away from them and they harassed, threw rocks at our windows.

Offender: Now I'm agoraphobic. I see a psychiatrist and take medication. The second I step outside I feel sick. I got beat up so much for no reason they scared me into my house. I convinced myself these people are everywhere. We call the superintendent of the building because we get threats. This is still going on.

Facilitator: Is this related to court?

Offender: These guys know I won't tell. I'd be dead next day, or badly beat up.

Source: Kenney, J. S., & Clairmont, D. (2009). Using the victim role as both sword and shield: The interactional dynamics of restorative justice sessions. *Journal of Contemporary Ethnography* (in press).

Offenders' Defensive Claims

Many designated offenders managed their emotions in line with institutional feeling rules and appropriated victim language defensively. They admitted the offence, claimed remorse and guilt, apologized, asserted that the incident had "ruined their lives," and listed the consequences they had suffered (e.g., losing jobs, parental respect, trust).They claimed that they had "changed," "feel bad," fear more trouble, and worked to improve themselves. Some claimed victimhood to evoke sympathy (Box 7.2). We call this the "I've already suffered so don't make it any worse" strategy.

Such enactment of contrition with suffering can be seen as a micro-political emotional tactic to put the offender in a better position, a strategic approach that shows how shame-guilt may be both associated with empathy (Harris, 2006) and used by offenders to manage victim claims.

Supporters reiterated that offenders had suffered consequences, adding vicarious redemption narratives (Maruna, 2001) that they had "learned" and "changed" in positive, responsible directions. Some added their own suffering, doubts, sympathy for the victims, and that they had already disciplined their child, hinting that anything else would be overkill. In a rock-throwing case (case #13):

> *Offender's father*: I'm greatly disappointed in him, but he worked all summer as punishment. He knew the gravity of the situation—that it could have been worse. I apologize too. It's been hard for me.

> *Offender's mother*: I apologize for [the offender]. I knew something was wrong right away. The boys are usually OK sleeping over with friends. He usually spends his time with sports. I spend money on that to keep him off the street. I initially blamed myself. I raised him a lot myself, but always made sure he went where he said. That night his friends stayed on base. Why they did it I don't know. I was hard on him and took everything away except hockey. Otherwise it would give him excuses and chances for trouble. He spent time playing hockey and worked to raise money for [attention-deficit hyperactivity disorder] by himself.

> *Victim 1*: I think that's excellent—to do something positive.

> *Offender's mother*: I told him "What little you have you're selling to help pay for the damage." He's tried since the beginning. If it had been me I'd have gone off the road. So he's had a rough year and isn't allowed to walk the street. He goes where he says. He's playing sports morning 'til night so there's no chance to get into trouble. I really apologize. I would have been furious. This whole thing has gone on far too long.

> *Victim 2*: This is more positive than going to court. I'm glad for the chance to learn from this.

Conversely, there were also offenders who tried to downplay their role, presenting accounts that they were victims of circumstance or "peer pressure." Many essentially disputed the facts:

> "A guy I was with called over [the victim]. My girlfriend said to him 'Don't do that, I know him.' First thing I knew someone hit him. My friend wanted me to have his stuff. I thought 'I can give it back tomorrow.' I was just there in the wrong place at the wrong time. Later, the police called that they were coming to get me if I didn't come in. It was all [the friend's] fault. He's not a friend no more" (case #2).

Others emphasized problems in their home life, dysfunctional family dynamics, victimization, abuse, addictions, or a disorder. One thus tried to excuse violence and property damage at home: "With bipolar disorder, my emotions are very intense. When I'm mad, I'm mad for hours or longer. It's not easy for me to calm down. My emotions are extreme. I don't need to be agitated more" (case #14).

A final "defensive" strategy was at times used when there were issues between offenders and "supporters." Beyond "selective memory loss," some sat sullenly, said little, and, in a crude bid at altercasting, gave the impression that no matter what they did—or do—they will be blamed (case #9):

> *Facilitator*: What is behind this? What do you think you have to do?
>
> *Offender*: [Silent, arms folded.]
>
> *School principal*: Make some good choices? Be honest? Do you really think you're being honest doing what you're doing? Does it really help? Or does it hurt you a bit too?
>
> *Offender*: [Sighs, stares at ceiling.]
>
> *Father*: [Emphatically] I'd really like an answer to that question.
>
> *School principal*: And, you know, it's not always who you're running with either.
>
> *Facilitator*: We're here to get a better understanding. What were you thinking then? Can you help me?
>
> *Offender*: No.

Facilitator: You know that stealing is wrong. Why do you do it?

Offender: [Inaudible.]

Facilitator: Could it be that you do it first and think about it after?

Offender: [Arms folded, no answer.]

Father: [Angrily] When I was a kid people stole out of necessity, but she has no reason. She even stole from our three-year-old. She has everything compared to what I had. I hate to judge her as I'd be judging myself, but no one else in the family does this. It gets me down. I swore I'd never ignore my kids, I've never hit her like my dad hit me, but I turned out better than this. We punish her, but it has no effect. I've tried my best to give her tools to make the right decisions and then I hear this horror story. I'm not handling this well!

Facilitator: Do you know what could happen if you keep getting into trouble with the law? Do you know about criminal records? How they can affect your life (e.g., not getting a job) ... [Silence continues] ... You need to make some good decisions or it will affect you when you're older.

Offenders' Assertive Claims

Offenders at times took a more robust stance, emotionally attempting to turn the table by claiming the victim was really the problem (e.g., "self-defence"). Such shaming provoked anger and hostility. As the exit was blocked by the threat of a return to court, a blame game soon emerged (case #14):

Facilitator: Do you want to make things better?

Offender: [Curtly] I'm dealing with it.

Mother: There have been no more holes in the wall.

Mother's boyfriend: But she can be nasty.

Mother: And she's jealous of [my boyfriend].

Offender: If you grew up with no father figure. He tries to control me! I never accepted her boyfriends and they never stayed over. He's the first overnighter. We lived with my grandparents and she couldn't.

Mother: [Laughing nervously] I didn't want her affected.

Facilitator: You were alarmed when the relationship started?

Offender: I wasn't allowed contact with my grandmother!

Mother's boyfriend: You were ignorant.

Offender: I'm not comfortable having a man telling me what to do when my whole life it was done by two females. He doesn't need to stick his neck in. [To mother's boyfriend] There's *nothing* you can tell me to do that I will do. [Mimicking him] "Don't fight with your Mom ..."

Mother's boyfriend: I do it politely.

Facilitator: Do you like [your mother's boyfriend]?

Offender: I think she can do better.

When victim and offender had no prior stormy relationship, offenders' supporters were more inclined to back them up, casting aspersions on victims regarding facts or responsibility. Some argued that victims unfairly "singled out" offenders, judged "guilt by association," provoked, or roughly handled them. In a case where a victim held an offender until the police came, the offender's father asserted: "I'm mad about how he was apprehended. I'm glad nobody was hurt" (case #13).

The forceful assertion of such claims, by a united front, at times threw victims off guard, prompting defensive posturing. More often conflict escalated, calling for facilitator intervention.

Victims' Parrying Claims

Victims also acted defensively, usually claiming that, by attending RJ, offenders had already accepted responsibility for their actions. Some victims also claimed necessity: the police that their actions were "not personal," they were "simply doing their job"; others claimed self-protection (case #13):

Offender: We ran because we were afraid you'd hurt us. When I was caught, I felt scared.

Offender's father: I heard you said if you were in the woods you'd have been rougher. It was intimidating.

Victim: I wasn't rough with him. So many kids have no appreciation for things, but will go after you if you do them wrong. I went after them, caught him, and protected myself in case he took a swing at me. I just held on hard enough to hold him. You don't know who you're coming across. I never threatened him. The police took a long time coming and didn't do much when they arrived. You need to take responsibility.

Victim's wife: He's a big kid you know.

Offender's father: I didn't appreciate a call from the police at 11 pm to pick up my son. This was a big surprise.

Victim's wife: I saw it. There was no violence. He just held on to him. I'm a mom. I wouldn't let anything happen. He's lucky it was us. Some really rough people could have caught him instead.

In other cases, when it was claimed that they were being too harsh, victims noted that offenders had been "given chances before" and that victims had repeatedly suffered and were justified in their suspicions (case #20):

Offender: [Angrily] It's not like I spent $2,000 on dope!

Victim: [Crying] I asked you about this and now you're saying different. I smell it in your room all the time!

Facilitator: Let's get back to the issue. If you two go at it we won't get anywhere. [To victim] How are you?

Victim: [Through tears] OK.

Facilitator: Do you want to talk from your perspective?

Victim: I checked my bank account and saw three checks went through. When I confronted him, he denied it, said I had to prove it. I had to go to the bank, the police station, close my account, and do an affidavit. They had to investigate. It took months to arrest him. Even then, he wasn't forthcoming about his actions. I *know* 90% of the money went to drugs [sobbing/emotion building]. Now he's moved out of the house!

Offender: [Attempts to interrupt/begins to say something.]

Facilitator: [Sternly] You'll get your turn.

Victim: There were at least 30 other incidents in the past two years as bad or worse. He's written checks before. He stole my car and totalled it. He's done B+Es. He's never had to suffer consequences for his actions or take responsibility. He's got a major drug problem and needs counselling. He's way down there somewhere [motions with her hand] ... I'd like to see him come out sometime before he ends up in jail for the rest of his life ... He's ...

Facilitator: You're worried about him.

Victim: I'm worried sick about him. Visitors to our house have money stolen out of their purses. You have to hold on to everything or it disappears from the house. It's all very drug-related. He needs to get off drugs, get some help and counselling. I can't help him ... [crying] I miss my son! I'm sorry to be so emotional!

Offender: [Begins to interrupt.]

Facilitator: [Emphatically] You'll have your turn!

Victim supporters often reinforced defensive tactics, for example, parents emotionally stating how their "innocent children" suffered: "It was just terrifying as a mother seeing your kid that upset and his friend all full of blood" (case #2). Others countered assertions by offender supporters (case #6):

Offender's mother: This is the first time [the offender] has done anything like this. He's quiet and mild-mannered. He must have been pushed.

Victim's mother: We've had incidents before and [the victim] has been beaten up every year. Other parents have told me stuff that [the victim] wouldn't, but I've seen the effects.

Offender's mother: [Interjecting] The police and school officials said this session was being held because both participated in the fight and [the offender] wasn't being blamed. He's aware his part in this was wrong.

Victim's mother: I've got no tolerance for fighting. [The victim] has always been picked on at school. I really fear for what kids bring in to school now. They're there to learn, not to fight.

Facilitator: Does [the victim's] history make this harder?

Victim's mother: [Emotionally] Yes, I understand that my son was a victim.

Facilitator: Well, a discrepancy exists in what we're dealing with, but the paperwork says that this is a pre-charge for [the offender]. Instead of going to court, let's work with what we have.

Offender's mother: [Grudgingly] OK ... but I'm not happy.

Contests and Outcomes

Competing rhetoric resulted in shame-based "victim contests," where each side effectively claimed to be the "real" or "biggest" victim to gain practical control. Three possible outcomes emerged: (1) the contest could escalate, identification with the victim identity by each side could harden, and the session be terminated, rescheduled, or sent back to court (three of 24 full victim/offender sessions); (2) facilitators could successfully intervene and enable parties to negotiate a contract (11 sessions); or (3) claims could cut common ground, the victim role could expand pragmatically, and parties could accept each other as having been victimized somehow, serving as a vehicle to resolve the case (10 sessions). Exemplary of the first of these

BOX 7.3:
THE UNFOLDING OF A VICTIM CONTEST (CASE #7)

Offender's mother: I took [the offender] from the [group home] to drive him to school. I told him not to hang around [another boy]. He flipped out and started yelling and insulting me in the car. I told him not to treat me like this. Soon I was running down the road chasing him. Then he hit me with something, went into our garage, started beating the door with a shovel, and broke the glass. Then he took off. My other son wanted to call the police.

Offender: [Disputes some details, then says] It really doesn't matter as they'll twist it all around against me anyway and I'll be blamed. I guess I'm the bad guy.

Offender's father: [Angrily] But you did swing the shovel at [your brother]!

Facilitator 2: Everybody calm down! [Things go quiet, all scowling.] OK, one at a time.

Offender's brother: I was holding [the door] and the glass got busted. I started out by saying that he shouldn't be hanging with [his friend]. He shouldn't have been outside.

Offender: Later I punched him and walked away.

Offender's brother: Really, anything could get him going.

Facilitator 1: [To offender] What do you have to say?

Offender: I might as well go with what he said. It will just turn around on me anyway.

Offender's mother: I've heard enough. I'm leaving. [Walks out; others look shocked.]

Offender's father: You're not coming home if you're hanging around with him!

Offender: [The other boy] had nothing to do with it. You're not supposed to take sides here! It's all your fault. Why are you always taking up for Mom?

Offender's father: I'm leaving. [Walks out.]

> *Facilitator 2:* [To both boys] How do you feel about your parents walking out?
>
> *Offender:* [Walks out, tears in eyes, exclaiming] I'm not the bad guy here!

Source: Kenney, J. S., & Clairmont, D. (2009). Using the victim role as both sword and shield: The interactional dynamics of restorative justice sessions. *Journal of Contemporary Ethnography* (in press).

outcomes was a case where a fight on the way to the session re-erupted (Box 7.3).

All parties assertively embraced victimhood to such an extent that positions hardened and no common ground could be cut. Unresolved shame, hostility, and anger made empathy impossible.

Successful intervention was seen in a case where two youth shot a pellet gun at a bus, injuring a teenage girl (case #5). The driver argued with the offender 1's mother over taking responsibility instead of shifting the blame to "peer pressure," and became angry when the youth "smirked" at him. Then:

> *Facilitator 1:* Why don't we take a break?
>
> [At this point offender 1's mother, the bus driver, and the girl and her mother remain, while offender 2's mother goes to the washroom. Facilitators and offenders exit and close the door. Facilitators can be seen conversing intently outside. The bus driver talks to offender 1's mother of the need to take responsibility. She replies that her son is 13 years old and has "an attitude" if confronted. After unrelated talk, most return, wait for offender 2's mother, and it is quiet. Offender 2's mother returns and things resume.]
>
> *Facilitator 2:* Well, [Facilitator 1] and I talked. RJ involves accepting responsibility. Both the police and the caseworker indicated that [both offenders] had already done so. [To victims] Are you willing to keep going, or would you like to stop the process and send the case back to court? It's your call.
>
> [Victims look at each other.]

Girl's mother: The process is fine. All I wanted to hear is they
   felt what they did was wrong with some conviction. I understand you're nervous. [Driver, clearly deflated, backs off.]

Offender 1's father: [Emphasizes to offender] You said you knew
   what you did was wrong.

Victim's mother: Now's your chance.

Offender 2: I'm sorry. I didn't mean to hurt anyone.

Offender 1: I want to apologize. It was wrong for me to listen
   and then go ahead with shooting at a bus.

Victim's mother: That's fine.

Bus driver: That's fine. They were nervous.

This strategy, grounded in institutional discourse, divided victims and enabled completion of the session. Facing court, the more symbolically potent victim spoke up, the driver's offensive was blunted, the offenders apologized, and terms seemingly satisfactory to all were worked out later on.

However, this category is complicated by whether resolutions following facilitator intervention are "meaningful"—whether parties merely "paper over" issues reflective of a settlement orientation, or if this enables one side to "win" and impose terms. Examples of both were evident.

Exemplary of three cases of "papering over" was the "bipolar" youth whose violence toward her mother and mother's partner damaged their home (case #14). Despite facilitators seeking common ground (e.g., "You're actually very similar"), the parties emotionally blamed each other throughout. A few chores were grudgingly negotiated after all were reminded of the court option, and saw it in their interests not to go to court if she continued treatment. One facilitator later stated: "Very little had really been resolved. Really, positions have hardened." A second added: "Nobody is under any illusions."

There were also five cases where facilitator intervention enabled one party to "win" a contest. In one, an offender had accepted responsibility on agency forms and the victim claimed to attend RJ on that basis, but the offender's camp openly disputed his alleged workplace theft (case #4). They argued that he was following existing payroll practices, had no intention of stealing, that the new manager who fired him unfairly "singled him out," and that "With proper training this wouldn't have happened," emotionally adding that he had suffered greatly. The victim objected "This isn't the story I was told," that the offender "had accepted responsibility," and emotionally stated that "If you had just trusted me and been open about your mistake, we wouldn't be here," adding that he too had suffered from resentful staff "siding" with the offender. The facilitator then stepped in. Hearing his point about responsibility validated, and a return to court raised, the victim pressed home his strategy and laid out his desired contract. Despite further objections about "excessiveness," his terms were adopted. The feeling of defeat from the offenders' camp was palpable.

These examples show that facilitator intervention can serve to officially resolve victim contests, but their meaningfulness may be suspect. They also illustrate that limiting clients' opportunities to tell their own stories by directing them to certain narratives, particularly invoking the use of "last resorts" (Emerson, 1981), can result in different outcomes. Such cases highlight issues of problem-solving versus settlement orientation, agency control in negotiations, transformative versus managed outcomes, and just how re-integrative RJ can be in such an institutional context.

The last category, where the victim role pragmatically expands to facilitate resolution, is seen in a case where, after hearing burglary victims speak of fear and violation, an offender and his mother recount harassment from his former friends, who believe he has "ratted" on them. Mutual feelings of victimization micro-politically paved the way for the dramatization of empathy (Box 7.4).

Interestingly, while this partially fits with Harris's (2006) argument that shaming that invokes emotions of guilt can be re-integrative and even associated with empathy, it is actually the enactment of mutual feelings of victimization that mediates this relationship, potentially cutting an area of common ground for empathy to be strategically experienced. Whether such feelings may be relatively lopsided, and the extent of manipulation involved, requires more study.

Strategic Interventions
Further tactical moves were also made by supporters, the police, and facilitators.

SUPPORTERS
Some supporters strategically claimed victimization beyond the formal complaint.

In one variant, "supporters" came down rather hard on uncooperative offenders, claiming that they had violated trust, "revived bad memories,"

BOX 7.4:

THE EXPANSION OF THE VICTIM ROLE SERVING AS A VEHICLE TO RESOLUTION (CASE #3)

Facilitator: Feelings of lack of safety are key tonight.

Offender: I feel exactly the same way as our home was broken into. I'm afraid to go out, even for appointments. We both panic. I hide my PlayStation 2 in case someone comes in.

Facilitator: What can you say to the victims?

Offender: It won't be me if anyone is going to break into your house.

Victim (father): I just wanted you to understand what we've gone through.

Offender: I'm sorry. I'll make it up to you in any way possible.

Facilitator: [To offender's mother] What about you?

Offender's mother: [Crying] I just can't believe today's kids. They aren't afraid of adults anymore. They have no respect. They're vicious. It's different from how I was brought up. They have no fear, respect, and I don't feel safe in my home.

Facilitator: We've talked of feelings and lost sentimental items. How do you feel?

Offender: I feel terrible. You seem like very nice people that wouldn't hurt anyone. At the time I didn't realize. I'm just very sorry it happened.

Victim (mother): His mom is right about kids' lack of respect for adults. I work in a school. It was good hearing from [the offender] and seeing how his life has been altered. I see a lot of bullying in the school I work in.

Facilitator: What help are you getting for the threats?

Offender: Not much. I'm thinking of moving away.

Offender's mother: The police are constantly in contact. I struggle when my son says don't call. We tried that, but it didn't work. Now I call, but we're still being terrorized.

Offender: I see these guys all around. I worry if I go on the bus. I worry they're everywhere. I know the situation [a local news story] where that bullied kid killed himself. I think about it every day. I don't know what to do. You tell the police and there's a problem. You don't tell and there's also a problem.

Victim (daughter): I just don't understand bullying.

Facilitator: Everyone here agrees on a lot. OK, let's start thinking about a contract, about what he can do to make amends. It seems like we have five victims tonight.

Source: Kenney, J. S., & Clairmont, D. (2009). Using the victim role as both sword and shield: The interactional dynamics of restorative justice sessions. *Journal of Contemporary Ethnography* (in press).

and "embarrassed" them, and that they have "tried" but "nothing seems to work," generally indicating that the offender should face the consequences or they "will never learn." One father listed his daughter's repeated theft, lying, drug use, and sexual activity, adding that he had called the police because "this has gone far enough." He claimed that his attempts to "teach her right from wrong" had failed, discipline was unsuccessful, that he "was at a loss," emotionally culminating with: "It all makes me feel like a failure as a father" (case #9). He received strong victim support and, given this alliance, the offender became compliant.

Such assertions were often coupled with excuses, denials, and distancing by supporters to shield themselves from responsibility, including claims that they were on medication, the incident occurred while they were away at work, and that they are single parents or without custody ("I can't watch him 24/7"). These stances were key either to constructing empathy with the victim or to forging an uneasy alliance of interests, making it hard for offenders to negotiate favourable terms.

There were also cases where criticism of the process brought opposing supporters together (case #13):

> *Victim:* This should have been dealt with long ago. I would have liked closure despite the contact ban. It's been very awkward. Getting that over with would have helped. It's also been awkward for [the two offenders].

> *Offender 1's father:* It was very embarrassing for me. It reflects on a parent how their kids behave. I don't like the fact that nobody told me the boys' teacher was one of the victims, and that he was going to be here. If I knew he was coming

I would have been sure that [offender 1] had apologized to his teacher by now.

Facilitator: Whether it's right or wrong , no contact is a standard police policy under our program.

Victim's wife: But how can that be when we live in the same community? There need to be exceptions. They were playing hockey on [the victim's] team for heaven's sake!

Offender 2's father: But we were told to avoid it.

Offender 3's mother: We were told specifically.

Offender 2's father: Give them the opportunity. They should have it.

Offender 3's mother: They had to face this every day.

Facilitator: I see this has been hard on the community.

THE POLICE

If the police were present, offenders' self-serving claims did not go unchallenged. Indeed, facilitators noted this. An example is the following case where a youth claimed "self-defence" after an altercation began nearby (case #15):

Facilitator: What would you have done if the cops weren't there?

Offender: I don't know.

Facilitator: I think that you had a lack of an inner policeman. You haven't said much—only about eight words.

Offender: It was pretty fast.

Officer 2: We all remember being 16/17 [years old]. The [community festival] draws a lot of people and raises a lot of money. Unfortunately, some youth drink and these things happen. But that ruins the event for everybody else. Why would the public want to come back again? And you don't even know what it's over! That's pretty stupid. You have to realize that we've got to wade into that mob scene and put ourselves at risk over something stupid. We could get hurt, especially if the mob turns on us. You're just lucky the victim wasn't hurt bad or you could be in front of a judge. What if he fell down and cracked his head? You'd have to live with that for the rest of your life. I know you weren't thinking, but you should look back and think. You lucked out.

Facilitator: So how's the learning going?

Offender: [Grudgingly] I thought I could throw some punches and get away. Now, I think about the people.

Facilitator: And?

Offender: [To the officers] I'm sorry about putting you people in danger over something stupid.

Facilitator: There's a stiffness in the air. Why?

Offender: I don't like cops.

Officer 1: Why?

Offender: They catch you for doing something wrong—not that I do things wrong.

Victim: That's ridiculous.

Officer 1: What if there's two guys just wailing on you? What if we weren't there?

Victim: I feel the stiffness too. You're not coming across as sincere. I think the others feel it too.

Similarly, when the contract came up, many offenders quickly suggested "community service hours." Here it was unsuccessful, and a police suggestion that the offender volunteer with brain-injured assault victims was endorsed over his objection that "I don't like seeing stuff like that."

BOX 7.5:
**FACILITATORS' STRATEGIC USE OF
UNCOMFORTABLE SILENCES (CASE #15)**

Facilitator 2: What's the ideal outcome here?

Offender: To get it over.

Facilitator 2: How can we help?

[Silence.]

Offender: [Grudgingly] Analyse the situation, ... talk why it
happened, how to prevent it.

[Silence.]

Facilitator 2: [The original facilitator, now the victim] wants to say
something.

Original facilitator/victim: I'm a volunteer. I facilitated [the
offender's] past mediation on assault/disturbing the peace, but
later learned that he hadn't been truthful about his involvement.
I support your statement about getting this over with/learning
from it. Yet, given the past mediation's results, you should be
required to show that you have learned something.

[Silence.]

Facilitator 2: How's that landing?

Offender: [Sheepishly] Fine. What do you want me to do?

Original facilitator/victim: We'll have to talk about what happened
and your explanation. I want to express my feelings, but I need
to hear from you first ...

[Silence.]

Offender: I said I didn't do it. But I told [a volunteer]. I thought I
could pull a fast one.

Facilitator 2: How's that plan working now?

Offender: Not so good.

Original facilitator/victim: I volunteered for this program as I believe in
it. My work deals with people in conflict. I don't like that. I prefer

to have people talk about their problems. That's what drew me to this—people getting to the heart of their problems. I've taken lots of training, invested lots of time. For the most part I like it and get lots out of it. But that brings us to your session where you said you were "in the wrong place at the wrong time." I had some doubts, but your parents were so supportive that it was hard to be hard on you. What was really bad was that a new observer was there [i.e., a potential volunteer facilitator]. When she told me you lied I felt that this was disrespectful to a program that has done a lot of good. Then, I thought of the new person, your parents, and felt bad for them. To be honest, I was pretty mad. I wasn't sure I'd want to participate, but I'd like to restore the honour of the program. It's up to you to take us there and demonstrate to us that you've learned.

[Silence.]

Facilitator 2: So, what do you say?

[Silence.]

Offender: I'd like to say sorry for violating trust, and ... [fidgeting] I'm kind of embarrassed, ashamed to put people through something unnecessarily.

Source: Kenney, J. S., & Clairmont, D. (2009). Using the victim role as both sword and shield: The interactional dynamics of restorative justice sessions. *Journal of Contemporary Ethnography* (in press).

FACILITATORS

While most facilitators took a largely "hands-off" approach, they were active with difficult issues, stressing offenders' need to "take responsibility," questioning the motivation for and consequences of their actions—and even questioning behaviour in sessions. They interrupted, tested thoughts and feelings, and asked if offenders had learned, how they could show they had learned, and what they might do the next time. They questioned openness and sincerity, and pushed offenders to answer or even apologize.

Two strategies were key: (1) drawing out uncooperative offenders in coordination with the victim; and (2) avoiding an unsuccessful outcome by using threats to cancel or postpone the session.

One coordinated strategy involved uncomfortable silences (Holstein & Gubrium, 2000) or questions about the "atmosphere," where facilitator questions were coupled with pointed victim input. This was exemplified in a case in which an offender lied in a prior session, then claimed not to remember (Box 7.5).

Another strategy we call "the velvet fist." This involves the facilitator, offender supporters, and victim(s), faced with sullen and taciturn offenders, evolving a coordinated strategy alternating between emphasizing harms caused by the offender's action and a "tough" caring for the offender. This cuts back and forth, softening-up offenders and laying the foundation to negotiate a resolution. In a case where three youth set a fire, the facilitator initially met vague, self-serving answers and "selective memory loss" (case #8). She asked the victims to describe the impact. They detailed other tragedies they had recently suffered, adding "We didn't need this in our lives at the time." Upon elaborating their loss of private space, sentimental items, and financial loss, the facilitator interjected "Now you're expecting a baby." Next, when prompted, the offender's supporters recounted how this brought back terrible memories of a childhood fire, "shattered faith" in the offenders, and how they feared for the offenders' safety when the police came to the door. One added that she had lost her job, recently suffered a fire, and now faces a lawsuit, so her daughter must "face the music."

> *Facilitator*: Look at all of the grief you've caused. Was it worth it?

> *Offender 2*: No.

> *Offender 3*: I don't even understand how you people [referring to the victims] can be here for this.

> *Female victim*: I didn't want to, but felt it was my duty. [To the offenders] I don't want you to become statistics. I want you to make something of your lives.

> *Facilitator*: That's very powerful considering the damage that was caused to you.

> *Offender 3*: Yes.

> *Facilitator*: [To victims] I'm amazed how you can still care for someone who caused you so much pain.

> *Female victim*: My husband's daughter was taken away too young. [To offenders] I realize that you only get one chance. Don't screw it up.

Offender 3: I'm really sorry. I never really understood.

Offender 2: I just regret doing it.

Facilitator: I hope so. What if a month from now a friend suggests doing something? Are you strong enough? Remember, next time you will go before a court. In fact, I would recommend that you not go through this program again because you've already had your chance. The repercussions of what you did were so serious. Remember, especially, these victims who said that they care about you.

Offender 1: [Who had been the most uncooperative] But we're just kids!

Facilitator: Ahhhh! But how does that make you less responsible? How you act affects how people treat you. Your uncle doesn't trust you now. The relationship has been damaged. Do you have $21,000? What do you have that you'd like to sell? Your snake? What's it worth? We wouldn't do that, but want you to see how quickly something you care about can be gone. Also, remember your actions close doors for yourselves. [To offender 1] I hope you know that, as blacks, we don't need to close any more doors. There's more blacks in prison and we face harsher sentencing. While all people do dumb things and can't get off the path, we always have to do better.

Offender 1: I have friends in [a local youth detention centre], it's not that bad.

Facilitator: Oh, that's just the beginning! It's a picnic compared to [nearby medium- and maximum-security prisons]. You're basically there on your own facing someone saying, quite literally, "Your ass is mine." You have to do it to keep on living. [To the female offender] It's no better for women. [To all] I want to help turn you around and help you from falling like dominoes like that. It's very easy to get in over your head without realizing it

[At this point, offender 1 becomes compliant and all negotiate a contract.]

However, the most common tactic was for facilitators to threaten a return to court or another session. These were last resorts that few wished to pursue, limiting offenders' chances to tell their stories and directing them to more acceptable narratives. This sometimes also divided allies, enabling sessions to move on.

Facilitator enactment of organizational imperatives against the backdrop of the justice system meant that offenders faced an uphill battle when vigorously disputing issues. Sessions were hardly voluntary mediations between equals: offenders faced a penalty if they did not make an agreement, although victims' interests in attending or negotiating were less well defined. Many sessions showed a high degree of agency control, emphasized settlement orientation more than problem-solving, and stressed a discourse of responsibilization. In fact, while facilitators may strongly impact outcomes, the 40 observed exhibited a wide variation in skills. At one end were two social workers whose ability to manage session dynamics stood out. Professionalism, use of voice, and problem-solving orientation enabled a more transformative experience. At the opposite end were a handful of minimally trained volunteers for whom "managing" sessions and reaching a settlement were effective priorities.[5] Most had developed a degree of skill on the job and could handle overt conflict, and efforts were made to pair up seasoned and novice volunteers. However, when resistance was not obvious, the variation in skill and organizational imperatives left RJ open to subtle domination.

Indeed, this was evinced by recriminations following sessions that were dominated by one party. In a school theft case where the principal was very vocal about the outcome, the facilitator did little to intervene (case #16). Later, the offender's mother, who originally wanted her son to be charged, made the following comments:

> *Offender's mother*: If it had been up to me, I'd have walked out. He was being very intimidating. He was being quite the asshole. Other kids were doing it, but [my son] gets singled out. If I wanted to take it to court and fight it, I would. But [the offender] did it, so I stayed...

> *Facilitator*: But he seems to care, and has offered to help.

> *Offender's mother*: He doesn't do his job properly and only cares about his paycheque. The problems at that school would be a lot less without him.

While RJ is portrayed as an "ideal speech situation" comprised of symmetrical, idealized mutuality, the verbal means of resolution may not be so ideal (Presser, 2004a). Such cases show a gap in ideals and practice. Subtle power dynamics must be managed for parties to see sessions as restorative. Facilitators must not be blinded by this ideal, taking a largely reactive, "hands-off" approach, nor become dominant in ways that render them tools of official responsibilization. They must be alert to both dynamics, sufficiently trained and skilled to intervene restoratively.

CONCLUSION

Until now, little has been known about the interpersonal dynamics of RJ sessions, with academics calling for research into practices and processes. If process is the heart of RJ, and means—not ends—are key, then our study of "how it works" begins to unpack the black box.

We have built on a series of key gaps in the literature. Research has shown that not all hypotheses derived from Braithwaite's (1999) theory have support, highlighting especially the role of emotion. Following qualification of the impact of re-integrative shaming on recidivism (Harris, 2006), we have corroborated that how shaming occurs impacts parties' emotions: some associated with potentially re-integrative outcomes, others with anger and resentment. Yet, the *mechanisms* underlying previous findings have been insufficiently explicated, most notably in sessions dealing with a variety of offences and with victims present (Harris, 2006). Given questions about participants' reported satisfaction, we have empirically revealed the interplay between organizational context, preferred institutional discourse, facilitator skill, parties, and supporters on one hand, and the active use of institutional resources, social problems resistance, strategic interventions and alliances, and the rhetorical manipulation of victim identity talk and emotion on the other. We have shown how emotions can facilitate both meaningful and "managed" outcomes, revealing that the victim role dramaturgically mediates their construction. It may be that how such micro-political shame management operates, and the extent to which it is institutionally versus participant driven, can explain both variations in recidivism (Gilligan, 2003) and attrition in victim satisfaction (Clairmont, 2005). Further, comparative studies are needed, both on these dimensions and between youth and adult offenders.

Our findings also indicate that how the victim role is employed, and how it mediates the emotions constructed, is linked to organizational context. Despite the "false understanding of utopia" idealized in RJ (Acorn, 2004, pp. 160–161), the organizational imperatives shown here mean that not all victim claims are equal—with "victims" being given relatively free rein, while "offenders" have more limited room to manoeuvre and are often treated as emotionally deviant when asserting victim claims. This not only corroborates concerns about the roles of ideology, program policy, power differentials, caseworker practices, and conference dynamics undermining client agency, but it also lends credence to claims that offenders' perspectives are not sufficiently addressed by RJ (Toews & Katounas, 2004). If the ability to construct "redemption narratives," at least initially of being "victimized by circumstance," are key to turning offenders' lives around (Maruna, 2001), then institutional discourse that hastily delimits these may interfere with constructing—and indeed managing—the emotions necessary to bring about meaningful outcomes (Harris, 2006), potentially breeding anger and resentment and undermining the restorative enterprise.

Indeed, while all but three of 24 of our sessions were "officially" resolved, all showed some evidence of "victim contests" and 11 required facilitator intervention to bring them to "official" resolution. Among these, there were indications of "papering over" in three cases and in five cases one side effectively "won" and "negotiated" the terms they desired. While corroborating Gray's (2005) findings that a narrow emphasis on moral responsibilization may undermine restoration and re-integration, our results go further by explicating the interactional roles, processes, coalitions, and emotions, along with the organizational context, in which this occurs. Not only do external links complicate negotiation, but the court alternative, and its emphasis by facilitators, victims, and supporters, renders it hardly surprising that contests emerged, often "managed" by facilitators, in order to achieve official "resolutions" that were more reflective of a settlement orientation and *realpolitik* than problem-solving. This may bode well for program statistics, but diverges significantly from the egalitarian, re-integrative philosophy of RJ. This raises questions as to whether RJ, operating under the umbrella of the justice system, can ever be predominantly re-integrative, rather than a watered-down, sometimes coercive form of an adversarial process with fewer procedural rights. Our findings call for comparative research on RJ programs with varying relationships to criminal justice institutions to see if this finding holds elsewhere.

While our research sheds light on the active, strategic role of supporters beyond the existing literature (Karp et al., 2004), it is to facilitators that it speaks most strongly. The range of skill at times had an impact on session outcomes, lending credence to concerns about competency, particularly the hierarchy of skills and shortcomings resulting from wide use of volunteers (Raye, 2004; Wonshé, 2004). A few facilitators were more professional and skilled in the use of voice than others. They also proactively engaged in problem-solving and sought more transformative outcomes. Many others, however, lower in experience and training, sat back, largely relied on scripted program narratives, let certain parties or supporters dominate, and reactively utilized the official rhetoric of last resorts when problems emerged. This was more reflective of a managed outcome and a settlement orientation. While better training and accreditation in "best practices" is the simple answer, comparative research is needed on: (1) the optimum, restorative balance of facilitator/participant control; and (2) the extent to which, despite further training, practices persist due to organizational factors.

Ultimately, we have revealed a far different picture than the frequently idealistic literature. While RJ may facilitate meaningful resolution for some, for others it may merely be "a ritual that we purposefully create with a view to eliciting a performance of the offender's compassion and remorse" (Acorn, 2004, p. 159). While we leave readers to judge the social utility of such programs, we hope our study encourages critical reflection and research in this key area of criminology.

ENDNOTES

1. For a more detailed review of the research literature underlying this chapter, see Kenney and Clairmont (2009).
2. Adults may deem it more crucial to communicate the significance of victimization to youth than to an adult offender, while all parties may be more receptive to the presentation of a young offender as victim.
3. We recognize that the terms "victim" and "offender" are multi-faceted social constructions. They are related to institutional politics of description, used as narrative resources by participants, and constitute pragmatic outcomes of social interactions with powerful implications for defining the situation. However, rather than awkwardly enclose these terms in quotation marks throughout this chapter to reflect this broader understanding, we either use the terms "designated" victim or offender, or write the terms as they ordinarily appear. Nevertheless, we urge readers to bear these considerations in mind.
4. See Chapter 1 for a detailed discussion of the methods underlying this study, demographic characteristics of the sample, and a breakdown of specific contract terms.
5. Training consisted of two days of workshops and study of the policy and procedures manual, followed by several session observations and a period of co-facilitation before, finally, taking the role of lead facilitator.

REFERENCES

Acorn, A. (2004). *Compulsory Compassion: A Critique of Restorative Justice*. Vancouver: University of British Columbia Press.

Anderson, L., & Snow, D. A. (2001). Inequality and the self: Exploring connections from an interactionist perspective. *Symbolic Interaction 24*(4), 395–406.

Boyack, J., Bowen, H., & Marshall, C. (2004). How does restorative justice ensure good practice? In H. Zehr & B. Toews (Eds.), *Critical Issues in Restorative Justice* (pp. 265–272). Monsey, NY: Criminal Justice Press.

Braithwaite, J. (1999). Restorative justice: Assessing optimistic and pessimistic accounts. In M. Tonry (Ed.), *Crime and Justice: A Review of Research* (pp. 1–127). Chicago: University of Chicago.

Clairmont, D. (2005). *The Nova Scotia Restorative Justice Initiative: Final Evaluation Report.* Halifax: Pilot Research.

Clark, C. (1990). Emotions and micropolitics in everyday life: Some patterns and paradoxes of "place." In T. D. Kemper (Ed.), *Research Agendas in the Sociology of Emotions* (pp. 305–333). Albany, NY: State University of New York Press.

Cormier, R. (2002, April). *Restorative Justice: Directions and Principles—Developments in Canada.* Paper presented at the 11th Session of the Commission on Crime Prevention and Criminal Justice, Vienna.

Dukes, F. (1993). Public conflict resolution: A transformative approach. *Negotiation Journal 9*(1), 45–57.

Emerson, R. M. (1981). On last resorts. *American Journal of Sociology 87*(1), 1–22.

Gilligan, J. (2003). Shame, guilt, and violence. *Social Research 70*(4), 1149–1180.

Gray, P. (2005). The politics of risk and young offenders' experiences of social exclusion and restorative justice. *British Journal of Criminology 45*(6), 938–957.

Gustafson, D. L. (2004). Is restorative justice taking too few, or too many, risks? In H. Zehr & B. Toews (Eds.), *Critical Issues in Restorative Justice* (pp. 299–310). Monsey, NY: Criminal Justice Press.

Harris, N. (2006). Reintegrative shaming, shame, and criminal justice. *Journal of Social Issues 62*(2), 327–346.

Herman, J. L. (2005). Justice from the victim's perspective. *Violence against Women 11*(5), 571–602.

Hill, R. F. A. (2002). Restorative justice and the absent victim: New data from the Thames Valley. *International Review of Victimology 9*(3), 273–288.

Hochschild, A. R. (1983). *The Managed Heart: The Commercialization of Human Feeling.* Berkeley, CA: University of California Press.

Hoffmann, E. A. (2001). Confrontations and compromise: Dispute resolution at a worker cooperative coal mine. *Law and Social Inquiry 26*(3), 555–596.

Holstein, J. A., & Gubrium, J. F. (2000). *The Self We Live by: Narrative Identity in a Postmodern World.* New York: Oxford University Press.

Holstein, J. A., & Miller, G. (1990). Rethinking victimization: An interactional approach to victimology. *Symbolic Interaction 13*(1), 103–122.

Karmen, A. (2001). *Crime Victims: An Introduction to Victimology* (4th ed.). Belmont, CA: Wadsworth.

Karp, D. R., Sweet, M., Kirshenbaum, A., & Bazemore, G. (2004). Reluctant participants in restorative justice? Youthful offenders and their parents. *Contemporary Justice Review 7*(2), 199–216.

Kenney, J. S. (2002). Victims of crime and labelling theory: A parallel process? *Deviant Behaviour 23*(3), 235–265.

Kenney, J. S., & Clairmont, D. (2009). Using the victim role as both sword and shield: The interactional dynamics of restorative justice sessions. *Journal of Contemporary Ethnography* (in press).

Kressel, K., Frontera, E., Forlenza, S., Butler, F., & Fish, L. (1994). The settlement-orientation vs. the problem-solving style in custody mediation. *The Journal of Social Issues 50*(1), 67–84.

Latimer, J., Dowden, C., & Muise, D. (2001). *The Effectiveness of Restorative Justice Practices: A Meta-analysis*. Ottawa: Department of Justice.

Loseke, D. R. (2001). Lived realities and formula stories of battered women. In J. F. Gubrium & J. A. Holstein (Eds.), *Institutional Selves: Troubled Identities in a Postmodern World* (pp. 107–126). New York: Oxford University Press.

Maruna, S. (2001). *Making Good: How Ex-convicts Reform and Rebuild Their Lives*. Washington: American Psychological Association.

Masters, G. (2002). In or out: Some critical reflections upon the potential for involving victims of youth crime in restorative process in England and Wales. *British Journal of Community Justice 1*(1), 99–110.

Miller, G., & Holstein, J. A. (1989). On the sociology of social problems. *Perspectives on Social Problems*, vol. 1, edited by J. A. Holstein and G. Miller, 1–16. Greenwich: JAI Press.

Nathanson, D. (1994). *Shame and Pride: Affect, Sex, and the Birth of the Self*. New York: W. W. Norton.

Nespor, J. (1986). Trouble at school: A case study of the economy of blame. *Urban Education 21*(3), 211–227.

Presser, L. (2004a). Justice here and now: A personal reflection on the restorative and community justice paradigms. *Contemporary Justice Review 7*(1), 101–106.

Presser, L. (2004b). Violent offenders, moral selves: Constructing identities and accounts in the research interview. *Social Problems 51*(1), 82–101.

Raye, B. E. (2004). How do culture, class, and gender affect the practice of restorative justice? (Part 2). In H. Zehr & B. Toews (Eds.), *Critical Issues in Restorative Justice, Part 2* (pp. 325–336). Monsey, NY: Criminal Justice Press.

Scheff, T., & Retzinger, S. (2000). Shame as the master emotion of everyday life. *Journal of Mundane Behaviour 1*(3), 303–324.

Strang, H. (2000). *Victim Participation in a Restorative Justice Process: The Canberra Reintegrative Shaming Experiments*. Doctoral thesis, Centre for Restorative Justice, Australian National University, Canberra.

Strang, H., Sherman, L., Angel, C., Woods, D., Bennett, S., Newbury-Birch, D., & Inkpen, N. (2006). Victim evaluations of face-to-face restorative justice conferences: A quasi-experimental analysis. *Journal of Social Issues 62*(2), 281–306.

Thoits, P. A. (1990). Emotional deviance: Research agendas. In T. D. Kemper (Ed.), *Research Agendas in the Sociology of Emotions* (pp. 180–203). Albany, NY: State University of New York Press.

Tjaden, P. G. (1994). Dispute processing in child maltreatment cases. *Negotiation Journal 10*(4), 373–390.

Toews, B., & Katounas, J. (2004). Have offender needs and perspectives been adequately incorporated into restorative justice? In H. Zehr & B. Toews (Eds.), *Critical Issues in Restorative Justice* (pp. 107–118). Monsey, NY: Criminal Justice Press.

Umbreit, M. (2001). *The Handbook of Victim–Offender Mediation: An Essential Guide to Practice and Research.* San Francisco: Jossey Bass.

Wonshé. (2004). How does the "who, what, where, when, and how" affect the practice of restorative justice? In H. Zehr & B. Toews (Eds.), *Critical Issues in Restorative Justice* (pp. 253–263). Monsey, NY: Criminal Justice Press.

Zedner, L. (2002). Victims. In M. Maguire, R. Morgan, & R. Reiner (Eds.), *The Oxford Handbook of Criminology* (pp. 419–456). Oxford: Oxford University Press.

CHAPTER 8

International Comparisons

INTRODUCTION

Much of this book has argued that victims—despite their potential for active coping, meaningful action, and input—have been socially and institutionally marginalized. Indeed, key institutions such as the criminal justice system have traditionally relegated them to a relatively powerless role.

Moreover, the many institutions that have emerged in the past few decades to apparently deal with this problem have often been: largely built around, and shaped by, existing institutional structures; not based on victims' interests, input, or consultation; and substantively limited at best and illustrative of "symbolic politics" at worst. As such, these have done little to alleviate the plight of victims, nor do they have much—if any—impact on the social and institutional power structures that make it so difficult for victims to deal with their situation.

Now that these matters have been outlined in some detail, and keeping the above considerations in mind, in this chapter we begin moving beyond Canada to consider victimization in developing countries. Specifically, the next section makes critical comparisons between the *de facto* and *de jure* positions of victims in Canada and Colombia, and suggests that there may be more similarities between the two countries than one might initially think.

DE FACTO AND DE JURE TREATMENT OF VICTIMS: CANADA VERSUS COLOMBIA
(with Alfredo Schulte-Bockholt)

For decades, people in many parts of the developed West felt relatively safe. Until very recently, North American society was characterized by a comparative sense of insularity—a feeling of being somehow cut off from the violence and mayhem in the rest of the world. Many would tune in to the nightly news and watch with disinterested detachment the political violence, civil wars, economic meltdowns, and ethnic and religious strife so evident else-where, but pay less attention to what is going on in their own backyard. In the aftermath of the September 11 terrorist attacks and the more recent eco-nomic meltdown, many in the West might feel a heightened sense of anxiety. However, there remains a sense that we are somehow set apart, that such things largely happen elsewhere.

A case in point is Colombia. Violence in Colombia kills tens of thousands of people annually. Between 1980 and 1990, the murder rate increased from two to 8.5 murders per 100,000 citizens annually (La vida no vale nada. C10). According to a Colombian police report, from 1996 to 1997 the annual num-ber of killings increased by 19% to 31,808 (Latin America rate of killing rising in Colombia. A12). There were over 32,000 murders in 2002, most of which resulted from criminal violence. Over 10,000 homicides were either politi-cally motivated or resulted from social-cleansing operations that victimize drug addicts, prostitutes, and homosexuals. Most of these killings have been attributed to right-wing paramilitary organizations. Colombia's 2005 murder rate of 39 per 100,000 people, or 17,331 homicides, made it one of the most perilous spots on the globe (Calvani & Liller, 2005; Nationmaster, 2007). In comparison, the US homicide rate in 2005—the highest in the developed world—was 5.6 per 100,000 persons, or 16,692 victims among a population of just under 300 million (Federal Bureau of Investigation, 2005).

Equally noteworthy is the violence that women in Colombia are sub-jected to, both in their homes and because of the civil conflict in their coun-try. As many as 41% of Colombia's women are victimized by their partners, and women also represent over half of the internal refugees who have fled war zones. A 2001 study by the non-governmental organization *Profamilia* asserted that one in five displaced women had suffered sexual violence, often resulting in unwanted pregnancies (Morgenstern, 2007; World Organization Against Torture, 2003).

It is often overlooked that Colombia is a society in civil conflict between government forces and various Marxist rebel organizations, most notably the *Fuerzas Armadas Revolucionarias de Colombia* (FARC). The present situation is best characterized as a protracted stalemate between military and guerrilla forces, in which neither side can destroy the other. Neverthe-less, the internal war is costing the country significantly in terms of military spending, economic losses, and the human casualties of the conflict ("Dina-mitados dos oleoductos," 1992; "Guerrilla economics," 1996).

An additional factor to be considered in the Colombian context is impu-nity, which is structural and systemic. The vast majority of reported conven-tional crimes routinely go unpunished, as do 100% of human rights violations perpetrated by the security agencies or their paramilitary allies (e.g., Giraldo, 1999).

When confronted with this, "common-sense" reasoning in the developed West typically points to how our societies, including their political and economic institutions, are characterized by the rule of law. The stock reasoning goes that we have a long tradition of political liberty, separation of church and state, and organized economic development, all carefully guided by the law. Therefore, we have both economic prosperity and dispute resolution institutions that enable us to prevent many of the problems that have occurred elsewhere. Of course, what we see often blinds us to what we do not see, and this mundane reasoning ignores the organized economic and political traditions of other societies, deep problems within our own economic, ideological, and political institutions, and the many fault lines in our own societies regarding class, race, and gender. Indeed, given the accelerated speed of globalization, such a limited perspective ignores the interactions and interdependencies between the developed West and so-called "trouble spots" in the rest of the world. Correspondingly, W. Gordon West (1989) suggested that using Western—particularly American—theoretical traditions to study crime in the developing world is similarly problematic.

This chapter aims to shed light on one small corner of this picture. Specifically, given that the themes of relative violence and victimization run through much of the above, we compare violence and victimization in Canada and Colombia. Keeping in mind the limitations of various data collection methods, we will: (1) report comparative crime and victimization data on Canada and Colombia, considering some of the problems with current explanatory frameworks; (2) review similarities and differences in the *de jure* treatment of crime victims in both jurisdictions; and (3) consider the *de facto* similarities and differences in how these play out in practice.

Such comparative research is becoming increasingly important in our rapidly globalizing world. Along with trade, markets, and the world economy, crime is becoming increasingly internationalized, and links are expanding both within and between countries. Further research may enable us to better trace links between crime and victimization in different countries, discover important empirical similarities between jurisdictions that are not immediately apparent when focusing on one country alone, highlight theoretical blind spots in our understanding of crime in our own countries, learn from others' experiences, and consider new strategies to deal with these problems.

METHODOLOGICAL CONSIDERATIONS

Before proceeding to discuss the data, it would be best to comment briefly on two methodological issues. First, we must comment on the choice of these two jurisdictions. Given that the relative sense of insularity noted above has traditionally been strongest in North America, and that Canada has traditionally been the target of less political antagonism around the world than the USA, it might be best to use our jurisdiction as a test case. Secondly, Canada and Colombia are commonly seen as very different economically, politically, culturally, and, perhaps most importantly, in relation to their levels of crime and victimization. While Colombia has commonly been considered one of the most dangerous countries on Earth, Canada has an international reputation as highly developed, stable, and possessed of a low crime rate, particularly by North American standards. Indeed, it has been at the top of the United Nations Development Index several times over the past decade. Like many developed European nations, the gap between rich and poor is not as problematic in Canada as it is in the USA. In many other respects, however, Canada has traditionally been seen as similar enough to the USA culturally, economically, and even in its political stability to render broader Western and North American criminological and victimological theories applicable. Hence, Canada may not only represent an extreme opposite to Colombia on many dimensions, but it also represents a more extreme comparison than the USA while still retaining enough points of similarity to other developed nations to render our discussion potentially relevant to researchers in America and parts of Europe as well. Using Canada and Colombia as "ideal types" in this fashion still leaves open many points of interest for jurisdictions that fall somewhere in between.

Another matter for comment involves the potential methodological difficulties involved when attempting to compare crime and victimization data from such apparently differing jurisdictions. For example, in relation to official police statistics, crimes are defined differently and there may well be different patterns of detection, reporting, recording, and official processing of incidents. Interactions between control agents, perpetrators, and victims may be grounded in different power structures and different perceptual biases, enforcement priorities may come into play, and so on. Indeed, there may well be political and other social influences on reporting crime statistics to international agencies. Conversely, utilizing survey data, such as that from the International Crime Victimization Survey, in an attempt to avoid the many problems posed by the activities of control agents, poses other problems (e.g., lack of honesty in answers, differing cultural interpretations of terms, faulty memories, respondents giving socially desired answers, sample selection, and choosing only certain common offences to the exclusion of others). Furthermore, both sources of data often tend to focus more on street crime than corporate crime, organized crime, or, particularly in this context, state crime.

It is very difficult to overcome such difficulties when using commonly available data sources, but that is true of many analyses. All that can be said is that, rather than reifying these sources of data as "the Truth," but instead critically cross-checking and comparatively reviewing them as social constructions, we hope to come to a better, more well-rounded account of the matters under investigation than might be possible otherwise. Certainly, however, broader conclusions must be qualified with these considerations in mind.

In the sections that follow, we compare identified patterns of violence and victimization in Canada and Colombia and the nature of institutional processing—including *de jure* and *de facto* differences therein.

COMPARATIVE DATA ON VIOLENCE, VICTIMIZATION, AND INSTITUTIONAL PROCESSING

Patterns of Violence and Victimization: Insufficient Explanations

At the outset we noted that the official homicide rate in Colombia is far higher than that in the USA (which itself has the highest figures in the developed world). Indeed, statistics on violent crime in Latin America are alarming generally. According to Rico and Chinchilla (2002), each year some 140,000 people are murdered, 28 million families are victimized by robbery or theft, and estimated economic losses due to crime amount to 14.2% of the region's GDP, or US$168 billion. Van Dijk (2000) observed that over half of Latin Americans are "multiple victims" who suffer an assault more than once a year. In its 2006 report, the Pan American Health Organization noted that the average homicide rate in Latin America was 25.3 per 100,000 in 2000–2004, which places the region among the most dangerous in the world. In addition, over 40% of women in the region face sexual or non-sexual violence more than once a year. Yet, as Van Dijk (2000) noted, in global terms "the prevalence rate of violence against women ... is at least three times higher than indicated by police figures," and even higher in Latin America (pp. 73, 77–78).

Despite these alarming statistics, the police are informed of relatively few crimes: reporting rates in 2000 were lowest in Latin America (27%) compared to North America (54%) and Western Europe (46%) (van Dijk, 2000). Many victims did not report crimes either because they felt the authorities would do nothing, or because they feared or disliked law enforcement. Compared to North America, residents of Latin America expressed little satisfaction with police efforts to control crime (65% vs. 25% satisfied residents, respectively) Indeed, compared to the citizens of other global regions, Latin Americans are the least impressed with law enforcement (Van Dijk, 2000). In 2000, only 32% of victims who reported offences were satisfied with how their cases were dealt with compared to 65% in North America. Female victims, especially, reported that the authorities did not treat them well and victimized them again (Van Dijk, 2000).

According to Rico and Chinchilla (2002), victimization reports provide a clearer picture than police statistics. A useful source of information is the International Crime Victimization Survey (ICVS), conducted in 1989, 1992, 1996, 2000, and 2004–5.[1]

In 2000, rates were highest in Latin America, where 46% of respondents reported at least one form of victimization in the preceding year—compared to an international average of 30% (Alvazzi del Frate, 2007). What is more, respondents felt the least safe in the streets of Latin America (57%), a figure that closely matches regional rates for contact crimes. Similar results can be found in data from earlier surveys, indicating a highly disproportional rate of victimization in the region (Alvazzi del Frate, 1998, 2007; Fairchild & Dammer, 2001).

Not surprisingly, according to the 2000 ICVS, corruption is most frequent in Latin America and Asia (Nieubeerta, de Geest, & Siegers, 2002). Schneider (1999), reporting on the results of the 1996 ICVS, noted that victimization related to the corruption of government officials is highest in Latin America (21.3%) and lowest in North America, Australia and New Zealand (1%), and Western Europe (0.7%). Hence, Latin Americans do not view "the police as a service to its citizens but rather as a distant and almost inaccessible agency, certainly not one to turn to for help and assistance" (Alvazzi del Frate, 2007, p. 241). Many feel "abandoned by institutions, lose confidence in the criminal justice system," all of which points to "a tear in the social fabric that, if not addressed as a matter of urgency, may generate further damage" (p. 243).

When comparing Canada and Colombia specifically, the latest available figures from the 1996 ICVS show Colombia having higher crime rates across the board (Table 8.1).

Thus, the percentages of respondents victimized by "any crime" over a five-year period in the urban areas of Colombia and Canada are 87.1% and 64.3%, respectively. The Colombian figure is, in fact, the highest among all 55 countries reporting (United Nations Office for Drug Control and Crime Prevention, 1999). The figures for other selected offence categories are shown in Table 8.1. In addition to significant differences in various property offences, perhaps most notable—given this book's focus on violent victimization—are the major differences in violent offences such as "contact crimes" and assaults on women. Of course, given the social context of the respondents, the real numbers are probably much higher.

Older statistics collected by the United Nations Criminal Justice Systems from law enforcement agencies worldwide show interesting differences

TABLE 8.1:
COMPARATIVE 1996 INTERNATIONAL CRIME VICTIMIZATION SURVEY RESULTS: CANADA VERSUS COLOMBIA (1992-1996 INCLUSIVE)

The % of the population experiencing these types
of crimes (as inferred from the sample)

	Total no. of cases	Car crimes	Burglary/ attempts	Other thefts
Canada	2,282	41.6%	19.7%	28.9%
Colombia	1,000	44.5%	39.1%	54.0%

	Contact crimes	Assaults (women)	Assaults (men)	Any crime
Canada	18.5%	7.7%	6.0%	64.3%
Colombia	50.6%	15.9%	8.3%	87.1%

Source: United Nations Office for Drug Control and Crime Prevention. (1999). *The Global Report on Crime and Justice.* United Nations. New York: Oxford University Press.

TABLE 8.2:
COMPARATIVE 1994 UNITED NATIONS CRIMINAL JUSTICE SYSTEMS CRIME RATES PER 100,000 POPULATION: CANADA VERSUS COLOMBIA

	Homicide	Sexual assault	Robbery	Burglary	Drug crimes
Canada	2.04	108.35	98.77	1,326.17	78.37
Colombia	78.59	5.59	82.52	24.72	N/A

Source: Fairchild, E., & Dammer, H. (2001). *Comparative Criminal Justice Systems.* Belmont, CA: Wadsworth: p. 32.

between Canada and Colombia in respect of the rates of homicide, sexual assault, robbery, burglary, and drug crimes (Table 8.2).

Thus in 1994 the reported homicide rate per 100,000 in Colombia was 78.59 versus 2.04 for Canada—an enormous difference. However, the official crime rates for other offences were much higher in Canada, save for "drug offences" where there were—not surprisingly—no figures reported for

Colombia (Fairchild & Dammer, 2001). Much of this, of course, has to do with differences in reporting conditioned by fear in Colombia, differing cultural priorities, and greater faith in the justice system and campaigns about sexual violence in Canada. It also reminds us again to be cautious of such statistics reported to the United Nations by official law enforcement agencies.

Castaneda's (1991) work is of help in contextualizing these numbers, succinctly summing up many of the structural, cultural, and institutional characteristics of Colombia in relation to crime and victimization. The following characteristics of Colombia were outlined (p. 105):

1. Collapse of the administration of justice, frequently described in terms of criminal impunity from prosecution, government inefficiency, high levels of crime, rampant corruption, and lack of security and protection for judicial officials, many of whom have been assassinated.

2. Inability of political parties and parliament to act as vehicles for expressing social demands.

3. Inability of juridical-institutional mechanisms to integrate and channel social struggles.

4. A growing, although dispersed, guerrilla challenge to the state and the military.

5. A breakdown of the state's monopoly over legitimate physical force, not only by guerrillas but also by "narco-paramilitary" groups.

6. Permanent tension between successive governments and cocaine entrepreneurs that has brought about paramilitary and "para-police" justice.

7. A generalization of forms of conflict, expressed in growing manifestations of physical violence from diverse social actors.

These factors alone indicate that Colombian levels of violence, crime, and criminal victimization are very high indeed when compared to Canada. Moreover, while reliable statistics are hard to come by under such conditions, it is telling that many writers have felt the need to explain the undoubtedly extreme levels of crime and victimization in Colombia. In doing so, they often emphasize the links between the above characteristics, evolving structural, institutional, and ideological inequalities in Colombian society, as well as links to international markets, capital formations, and pressures from the US Government (Camacho, 1992; Castaneda, 1991; Commission for the Study of the Violence, 1992; Knoester, 1998; Molano, 1992; Pecaut, 1992; Pizarro, 1992).

On the surface, then, Colombian patterns of violence and victimization exhibit numerous structural, cultural, and institutional differences from developed societies such as Canada, which, at first glance at least, suggest that the common-sense views held by many here are correct. Such characteristics, existing against the backdrop of profound social inequalities, might suggest the hasty conclusion that such countries are really quite different. We jump to no such conclusions.

There are several reasons for this. First, despite the evident violence in Colombia, one cannot ignore the structural, cultural, and institutional violence that exists in developed countries such as Canada, nor how these may also be linked to international markets and capital formations (e.g., the complexities of the drug trade cut across both areas). Second, critical criminologists have long pointed out that violence in our societies is often a reflection of structured social inequalities (Currie, 1997; Galtung, 1969; Pfohl, 1994). Cultural blindness, aided and abetted by a ruthless ethic of individualism, merely allows this to march on unopposed. Third, while the impact of our imperfect criminal justice institutions on violence is often downplayed or ignored by the Western public, radical criminologists have long considered it significant (Chambliss & Seidman, 1971; Taylor, Walton, & Young, 1973; Quinney, 1974, 1977). The argument might be made, therefore, that Colombia is an extreme example of what Canada and other developed societies are also experiencing, albeit to a lesser degree. Indeed, the significant interrelations between such jurisdictions cannot be ignored.

Yet there is a problem with this reasoning. Considering the vast differences in wealth, Western structural theories suggest that there would be far more victimization among the poor in Colombia than in Canada. Certainly the poor are victimized greatly in Colombia, and some at their own hands. Yet, as the above indicates, this is far from the whole story. The big problem is that much structural victimization theory suggests that those pushed to the margins of society turn on each other in private settings (e.g., domestic violence), indirectly translating structural violence into interpersonal violence (Galtung, 1969). To the extent that this characterization of structural victimization is true, it is quite inaccurate in the context of state violence. In Colombia, victims and victimizers must be more carefully distinguished. Organized victimization of the poor must be distinguished from disorganized victimization by the poor. Structural violence is rarely so indirect in the Colombian context, nor so disorganized.

If, instead, we attempt to compare patterns of victimization in these two jurisdictions interactionally, using theories from developed countries that emphasize victim precipitation (Wolfgang, 1958), situated transactions (Luckenbill, 1977), lifestyle (Hindelang, Gottfredson, & Garofalo, 1978), or routine activities (Cohen & Felson, 1979), we again find patterns of correspondence and divergence. On one hand, such approaches cannot be summarily dismissed in the study of Colombia. The potential utility of broadening the scope of theories beyond the micro level, such as by focusing on provocative acts, escalating "character contests," or even outright battles for control between various institutional and organizational parties (e.g., judges, government officials, paramilitaries, and organized drug cartels), is but one example. Another example is the routine-activity theory, which focuses on the structure of criminal opportunities in a particular area containing victims, offenders, and the presence/absence of "capable guardians" (i.e., presumably this term could be re-conceptualized to include the breakdown of the civil administration of justice, thus hypothetically encouraging high levels of victimization). Such variations, similarities, and differences in the structure of criminal opportunities between the two jurisdictions may be significant and cannot be ignored.

Nevertheless, the sheer amount of organized violence and victimization experienced in Colombia suggests that situation-oriented comparisons are currently insufficient. Moreover, we cannot ignore the fact that, as presently formulated, such approaches do not technically cover the situations described (e.g., the notion of "capable guardians" currently refers only to individuals such as family members, friends, the police, and so forth, but becomes meaningless in Colombia where the police are often the problem and—in the public's mind at least—the term implies the presence of half a dozen bodyguards who protect ordinary citizens going about their daily routines. Indeed, most Colombians cannot afford such protection and live in constant fear of victimization).

In the end, we argue that, as presently formulated, many theoretical accounts of crime and victimization are quite insufficient to frame comprehensive empirical comparisons between the two jurisdictions—and, by extension—between the developed and developing world. Indeed, the data themselves are frequently problematic. Nevertheless, this review, if nothing else, suggests that there may be tentative parallels to build upon. To do so, we need to broaden our focus and consider the comparative roles of criminal justice institutions.

Institutional Processing

Any comparative analysis of crime and victimization in the two jurisdictions must actively focus on the role of interactions between individuals and criminal justice institutions. There has been some work on the legal structure of these institutions in North America, particularly how "legal fictions" translate into multiple bureaucratic structures that strictly limit the victim's role (Kenney, 1995). There has also been interactionist, observational research illustrating how individuals' interactions in North American criminal justice contexts are often experienced as disempowering and re-victimizing (Kenney, 1998, 2002). While such ethnographic work in the Colombian context is scarce, the available information indicates that individual encounters with the justice system are experienced as far from empowering (Knoester, 1998). Hence, it is important to examine the legal position of victims in Colombia, and the available materials on their interactions with criminal justice institutions, to compare the *de jure* and *de facto* position of victims in these two jurisdictions.

THE *DE JURE* POSITION OF VICTIMS IN NORTH AMERICA AND COLOMBIA

As noted in Chapter 4, the fundamental principle underlying British, Canadian, and US legal institutions is that a criminal proceeding is an adversarial process between two—and only two—parties: the state and the accused. The victim is not a party to the proceedings, and has no legal standing to dispute decisions of the prosecutor (e.g., whether to prosecute or to make a plea bargain). The prosecutor works for the state and is not the victim's lawyer (Kenney, 1995). The victim has only two roles to play in this scenario: (1) to call the police to report the crime; and (2) to act as a witness for the prosecution if called. The traditional response to victims who complain about this lack of a recognized role is to suggest a civil lawsuit for damages against the offender (e.g., Fred Goldman vs. O. J. Simpson).

Of course, some would argue that this situation has been considerably softened in recent years since the rise of the victims' movement. There have been numerous policy initiatives such as criminal injuries compensation, the introduction of victims' services programs, moves toward restorative justice, and so on. Yet some argue that victims' organizations were not the primary impetus for these initiatives (Rock, 1990), and such initiatives have been criticized as inadequately funded, built around the power structure of the existing criminal justice system, under-utilized, and mere examples of "symbolic politics" (Elias, 1983). Indeed, they may have counter-intuitive effects that potentially exacerbate claims to victim identity (Kenney, 2002). None addresses the fundamental fact that, in the vast majority of cases, the central organizational axis of criminal justice institutions remains that between the offender and the state, with very little formal part for victim involvement.

This situation contrasts sharply with the role of victims in countries with differing legal traditions. Legal systems that grew out of Roman law did not develop so sharp a distinction between criminal and civil matters. Thus, in France, as well as in some other "civil law" countries, the victim may, at his or her option, join a civil to a criminal proceeding, and these are then conducted together in the criminal court (Glendon, Gordon, & Osakwe, 1984; Mawby & Walklate, 1994). Victims are given access to legal aid and legal representation, and are able to be a part of the process at bail and during the trial, sentencing, and (more recently) parole proceedings. A similar type of representation and merger of claims is permitted under the legal systems of many of the former socialist countries (Glendon et al., 1984).[2] For our purposes, it is instructive to point out that this more accommodative civil law tradition underlies the legal institutions of the Spanish empire in what is now Colombia, and that Colombia and other Latin American countries turned to the clear French revolutionary codes as the inspiration for their legal institutions (Glendon et al., 1984). Hence, in a *de jure* sense at least, Colombian criminal procedure has traditionally been more open to participation by victims of crime.

It is yet important to consider more recent legal developments. Probably the most important was the 1991 introduction, under American pressure, of a new constitution. Among other things, this constitution attempted to protect Colombian judges from the escalating violence and intimidation that threatened them from numerous directions during the 1970s and 1980s. In effect, the constitution instituted "faceless courts," a parallel, secret justice system that formally eliminates human rights guarantees of due process. Individuals may now be found guilty on the testimony of secret witnesses and a judicial police report without evidence being placed before a judge— and after the accused has already been detained for a significant period time (Knoester, 1998). In addition, the new constitution created a prosecutor general who is responsible for high-level judicial appointments and who has the exclusive power to decide which cases go to trial (Knoester, 1998). In effect, this placed Colombian courts largely under the control of the military in an environment of political corruption and widespread violence.

Hence, while the Colombian legal system is historically grounded in a tradition of relative procedural advantages for victims in the criminal justice process compared to common-law jurisdictions such as Canada, changes following the introduction of a new Colombian constitution in 1991 introduced a repressive element to the administration of justice. Indeed, over 40% of Colombia's court cases are tried by these "faceless courts" (Knoester, 1998). Of course, it may be retorted that these changes are primarily directed at the accused, and there may indeed be an attraction for some victims in anonymously prosecuting an offender. Indeed, the introduction of such courts in Colombia was initially designed to stop drug traffickers from killing judges. However, the practice leaves everybody but the defendant unidentified and allows hearsay as evidence. Indeed, it has deteriorated into an instrument for the repression of legitimate political organizations, such as labour unions and community groups (Weiner, 1996).

Thus, given the extensive social and political violence in Colombia, coupled with the corruption of key officials and the power of the military, most victims of crime without powerful connections would probably be wise to stay clear of the criminal justice system. This is given further urgency when we consider that who, indeed, is a victim in such an environment becomes a matter of considerable debate, and that these institutions themselves are frequently utilized to victimize individuals or groups that are out of favour with those in positions of power.

THE *DE FACTO* POSITION OF VICTIMS IN NORTH AMERICA AND COLOMBIA

These matters lead us next to compare the *de facto* position of victims in the two jurisdictions. Looking first at Canada, it would appear that the treatment of victims varies considerably depending upon their social background. Thus, Hagan (1983) found significant differences in both influence on, and satisfaction with, the Canadian criminal justice process between organizational (i.e., corporate) and individual victims of crime. Indeed, his research indicated that there is an "organizational domination" of criminal law whereby relatively powerful organizations, sharing bureaucratic and structural affinities with the criminal justice system, tend to be both more successful in pursuing a prosecution against an offender and more satisfied with the results:

> "When most of us think of crime, we begin by thinking of attacks against persons and their property. Indeed, most of us probably think of the criminal law as a protection against such attacks. It is not surprising, then, that as attention has been focused on victims of crime in recent years, it focused on innocent and frequently defenseless individuals who have experienced serious and often permanent injuries. Our research originally was designed to trace the experiences of these individuals and others in the criminal justice system. We were anxious to determine the nature of the victims' involvement in, perceptions of, and influence on the operations of this system. However, we soon found that many, if not most, of the victims who successfully pursued their cases through the criminal justice system were not individuals, but rather organizations, particularly commercial organizations. This finding was not only unexpected, and potentially important, but also ironic" (Hagan, 1983, p. 1).

Of course, none of this should be any surprise to victimologists with a critical perspective. It has been noted that race, class, and gender influence patterns of victimization and have an impact on victims' experiences of and their likelihood of successful redress in the criminal justice system (Mawby and Walklate, 1994). Indeed, the emphasis on formal rationality in the criminal justice system, coupled with strategic points of discretion, tends to legitimize the system while ideologically obscuring such inequalities (Pfohl, 1994).

Some have gone further in this regard and have discussed some of the recent changes that have been put in place to address victims' concerns with the existing criminal justice system. It has been argued that major criminal justice programs aimed at fulfilling "victims'" needs have been set up without regard to, or even investigation into, their expressed needs (Shapland, Willmore, & Duff, 1985). Considering this, some have argued that "victims'" interests were never the motivating force behind new initiatives (Rock, 1990). In this respect, some have asserted that "victims" were merely being used by a right-wing, law and order constituency to further their agenda (Mawby & Gill, 1987); others that "victim" services really serve official needs, not "victims'" needs (Elias, 1983; Kenney, 2002). All of this raises questions about the symbolic "reality" being enacted—and the differential extent to which "victims'" interests are served by the Canadian criminal justice system.

It is instructive to compare this with the situation in Colombia. In its *Third Report on the Human Rights Situation in Colombia*, The Inter-American Commission on Human Rights of the Organization of American States (1999) refers to the situation in Colombia as one of "impunity," where 97–98% of crimes go unpunished and approximately 74% go unreported. The situation is even worse in cases where human rights violations are involved (where virtually 100% of crimes go unpunished). It elaborates:

> "Impunity in Colombia is structural and systemic. It is not simply a question of leaving numerous individual crimes unpunished. Rather, the issue is one of the creation of an entire system of impunity which affects the culture and life of the nation even for those individuals who are not directly affected by human rights violations or other crimes. Most international observers agree that this high level of impunity is itself one of the most serious human rights violations occurring in Colombia" (Inter-American Commission on Human Rights, 1999, Chapter V, Nos. 12, 14, and 16).

While one might be quick to point out that the system in Canada is not one of "impunity" in the sense of state-organized violence, similarly in Colombia, it has similarly been pointed out that powerful organizations, such as corporations and organized crime, have enormous advantages that individual criminals do not have, and that these translate into greater criminal gains (Hagan, 1996). Indeed, organizations find the criminal justice system more responsive to their needs than individuals (Hagan, 1983). Moreover, one must realize that the ICVS has shown that, in the four times it has been conducted in Canada between 1989 and 2000, an average of only 55% of crimes were reported to the authorities, and that the least reported crimes tended to be violent ones directed against individuals: assault and sexual assault (Besserer, 2002). Furthermore, the 1993 General Social Survey showed that only 33% of offences against the person in Canada were reported (Canadian Centre for Justice Statistics, 1999). Concern about the ability of the authorities to do anything, as well as questions about the handling of such incidents by the criminal justice system, emerged as significant. As in Colombia, for those many victims who feel that the system will not respond in a helpful fashion to such crimes, impunity may occur in effect if not in systemic intent. For the un-prosecuted and un-punished offender, moreover, the difference is non-existent.[3]

Second, while there is much talk of human rights violations in the Colombian context, it has already been noted that victims have few—if any—legal rights in Canada (reflecting the legal necessities of offenders' constitutional rights and institutional traditions leaving victims without party status). Those rights that victims have tend to be asserted differentially by organizations, and gender, race, and class inequities in processing are significant. If victims' rights may be seen as human rights (much as feminists argued that "women's rights are human rights"), then we may see a parallel between Canada and Colombia. While there is a greater probability of criminal justice officials exercising prosecutorial discretion in favour of "justice" for those in powerful structural conditions, there is relative impunity against the structurally disadvantaged.

Third, in all of this one must remain cognizant of one of the key underlying themes of critical victimology: an orientation toward power and how it intersects with the construction of social reality (Mawby & Walklate, 1994). Thus, there is the issue of ideological obfuscation. In Canada, this is achieved by the formal, individualistic principle that all victims may come forward and have their complaints looked into equally by the authorities, who ostensibly make impartial, rational decisions regarding the prosecution of the case. This classical, bureaucratic equality obscures the functional inequalities engendered by structural inequities of gender, race, class, and organizational position (Kenney, 1995; Pfohl 1994), pragmatically translated through multiple points of discretion in official processing (Goff, 2004; Gomme, 2007), and glossed over by symbolic "programs" that serve official needs more than victims' needs (Kenney, 2002). This system, as most bureaucracies do, frequently responds to complaints by placing responsibility on the victim for not meeting the necessary requirements, or for demanding "impractical" things that fall outside of established procedures or legal or fundamental constitutional frameworks (e.g., that could impact offenders' legally necessary, constitutionally guaranteed rights).

In Colombia ideological obfuscation is similar to some extent (i.e., formally equal bureaucratic rules for victims coming forward, discretion applied in favour of more powerful groups by the official justice system, while responsibility for the system's failures may be placed on the victim). Yet in Colombia the breakdown of state authority in many areas, along with rampant corruption, criminal infiltration, state repression, revolutionary movements, paramilitarism, and international pressure—all in a broader structural context of a state unable to successfully mediate societal conflicts—makes the Canadian approach largely impracticable. However, these very conditions provide the authorities with multiple functional excuses—but not justifications—for similar outcomes, also revolving around the idea of "practical necessity." Harsh constitutional measures—again favouring the state over victims, allowing official interpretations of justice, privileging some rights over others,[4] and leaving many victims without redress—are claimed to be "necessary in an insurgency."

While some, such as Giraldo (1999), have thus characterized Colombia as a "schizophrenic state" where "process truth" gets separated from the "actual truth" that one can access outside of judicial files, we would ask: (1) how is this different, except in form or emphasis, from what is going on in Canada?; and (2) could it not be that in both Canada and Colombia agents of the state are able to "gerrymander" responsibility by manipulating the rhetorical boundary between formal equality and "practical necessity"—both within legal and constitutional arrangements and in relation to the structures of society at large—in such a way that obfuscates very real inequalities in the administration of justice for victims? We would argue that it is in fact the institutionalization of the state's ability to differentially gerrymander between areas where formal equality and responsibility apply (but may be limited by bureaucratic discretion in relation to various groups) and those where "practical necessity" socially and constitutionally requires otherwise that represents the greatest point of similarity between Canada and Colombia. For many victims the effect is similar—it is merely the form that differs.

CONCLUSION.

Drawing upon earlier chapters' critical analysis of victims' powerless role in the Canadian criminal justice system, their frequent re-victimization via various procedures and outcomes, and the organizationally based, ineffective, and largely symbolic programs put in place to assist them, in this chapter we have attempted to draw parallels between our system and those of Colombia. We have argued that the parallels are greater than one might expect at first glance: that victims in both countries suffer greatly from crime, do not have enforceable legal rights, often fail to report crime because of a feeling that nothing will be done, tend to be re-victimized by the criminal justice system, and that the interests of the powerful and of organizations take precedence over victims of violence regardless of formal bureaucratic equality.

Perhaps more importantly, the legal institutions of both Canada and Colombia exhibit an ability to avoid addressing the above matters through a smokescreen of ideological obfuscation. In Canada this occurs through official espousal of (and common-sense belief in) the principle of formal equality before the law, where all victims may ostensibly come forward and have their concerns addressed—which is quietly not played out in practice. Not only are some "more equal than others," but legal rights—including "equality"—are constitutionally applied to offenders over victims by virtue of "legal necessity." Largely symbolic programs have been put in place for victims, which have resulted in better public relations but little, if any, substantive gains. In Colombia, ideological obfuscation also occurs through the separation of process "truth" from outcome, but there the institutionalization of ongoing conflicts serves as an excuse for the failure of the system to work effectively for all. In both cases, the legal system has an institutionalized ability to gerrymander between responsibility and necessity, producing outcomes that leave victims—particularly those without power or status—effectively without redress. Indeed, Dr. Schulte-Bockholt and I are further developing our thoughts on this matter in a forthcoming paper on state crime, victimization, and various "racket regimes" tied into globalization.

Of course, this chapter represents but a few tentative thoughts. Ultimately the levels of analysis need to be better integrated, theoretical assumptions worked out, methodological difficulties minimized, and theoretical tools refined in a more comprehensive fashion. Only then will we be able to effectively compare patterns of and responses to victimization across jurisdictions more generally. However, through removing the blinkers of past traditions and engaging in carefully grounded research it is hoped that future researchers will ultimately be able to better construct comparative studies of victimization and institutional responses to victimization between jurisdictions and across development contexts. At the very least, our preliminary foray into victimization in Canada and Colombia helps to undercut some of the common-sense ways by which many in the developed West have traditionally set themselves apart from the rest of the world.

Given recent events, we would suspect that more in the West are starting to wake up to these broader issues. By carefully considering the factors, similarities, and differences outlined in this chapter in relation to the contexts studied, researchers may begin to frame better accounts of state responses to victimization. While this is but a first step, and more study is certainly needed, only by removing the blinkers of past theoretical traditions, considering such issues, and engaging in careful research can we ever hope to construct comparative studies of victimization and state responses—both between these two jurisdictions, and in other development contexts as well. This represents but a beginning, a signpost as it were, pointing out a direction to follow. Hopefully, other researchers will take up the challenge and broaden our narrow path in the future, examining where it leads, where it meets roadblocks, and so on. By their very nature, the examination of such issues can be a challenging road both in the developed and developing worlds. Hopefully, this preliminary foray has helped to make the route a little clearer. If we have achieved this, then we have accomplished our goal.

ENDNOTES

1. Results of the 2004–05 ICVS do not provide information on Colombia and fail to provide sufficient regional comparisons.

2. While far from perfect, not uniformly implemented, and possessed of their own problems, these procedures do provide a certain flexibility that is not available in common-law countries.

3. It may be useful to consider state crime and impunity in light of the traditional legal distinction between acts of commission and omission. While actively organized state violence, as in Colombia, may be reasonably seen as a state crime of commission, allowing criminal acts to occur with impunity (i.e., with little to no response from the justice system) may be a state crime of omission. Given the overlap discussed between Canada and Colombia, it is possible that Colombia is characterized by both forms, while, to the extent that impunity effectively exists here, Canada is characterized by state crimes of omission.

4. The difference in this respect is that, in Canada, the rights of the accused are constitutionally privileged over those of victims; in Colombia, the rights of the accused on the state's side are legally privileged over those of their victims, while the rest are subject to victimization by the state without effective legal protections.

REFERENCES

Alvazzi del Frate, A. (1998). *Victims of Crime in the Developing World*. Rome: United Nations Interregional Crime and Justice Research Institute.

Alvazzi del Frate, A. (2002). Criminal victimization in Latin America. In P. Nieuwbeerta (Ed.), *Criminal Victimization in Comparative Perspective* (pp. 101–115). The Hague: Boom Juridische uitgevers.

Alvazzi del Frate, A. (2007). Victimization: An international perspective. In R. Davis, A. Lurigio, & S. Herman (Eds.), *Victims of Crime* (pp. 233–252). Los Angeles: Sage.

Besserer, S. (2002). Criminal victimization: An international perspective. Results of the 2000 International Crime Victimization Survey. *Statistics Canada—Catalogue no. 85-002-XPE, 22*(4), 1–19.

Calvani, S., & Liller, S. (2005). *Violence, Crime, and Illegal Arms Trafficking in Colombia*. United Nations Office on Drugs and Crime. New York.

Camacho, A. (1992). Public and private dimensions of urban violence. In C. Bergquist, R. Penaranda, & G. Sanchez (Eds.), *Violence in Colombia: The Contemporary Crisis in Historical Perspective* (pp. 241–260). Wilmington, DE: Scholarly Resources.

Canadian Centre for Justice Statistics. (1999). *The Juristat Reader: A Statistical Overview of the Canadian Criminal Justice System*. Toronto: Thompson.

Castaneda, G. (1991). Institutional crisis, parainstitutionality, and regime flexibility in Colombia: The place of narcotraffic and counterinsurgency. In M. K. Huggins (Ed.), *Vigilantism and the State in Modern Latin America* (pp. 105–123). New York: Praeger.

Chambliss, W., & Seidman, R. (1971). *Law, Order, and Power*. Reading, MA: Addison-Wesley.

Cohen, L. E., & Felson, M. (1979). Social change and crime rate trends: A routine activities approach. *American Sociological Review 44*, 588–608.

Commission for the Study of the Violence. (1992). Organized violence. In C. Bergquist, R. Penaranda, & G. Sanchez (Eds.), *Violence in Colombia: The Contemporary Crisis in Historical Perspective* (pp. 261–272). Wilmington, DE: Scholarly Resources.

Currie, E. (1997). Market, crime, and community. *Theoretical Criminology 1*(2), 147–172.

Dinamitados dos oleoductos. (1992, October 24). *El Tiempo*, p. 10A.

Elias, R. (1983). Symbolic politics of victim compensation. *Victimology 8*(1–2), 213–224.

Fairchild, E., & Dammer, H. (2001). *Comparative Criminal Justice Systems*. Belmont, CA: Wadsworth.

Federal Bureau of Investigation. (2005). *Crime in the United States 2005*. Washington: Federal Bureau of Investigation. Available from: www.fbi.gov/ucr/05cius/data/table_01.html.

Galtung, J. (1969). Violence, peace, and peace research. *Journal of Peace Research* 6(3), 167–191.

Giraldo, J. (1999). Corrupted justice and the schizophrenic state in Colombia. *Social Justice 26*(4), 31–54.

Glendon, M., Gordon, M., & Osakwe, C. (1984). *Comparative Legal Traditions*. St. Paul, MN: West Publishing Company.

Goff, C. (2004). *Criminal Justice in Canada* (3rd ed.). Toronto: Thompson-Nelson.

Gomme, I. (2007). *The Shadow Line: Deviance and Crime in Canada*. Toronto: Thomson-Nelson.

Guerrilla economics. (1996, January 13). *The Economist*, p. 40.

Hagan, J. (1983). *Victims before the law: The Organizational Domination of Criminal Law*. Toronto: Butterworths.

Hagan, J. (1996). White-collar and corporate crime. In R. Linden (Ed.). *Criminology: A Canadian Perspective* (pp. 495–520). Toronto: Harcourt Brace Jovanovich Canada.

Hindelang, M., Gottfredson, M., & Garofalo, J. (1978). *Victims of Personal Crime*. Cambridge, MA: Ballinger.

Inter-American Commission on Human Rights (IACHR). (1999). *Third Report on the Human Rights Situation in Colombia*. Washington: IACHR.

Kenney, J. S. (1995). Legal institutions and victims of crime in Canada: An historical and contemporary review. *Humanity and Society 19*(2), 53–67.

Kenney, J. S. (1998). *Coping with grief: Survivors of murder victims*. Unpublished doctoral thesis, McMaster University, Hamilton, ON.

Kenney, J. S. (2002). *Unintended Consequences: The Impact of Government Victim Services on Claims to Victim Identity*. Unpublished manuscript, Saint Mary's University, Halifax.

Knoester, M. (1998). War in Colombia. *Social Justice 25*(2), 85–109.

Latin America rate of killing rising in Colombia. In: *The Globe and Mail*. May 5, 1998: A12.

La vida no vale nada. In: El País. Cali, Colombia, Nov. 22, 1992: C10).

Luckenbill, D. (1977). Criminal homicide as a situated transaction. *Social Problems 25*, 176–186.

Mawby, R. I., & Gill, M. L. (1987). *Crime Victims: Needs, Services, and the Voluntary Sector*. London: Tavistock.

Mawby, R., & Walklate, S. (1994). *Critical Victimology*. London, Sage.

Molano, A. (1992). Violence and land colonization. In C. Bergquist, R. Penaranda, & G. Sanchez (Eds.), *Violence in Colombia: The Contemporary Crisis in Historical Perspective* (pp. 195–216). Wilmington, DE: Scholarly Resources.

Morgenstern, V. (2007, winter). New rights, old wrongs. *MS. Magazine*, Morgenstern, V. (2007). Available at http://www.msmagazine.com/winter2007/newrights.asp

Nationmaster. (2007). *South America. Colombia*. Available from: www.nationmaster.com/country/co-colombia.

Nieuwbeerta, P., de Geest, G., & Siegers, J. (2002). Corruption in industrialized and developing countries. In P. Nieuwbeerta (Ed.), *Criminal Victimization in Comparative Perspective* (pp. 162–182). The Hague: Boom Juridische uitgevers.

Pan American Health Organization. (2006). *Health Situation in the Americas. Basic Health Indicators*. Washington: Pan American Health Organization. Available from: www.paho.org/English/DD/AIS/BI-brochure-2006.pdf

Pecaut, D. (1992) Guerrillas and violence. In C. Bergquist, R. Penaranda, & G. Sanchez (Eds.), *Violence in Colombia: The Contemporary Crisis in Historical Perspective* (pp. 217–240). Wilmington, DE: Scholarly Resources.

Pfohl, S. J. (1994). *Images of Deviance and Social Control: A Sociological History*. New York: McGraw-Hill.

Pizarro, E. (1992). Revolutionary guerrilla groups in Colombia. In C. Bergquist, R. Penaranda, & G. Sanchez (Eds.), *Violence in Colombia: The Contemporary Crisis in Historical Perspective* (pp. 169–193). Wilmington, DE: Scholarly Resources.

Quinney, R. (1974). *Critique of the Legal Order: Crime Control in Capitalist Society*. Boston: Little, Brown.

Quinney, R. (1977). *Class, State, and Crime: On the Theory and Practice of Criminal Justice*. New York: David McKay.

Rico, J., & Chinchilla, L. (2002). *Seguridad ciudadania en América Latina*. México DF: Siglo Veintiuno Editores.

Rock, P. (1990). *Helping Victims of Crime: The Home Office and the Rise of Victim Support in England and Wales*. Oxford: Oxford University Press.

Schneider, H. J. (2000, August). *Victimological Developments in the World during the Last Three Decades: A Study of Comparative Victimology*. Paper presented at the Xth International Symposium on Victimology, Montreal, Canada.

Shapland, J., Willmore, J., & Duff, P. (1985). *Victims and the Criminal Justice System*. Aldershot: Gower.

Taylor, I., Walton, P., & Young, J. (1973). *The New Criminology: For a Social Theory of Deviance*. London: Routledge and Kegan Paul.

United Nations Office for Drug Control and Crime Prevention. (1999). *The Global Report on Crime and Justice*. United Nations.

van Dijk, J. J. M. (2000). Criminal victimisation: A global view. In P. Garonna & U. Zvekic (Eds.), *Surveying Crime: A Global Perspective* (pp. 63–95). Rome: United Nations Interregional Crime and Justice Research Institute.

Walklate, S. (2000). Researching victims. In R. D. King & E. Wincup (Eds.), *Doing Research on Crime and Justice* (pp. 183–201). Oxford: Oxford University Press.

Weiner, R. (1996). War by other means: Colombia's faceless courts. *NACLA Report on the Americas 30*(2), 31–37.

West, W. G. (1989). Towards a global criminal justice problematic. *The Journal of Human Justice 1*(1), 99–112.

Wolfgang, M. (1958). *Patterns in Criminal Homicide*. Philadelphia: University of Pennsylvania Press.

World Organization against Torture. (2003, November 11). Violence against women in Colombia a continuing concern [Press Release]. Geneva: World Organization against Torture. Available from: www.omct.org/index.php?id=EQL&lang=eng&articleSet=Press&articleId=3786.

CHAPTER 9

Conclusion

Being a young discipline, many areas of victimology remain virgin territory and have yet to be explored by inquisitive and adventurous researchers. The coming years will witness a growing realization that action not backed by research is a mere ideological exercise, and that practice not grounded in theory is dangerous and potentially harmful. (Fattah, 2000, p. 40)

At this point it is appropriate to consider the key threads that tie together the various chapters in this book, discuss some things that may be changing, and identify key areas for future research.

COMMON THREADS

First, I feel that this book has, in some small part, responded to Fattah's (2000) call that, due to the "diminishing returns" of large-scale quantitative methods such as victimization surveys, where many of the same well-worn patterns tend to be repeated, the victimology of the future will need to place more of an emphasis on qualitative research. Thus, I have attempted throughout to emphasize the qualitative aspects of victimized individuals' lived experiences. As we have seen, these help to highlight questions about unexamined assumptions, official accounts, ideologies, and programs.

However, as with the study of deviance, the study of criminal victimization poses difficult methodological challenges (Gomme, 2007). While the difficulties with traditional quantitative approaches such as victimization surveys have been discussed in detail elsewhere (Gomme, 2007), and the pros and cons of qualitative methods are well known (Berg, 1995; Gomme, 2007), the studies in this volume highlight further specific issues faced by qualitative researchers who are dealing with those suffering from emotionally upsetting forms of victimization (see Appendix A for a detailed discussion). While qualitative researchers are able to obtain far more detailed and meaningful data on victims' lived experiences, great care must be taken with regard to research ethics, accessing subjects, interviewing and ethnographic observation, careful use of language, transcription, analysis, and presentation of results. Indeed, it is important to consider researchers' experiences in all of this, as these sometimes reflect and shed useful light on the data encountered. I hope the discussion in this regard encourages qualitative researchers to build on my observations, strategies, and methodological insights, particularly by providing accounts of their own research experiences in other qualitative analyses of more far-ranging victimological contexts.

Second, the research in this book indicates that Canadians who have been victimized by crime often embark on a difficult path, facing a great deal of misunderstanding in social, institutional, and even academic circles. Thus, on one hand it indicates that the impacts of victimization (and indeed the issue of what constitutes a "real" victim) can be problematic, particularly given that claims of victimization can serve pragmatic purposes in social interaction; while on the other hand it identifies fundamental dimensions of the self that may be impacted by victimization and potentially obfuscated by such considerations. Adding to such misunderstandings is my finding that coming to terms with victimization is inextricably entwined with often problematic social factors. These include things such as gender-role socialization, negative social reactions, and institutional context, all of which are key elements in the reconstruction of the self in relatively active or victim-centred forms. In particular, the criminal justice system has traditionally provided little place for the victim, other than as a witness, and the limited initiatives ostensibly taken to improve victims' experiences have essentially been built around this existing structure, suggesting both symbolic politics and raising the spectre of unmet needs. Indeed, not only do supposedly innovative programs such as restorative justice often reinforce the victim role, but private victim support services, built around their own institutional goals, may also do so in other ways. All have some impact on coping—and it is sometimes a negative impact. Indeed, as Chapter 8 in part draws out, such a social and institutional situation, whether based on misunderstanding, neglect, institutional interest, or structural interest, contains the potential for re-victimization and does not put us in good company internationally. If these may be factored into my discussion of agency in Chapter 3, I would argue that, while not entirely obfuscating coping ability, on balance, they often coalesce in ways that inhibit it. What are we to make of this?

I contend that many of these findings may be usefully tied together through the analogous use of a concept from medical sociology. Illich (1976) argued that medical practice, set up to help individuals to return to good health, may in some instances be iatrogenic (i.e., creating disease and illness even as it provides medical assistance). If we broaden Illich's ideas beyond the institutional setting, it could be argued that many of the social and academic misunderstandings of victim experiences, negative reactions, institutional marginalizations, token programs, and counter-intuitive impacts enhancing victim claims have parallel iatrogenic impacts on victimized individuals, creating or enhancing victimization through social reactions and misguided attempts to help.

To elaborate, Illich broke iatrogenesis down into three subcategories: clinical, social, and structural:

> "[It is] clinical, when pain, sickness and death result from the provision of medical care; it is social, when health policies reinforce an industrial organization which generates dependency and ill health; and it is structural, when medically sponsored behaviour and delusions restrict the vital autonomy of people by undermining their competence in growing up, caring for each other, and aging" (Illich, 1976, p. 165).

While a parallel with clinical iatrogenesis may be seen with some of the social reactions to victimization in Chapter 3, where labels were at times applied and reinforced through the ostensible provision of support, it is in the institutional context that clinically iatrogenic results are most prominent. The traditional criminal justice system, ostensibly society's source of justice when things go wrong, marginalizes and often re-victimizes those who have been victimized by crime. The token institutional responses to victims' concerns, detailed in Chapter 6, are built around the existing re-victimizing structure, and can reinforce the powerlessness of the victim role even when trying to help. Add the reinforcement of victim claims by private-support groups, shelters, outreach services, and restorative justice, and, despite these being variously helpful in some respects, the potential range of counter-intuitive and indeed clinically iatrogenic impacts looms large.

Next, social iatrogenesis occurs when policies reinforce an organization that produces dependency and poor health (Illich, 1976). Much of the above may be read in this light as well. In our "risk society" (Giddens, 1990, 1999), where "risks are increasingly globalized and generalized in ways which are seen as out of the individual's control, bolstering the social and political significance of institutions and expert knowledge" (Howson, 1998, p. 196), there is a growing series of medical specialties and interventions that focus on "prevention," early detection, and screening out potential problems (Clarke, 2008). I would argue that social reactions to victimized individuals (which often encouraged seeking help) and the historical expansion of general and specialized victim programs to serve their ostensible needs are part and parcel of this risk society. Organizers, justifying their existence and using victims as symbolic tokens (Giddens, 1999), may claim that programs have been set up to prevent or offset additional negative events that "might happen" were they not there. However, the ambiguity of the term "victim" and programs' varying, often limited attention to victims' expressed needs, limits on expert knowledge, and reflection of their organizational background often result in limited assistance being offered. This is perhaps most notable in the criminal justice system, where the existing organization is strengthened and yet assistance is limited, and may even have counter-intuitive, disempowering impacts while fostering dependence on the system. It is also seen in the various ways in which victim claims, and indeed dependence, are at times fostered in support groups and other programs.

Finally, structural iatrogenesis involves the loss of individual autonomy and the institutional creation of dependency (Illich, 1976). This is seen in the interaction of various social and institutional factors, outlined in Chapter 3, that may limit or "hem in" the exercise of human agency. Again, to the extent that social images of victims, ideologies, structurally prominent programs, and services either explicitly or implicitly emphasize need, weakness, and the need for intervention to justify their existence, then the structurally iatrogenic fostering of such victimization claims may be an issue.

My focus on this token and potentially iatrogenic nature of social and institutional responses to victimization, particularly in a Canadian context, not only serves to tie together many of the findings in this book, but also assigns them a special place in the broader victimology literature today. It is an area that certainly bears further investigation.

ONGOING CHANGES

All the same, some might argue that things are starting to change for the better. Programs and services are always changing, and laws are regularly amended. To focus on but one example, beyond my outline and critique of general criminal justice responses to victims, governments have been busy instituting a variety of more specific changes for particular types of victims.

The Federal Government, for example:

1. Passed Bill C-89 in 1988, amending the Criminal Code to allow victim impact statements at sentencing, in camera hearings, improved restitution and return of property to victims. It introduced the Canadian Statement of Principles of Justice for Victims of Crime, enabled courts to order a ban on publishing the identity of witnesses, and imposed a "victim fine surcharge" on fines, which are directed into the "Victims Fund."

2. Instituted a more open position by Correctional Services and the Parole Board regarding the release of certain information on offenders, including a toll-free number to call for information (until the early 1990s, information requests by victims were often opposed under the old Privacy Act).

3. Passed legislation regulating the use by defence counsel of the victim's prior sexual history in sexual assault cases. Although the constitutionality of the original provisions was successfully challenged, the federal government passed modified legislation in 1992. While upheld by the Supreme Court in 2000, this has nevertheless remained a hot issue with defence lawyers.

4. Passed legislation in 1993 making criminal harassment ("stalking") an offence. Prior to this all that existed were the notoriously ineffective "peace bonds."

5. Introduced further restitution provisions to the Criminal Code authorizing a sentencing judge to award damages for bodily injury, loss of income or support "where the amount is readily ascertainable," and enabling the victim to later enforce it as a civil judgment (the older provision only applied to property damage, and was little known and little used). This still faces the enforcement problems of civil lawsuits noted in Chapter 6.

6. Introduced a national sex offender screening system in 1994 enabling community organizations to access the criminal records of potential applicants for positions of trust with children and vulnerable adults. The same year Bill C-7 established a special flagging system within the Canadian Police Information Centre for offenders pardoned of such offences.

7. Passed legislation in 1995 facilitating the use of DNA evidence in criminal proceedings. This was strengthened in 2000 with the passage of the DNA Identification Act, which established a national databank and retroactively required offenders of a series of serious, violent offences to provide samples to help facilitate criminal investigations.

8. Passed Bill C-37 in 1995, which amended the Young Offenders' Act to increase sentences for those convicted of murder in Youth Court. This was followed in 2003 with the introduction of the Youth

Criminal Justice Act, which, while diverting most youth away from the formal court process, theoretically favors harsh penalties for serious, violent offences and gives victims limited opportunities to participate in the youth justice process.

9. Passed Bill C-72 in 1995, which limits the use of the drunkenness defence.

10. Passed Bill C-41 (the "Hate Bill") in 1995 to increase sentences for crimes committed specifically against identifiable minorities as a result of hatred toward that group.

11. Passed Bill C-68 on gun control in 1995. This increases penalties for illegally importing firearms and for the use of guns during the commission of a crime. It also sets up a national firearms registry. It was strengthened in 1997 with the creation of new offences related to the unauthorized possession, transfer, importing, or exporting of firearms and their use in a criminal offence. By 2003 all owners and users were required to have a licence and all guns had to be registered. In 2006 mandatory minimum sentences for firearm-related offences were increased.

12. Passed legislation in 1996 to somewhat tighten up eligibility for judicial review hearings for murderers under s.745 (the "faint hope clause") of the Criminal Code.

13. Passed legislation in 1996 to create a new category of "long-term offender" mandating tougher supervision. This is in addition to 1986 amendments tightening the notorious "mandatory supervision" program. In 1997 a dated "dangerous offender" provision of the Criminal Code was strengthened, mandating automatic indeterminate sentences for those so declared. In addition, the federal government and several provinces have been looking at electronic monitoring for violent as well as non-violent offenders.

14. Passed anti-gang/criminal conspiracy legislation in 1997 as a result of the Quebec biker war. This expanded the investigatory powers of police officers in such cases (e.g., electronic surveillance), limited bail, increased sentences, created new offences (e.g., re: use of explosives), and enabled the seizure of the proceeds of crime. In 2001 further amendments were added criminalizing participation

in a criminal organization, benefiting from a criminal organization, and directing others to commit crimes.

15. Passed amendments to the Criminal Code in 1999 commonly referred to as the "Federal Victims' Bill of Rights." This includes increased, but carefully limited opportunities for victim input on matters such as bail and parole hearings, as well as removing the discretion of the judge such that victims will henceforth have a "right" for victims to make a victim impact statements.

16. In 2001 passed new anti-terrorist legislation extending police powers of investigation and detention, creating tougher sentences and parole supervision, and introducing new offences of knowingly participating in, contributing to, or facilitating the activities of a terrorist group.

17. In 2002 introduced Bill C-15A to better protect children from cyber-predators.

18. In 2002 introduced Bill C-16, following two years of intense pressure, to establish a National Sex Offender Registry. Coming into effect in 2004, this retroactively required all convicted sex offenders to register their addresses shortly after conviction, with local law enforcement when they move, and to provide information such as a name change.

19. In 2003 revised and updated the Canadian Statement of Basic Principles of Justice for Victims of Crime.

20. Established the National Office for Victims in 2005, a central resource for victims of offenders under federal responsibility.

21. In 2005, following its earlier introduction of the Victims Fund, began providing financial assistance to victims to attend National Parole Board hearings.

22. In 2007, enhanced the Victims Fund to enable the provision of emergency financial assistance to Canadians victimized abroad.

23. In 2007, established the Office of the Federal Ombudsman for Victims of Crime in 2007.

Provincial Governments have also been active. For example, they have:

1. Long since introduced Criminal Injuries Compensation Programs, though after 1992 types of compensation have been cut back and boards amalgamated with workers' compensation or victims' services programs.

2. Introduced victim-witness programs in police and Crown Prosecutors offices across the country. These programs generally provide workers who help provide information, counsel witnesses as to what to expect in court, and who may, in some instances, attend court with victims. As noted, they do not change the procedural power of the victim.

3. Passed so-called "victims' bills of rights," which typically list things like "the victim should be treated with compassion and fairness," but specifically deny any legally enforceable remedy should this not be the case.

4. Increasingly trained police forces to deal with situations where they must inform someone of the death of a loved one, and to provide information as to where services may be available for victims of violent crime generally.

5. Several provinces, for example, Ontario and Manitoba, have introduced legislation giving police chiefs and provincial correctional officials the right to publicize the names of sex offenders and other criminals released into their community who they believe pose a threat. In addition, Ontario has introduced legislation preventing offenders from hiding their criminal records by officially changing their names.

6. Many provinces, in concert with their victims' services programs, have introduced computerized systems to inform victims of the progress of an offender's trial.

7. Some provinces with provincial parole systems (e.g., B.C.) have announced that victims will be permitted to make oral submissions at parole hearings (previously, victims had to apply to attend hearings, and, as they were generally permitted only written submissions, could not effectively address or respond to matters that emerged therein).

8. Many provinces have introduced "zero-tolerance" policies in relation to domestic violence, often referred to as pro-arrest and pro-charge policies.

9. Several provinces (e.g., Ontario in 2001) introduced provincial sex offender registries.

10. Several provinces (e.g., Alberta, P.E.I., Saskatchewan) have strengthened civil restraining orders, even experimented with preventative detention in domestic violence cases.

Finally, there is one interesting emerging development:

1. A slowly developing trend where victims apply to have private counsel act on their behalf as "intervenors" in the criminal justice process. Thus, it has become common, since *R. v. O'Connor* (1995) 44 C.R. (4th) 1, 103 C.C.C. (3d) 1 (S.C.C.), and 1999 legislation by the Federal government, for Canadian judges to grant standing to private lawyers representing victims in sexual assault cases. These lawyers appear in order to specifically assert their client's right to privacy with respect to documents such as personal diaries and confidential psychiatric records. Courts have construed this exception narrowly, and in most other respects the victim does not have procedural rights in criminal court.

Taken together, such changes have made minor progress toward alleviating the victim's plight when facing the criminal justice system. However, the substantive vs. symbolic impact of these initiatives may frequently be questioned, since many still focus on the offender and are built around the existing system. It must be remembered that the victim is still not a party to the proceeding, and thus has comparatively few enforceable rights in a process that remains dominated by the state and defence counsel. Thus, caution and a critical eye still urged.

FUTURE RESEARCH

At this point, I would like to turn my attention to several key areas where I feel that future researchers can make a significant contribution to the victimological literature.

First, the initial impact of victimization and its relationship to victim claims is still poorly understood, and this may be part of the reason behind both problematic social reactions and the varying constructions of victim needs underlying specific programs. Thus my preliminary findings in this respect call out for comparative research in relation to a greater diversity of offences, victim backgrounds, and offence contexts to see whether these findings hold, and to what extent they may be qualified empirically. Indeed, my findings highlight the difficult question of what, in fact, constitutes a "real" victim found in the work of Viano (1989) and Holstein and Miller (1990), calling for researchers to find innovative ways to move beyond unhelpful terms such as "objective" and "subjective" measures—and their corresponding pitfalls of "expert" diagnoses and individual impression management—by highlighting the construction of reality and its pragmatic implications occurring in the social context at hand.

Next, Chapter 2 has highlighted the lived experiences of individuals who have experienced, claimed, and even embraced the victim identity in homicide cases, particularly the various fundamental dimensions of the self that may be impacted by crime. I strongly urge future researchers to study these metaphorical claims—and how they may be elaborated, varied, or discounted—in other types of victimization contexts (e.g., various violent vs. property crimes); in other bereavement contexts (e.g., terminal illness, car accidents, suicide); and in the experiences of individuals in the throes of other "life crises" (e.g., divorce, bankruptcy, terminal illness). Indeed, future research should comparatively investigate the evolution of those aspects of the self that remain following various crimes and how these evolve in inter-action with such metaphorical claims.

Finally in this respect, metaphors of loss often serve a pragmatic purpose in social interactions, acting not only as announcements in the process of role-making and role-taking (Hewitt, 2000), but also as emotional place markers and place claims (Clark, 1990), assisting individuals to rhetorically control the definition of the situation when micro-political claims to victim status are in question. Again drawing attention to both the question of what constitutes a "real" victim and the pragmatic construction of victimization in interactions, I call upon researchers to compare how metaphors are used both in other kinds of victimization (e.g., domestic violence, fraud) and in other types of micro-political interaction (e.g., spousal relationships, office politics). Researchers should also move beyond the micro-political realm described here and examine how these metaphors are utilized in the pol-itical process of social problem construction more generally. This is signifi-cant, considering that a sizable number of my interview respondents had affiliations with victims' rights organizations with a political agenda.

Next, given my focus in Chapter 3 on how the social self is both recon-structed and struggles to reconstruct itself in various social contexts, I feel it would be useful for future researchers to move beyond homicide and focus on factors such as parallel victim labelling processes, socially organized gender dynamics and grief cycles, and the construction of human agency to cope in other victimization and bereavement contexts. Questions might include: whether grief cycles are found in all types of bereavement, or merely in those where death is sudden and violent? Or is some element of intention also necessary, such as in suicide? Do they vary on the basis of victim relationship? Or by culture? What is their relationship to the diagnosis of "mental disorders"? What are the epidemiological patterns? In which social and institutional contexts is human agency best fostered among victimized individuals? Indeed, further focused, observational studies of "volitional gerrymandering" by various types of victims in differing social contexts would be most illuminating.

Given the central role and significantly negative impact of the Canadian criminal justice system described in Chapter 4, where the "legal fiction" that criminal law is a matter between the accused and the state ironically relegates victims to the lived construction of a precarious reality, ongoing tinkering with criminal law and procedure in areas of victim concern calls for ongoing research on how things might be changing. Such research is necessary to track what differences, if any, these initiatives are making to victims' experiences in the criminal justice system. Indeed, research on comparative criminal justice systems and their approaches to the role of the victim is also called for.

We have highlighted the strategic management of emotion, especially as related to the criminal justice system, as the missing ingredient in the emergence of the Canadian victims' rights movement. Therefore, our work suggests that attention should be paid to the careful emotional balancing act between organizational and public contexts in the study of other emerging social movements. Moreover, now that the movement's emergence has been charted, more attention needs to be focused on the characteristics, successes, failures, and organizational trajectories of other victims' groups. For example, I have seen victims' groups emerge, flourish for a time, and then fold (e.g., CAVEAT in the 1990s). It would be interesting for future researchers to examine whether a breakdown of this emotional balancing between organizational and public contexts, along with victim hierarchies, plays a role in what appears to be a limited lifespan for such groups. On the other hand, what role does government—and government funding—play in more enduring organizations, and how much does government input compromise group goals? Finally, given that questions have been raised about the relative influence of the victims' movement on emerging programs and services for victims (Elias, 1983; Rock, 1990), there should be further study to determine the degree to which the movement has impacted the development of such initiatives.

As institutions, programs, and services have been central to this book, it should come as no surprise that I argue for an ambitious research agenda in this regard. Thus, since the term "victim" is open to diverse interpretations (Weed, 1995), and victim policies may primarily reflect prior institutional and organizational contexts, more research, on a more diverse group of victim programs, should be performed to determine how much this pattern holds or varies—with an emphasis on newly emerging programs. Next, given public programs' often limited response to victims' substantive interests, and that the theme of "symbolic politics" (Elias, 1983) has been found to be more applicable than originally formulated in relation to criminal injuries compensation, more research, on a more diverse group of victim programs, should be performed to determine how much this prevalence of symbolic politics holds or varies elsewhere, with a particular emphasis on its impact on various clientele groups. Indeed, research should consider whether it is possible that anything can be done within our current system—or can be found in others—to effectively improve the lot of victims. Finally, given the reality of varying counter-intuitive, interactional impacts of various victim support services that potentially risk therapeutic gain (Winkel & Renssen, 1998), researchers should consider a wider variety of victim programs and services to identify best practices whereby supportive assistance may be increased and these attendant problems minimized. The need for research in this area is most pressing (Fattah, 2000). The research goal should be practical: better victim services for all.

Turning to restorative justice, beyond considering whether there are any differences in interactional dynamics between restorative justice programs dealing with youth and adults and in those dealing with more serious, violent offences, future research should: (1) examine whether differences in the above dynamics occur in variously organized programs; (2) review the roles played by ideology, program policy, power differentials, caseworker practices, and conference dynamics undermining client agency; (3) consider programs with varying relationships to criminal justice institutions to see whether restorative justice, operating under the umbrella of the justice system, can ever be predominantly re-integrative, rather than primarily emphasizing formal settlement; (4) review further the strategic role of supporters; (5) consider the impact of varying degrees of facilitator skill, particularly in relation to the optimum, restorative balance of facilitator/participant control and the extent to which, despite training, settlement-oriented practices persist because of organizational factors; and (6) in all of this, consider the degree to which micro-political shame management fails, thereby facilitating anti-social as opposed to restorative outcomes.

Next, further research should move beyond the Canadian experience and expand international comparisons. Considering the uncomfortable parallels we have drawn between Canada and Colombia, where there is an institutionalized ability for the legal system to gerrymander between responsibility and necessity producing outcomes that leave victims—particularly those without power or status—effectively without redress, future researchers should attempt to compare patterns of and responses to victimization across jurisdictions more generally. Of course, levels of analysis need to be better integrated, theoretical assumptions worked out, methodological difficulties minimized, and theoretical tools refined in a more comprehensive fashion. Yet by removing the blinkers of past traditions and engaging in carefully grounded research, it is hoped that future researchers will ultimately be able to better construct comparative studies of victimization and institutional responses to victimization between jurisdictions and across development contexts.

It is the question of human agency, finally, that I feel compelled to return to in the end. Given the experience of a horrific crime such as homicide, and that both legal institutions and many medical, psychiatric, and counselling approaches often either marginalize agency or emphasize passive approaches,[1] if some evidence of human agency can be found in such a context, then it can likely be found anywhere. Yet, despite signs of hope in the various coping strategies chosen, learned, or innovated by survivors, the many social and institutional factors above often serve to *limit* their ability to cope, to hem their agency in. While some fall back on emphasizing different aspects of the victim role, even politically, changes to the criminal justice system illustrate that the victims' movement has achieved limited success. These and other respondents' comments about helping agents such as therapists, support groups, and public and private victim support programs lend credence to Fattah's (2000) doubts about some common approaches to counselling victims.[2] Not only do these potentially compress agency into a relatively narrow realm, bearing potentially iatrogenic effects, but they also echo Conrad and Schneider's (1980) discussion of the negative implications of the medical model. These would particularly include reliance on "experts," the individualization and de-politicization of social problems, and the fostering of dependence and—by extension—the potential reinforcement of victim claims as a means to facilitate action. There is a pressing need to sort these matters out, and for further comparative research in differing victimization contexts and beyond to find methods of expanding victims' rights, agency, and coping abilities while minimizing the problems identified herein.

A PERSONAL CODA

Writing this book has been a long, sometimes difficult, but rewarding road to travel. While it is critical in many respects, I do hope that some of the thoughts here not only provoke, but also raise critical questions in turn. Questioning assumptions and accepted parameters often leads to hypotheses and then to further research, adding to our knowledge of victimized individuals and the various social and institutional contexts that they encounter throughout their experience.

I have come to believe that the social, institutional, and particularly the legal matrix faced by victimized individuals is often a big part of their problem. Victims need to find ways to engage in effective political action for more institutional and legal options that both help to expand agency and effectively balance their rights against those of others, rather than entirely limit them *by* the rights of others. For example, one might ask why, if we have built up considerable experience in balancing the offenders' rights against the state and the limits of one right against another since the introduction of the Canadian *Charter of Rights and Freedoms* a mere quarter-century ago, can we not then balance in more substantive and procedural rights for the victim? Could constitutional rights for victims be a goal worth fighting for, or is this simply pie in the sky? Fighting for such increased options—if both the will and structure of political opportunities permit—will not be easy, and past attempts at constitutional amendment show that victims undoubtedly face daunting obstacles. Still, enabling them to expand their agency beyond the narrow band to which they have been socially and institutionally confined would likely help to avoid their marginalization, re-victimization, and some of the counterproductive trauma and shaming, and be of service to us all.

As we come to the end of this book one particular conversation springs to mind. In 2004, I asked a highly placed lawyer his opinion about the equity of a new criminal justice program, widely promoted as a means of "bringing victims back in"—but without providing victims with similar rights to those of the offender. He responded that the victim "has no rights anyway," so is not losing anything in the program. This is a telling comment on our system, and I hope the presence of such ingrained attitudes will provoke further discussion, debate, research, activism, and innovation in Canadian victimology. While I am not persuaded that a greater procedural role for victims would be the whole solution (or even be seen as desirable for some), I am convinced that limiting options through the continued enforcement of such formal inequity is problematic—both in symbolic and practical terms—for their experiences. Without much more than symbolic options, and without the efforts of future researchers and activists on many of the issues raised in this book, Canadian victims of crime are likely to continue facing many of the same challenges for some time to come.

ENDNOTES

1. Psychological understandings of victims generally reflect three themes: (1) attempts at differentiating the "symptoms" of "post-traumatic stress disorder" from other "mental disorders" (Meadows, 2001; National Institute of Mental Health, 2001); (2) a focus on temporal "stage models" of the grieving process (Casarez-Levison 1992; Young, 1991); and (3) an emphasis on the therapist's role in helping individuals to accomplish various tasks leading to recovery (Klass, 1988; Worden, 2001). All imply that, due to the debilitating nature of victimization, relatively powerless individuals either need professional attention or, in less severe cases, must pass through certain stages over time (Attig, 1991). Indeed, the task model still implies a need for therapeutic direction and control (Klass, 1988). To the extent that such inhibitory assumptions come into play, these current models may be criticized around the theme of agency.

2. While mental health and human service professionals often assert that intervention should be based on the voluntary participation of victims presented with options, others claim that a more active, interventionist agenda is at play (Dineen, 1996). While some emphasize passivity and helplessness, others argue that victims have natural coping skills that are usually effective (Fattah, 2000). Indeed, it has been argued that the provision of services plays a part in determining victims' needs, and that expert-led innovations in the provision of support have an impact on victim expectations (Zedner, 2002).

REFERENCES

Attig, T. (1991). The importance of conceiving of grief as an active process. *Death Studies 15*, 385–393.

Berg, B. (1995). *Qualitative Research Methods for the Social Sciences*. Needham Heights, MA: Allyn & Bacon.

Casarez-Levison, R. (1992). An empirical investigation of the coping strategies used by victims of crime: Victimization redefined. In E. C. Viano (Ed.), *Critical Issues in Victimology: International Perspectives* (pp. 46–57). New York: Springer.

Clark, C. (1990). Emotions and micropolitics in everyday life: Some patterns and paradoxes of "place." In T. D. Kemper (Ed.), *Research Agendas in the Sociology of Emotions* (pp. 305–333). Albany, NY: State University of New York Press.

Clarke, J. N. (2008). *Health, Illness, and Medicine in Canada*. Toronto: Oxford University Press.

Conrad, P., & Schneider, J. (1980). *Deviance and Medicalization: From Badness to Sickness*. Columbus, OH: Merrill.

Dineen, T. (1996). *Manufacturing Victims: What the Psychology Industry Is Doing to People*. Toronto: Robert Davies.

Elias, R. (1983). Symbolic politics of victim compensation. *Victimology 8*(1–2), 213–224.

Fattah, E. A. (2000). Victimology: Past, present, and future. *Criminologie 33*(1), 17–46.

Giddens, A. (1990). *The Consequences of Modernity*. Cambridge, UK: Polity Press.

Giddens, A. (1999). Risk and responsibility. *The Modern Law Review 62*(1), 1–10.

Gomme, I. (2007). *The Shadow Line: Deviance and Crime in Canada*. Toronto: Thomson-Nelson.

Hewitt, J. P. (2000). *Self and Society: A Symbolic Interactionist Social Psychology*. Boston: Allyn and Bacon.

Holstein, J., & Miller, G. (1990). Rethinking victimization: An interactional approach to victimology. *Symbolic Interaction 13*(1), 103–122.

Howson, A. (1998). Surveillance, knowledge, and risk. *Health 2*(2), 195–215.

Illich, I. (1976). *Limits to Medicine*. Toronto: McClelland & Stewart.

Klass, D. (1988). *Parental Grief: Solace and Resolution*. New York: Springer.

Meadows, R. J. (2001). *Understanding Violence and Victimization* (3rd ed.). Upper Saddle River: Pearson.

National Institute of Mental Health. (2001). *Post-traumatic Stress Disorder: A Real Illness*. Bethesda, MD: National Institute of Mental Health: Publication #00–4675.

Rock, P. (1990). *Helping Crime Victims: The Home Office and the Rise of Victim Support in England and Wales*. Oxford: Clarendon Press.

Viano, E. C. (1989). Victimology today: Major issues in research and public policy. In E. C. Viano (Ed.), *Crime and Its Victims: International Research and Public Policy Issues* (pp. 3–14). New York: Hemisphere.

Weed, F. (1995). *Certainty of Justice: Reform in the Crime Victim Movement*. New York: Aldine de Gruyter.

Winkel, F. W., & Renssen, M. R. (1998). A pessimistic outlook on victims and an "upward bias" in social comparison expectations of victim support workers regarding their clients. *International Review of Victimology 5*, 203–220.

Worden, W. (2001). *Grief Counselling and Grief Therapy* (3rd ed.). New York: Springer.

Young, M. A. (1991). Survivors of crime. In D. Sank & D. I. Caplan (Eds.), *To Be a Victim: Encounters with Crime and Injustice* (pp. 27–42). New York: Plenum.

Zedner, L. (2002). Victims. In M. Maguire, R. Morgan, & R. Reiner (Eds.), *The Oxford Handbook of Criminology* (3rd ed., pp. 419–456). Oxford: Oxford University Press.

Key References and Further Reading

CHAPTER 2

Dauvergne, M. (2008). Crime statistics in Canada, 2007. *Statistics Canada—Catalogue no. 85–002-X, 28*(7). A good source on victimization data as reported to and recorded by the police.

Gannon, M., & Mihorean, K. (2005). Criminal victimization in Canada, 2004. *Statistics Canada—Catalogue no. 85–002-XPE, 25*(7). Provides the most recent Canadian self-report data from the 2004 General Social Survey.

Holstein, J. A., & Miller, G. (1990). Rethinking victimization: An interactional approach to victimology. *Symbolic Interaction 13*(1), 103–122. A key source outlining the idea of victimization as a social construction.

Kennedy, L. W., & Sacco, V. F. (1998). *Crime Victims in Context*. Los Angeles: Roxbury. Chapter 8, "The Aftermath of Victimization: The Victimization Experience" (pp. 163–178), sets out the range of psychological and material losses that may be experienced in the aftermath of victimization.

Viano, E. C. (1989). Victimology today: Major issues in research and public policy. In E. C. Viano (Ed.), *Crime and Its Victims: International Research and Public Policy Issues* (pp. 3–14). New York: Hemisphere. Outlines a four-stage model for the determination of "real" victim status.

CHAPTER 3

Attig, T. (1996). *How We Grieve: Relearning the World*. New York: Oxford University Press. An excellent source on bereavement, with an emphasis on grief as an active process.

Clark, C. (1987). Sympathy biography and sympathy margin. *American Journal of Sociology 93*(2), 290–321. Drawing upon a broad research literature, Clark outlines a theory of the normative organization of sympathy and its expression.

Conrad, P. , & Schneider, J. (1980). *Deviance and Medicalization: From Badness to Sickness*. Columbus, OH: Merrill. A classic that considers the historical trend toward constructing more and more problems in medical terms, along with the implications.

Cook, J. A. (1988). Dad's double binds: Rethinking father's bereavement from a men's studies perspective. *Journal of Contemporary Ethnography, 17*(3), 285–308. A useful sociological account of how gender impacts bereavement, particularly for men.

Taylor, S., Wood, J., & Lichtman, R. (1983). It could be worse: Selective evaluation as a response to victimization. *Journal of Social Issues 39*(2), 19–40. An excellent explanation of the key concepts of labelling theory as applied to victimization.

CHAPTER 4

Grossman, M., & Kane, C. (2004). Victims of crime and the Canadian justice system. In J. Roberts & M. Grossman (Eds.), *Criminal Justice in Canada* (pp. 106–119). Toronto: Thompson-Nelson. A general discussion of the role of the victim in the Canadian criminal justice system, with a brief introduction to some of the policy initiatives taken in recent years for victims.

Joutsen, M. (1987). Listening to the victim: The victim's role in European criminal justice systems. *Wayne Law Review 34*, 95–124. A comparative perspective on the legal role of the victim in the criminal justice systems of continental Europe.

Karmen, A. (2001). *Crime Victims: An Introduction to Victimology*. Belmont, CA: Wadsworth. Chapter 4: "Victims and the Criminal Justice System: Cooperation and Conflict," pp. 139–186, provides a detailed discussion of the various issues that victims face in their dealings with the criminal justice system, particularly in the American context.

Wallace, H. (2007). *Victimology: Legal, Psychological, and Social Perspectives*. Boston: Allyn and Bacon. Chapter 3: "The Criminal Justice System and Victims," pp. 39–60, provides a detailed procedural overview of the victim's role in the American criminal justice system.

Zedner, L. (2002). Victims. In M. Maguire, R. Morgan, & R. Reiner (Eds.), *The Oxford Handbook of Criminology* (pp. 419–456). Oxford: Oxford University Press. Between p. 435 and p. 443, Zedner provides a good discussion of the victim's position in the British criminal justice system, along with some recent developments.

CHAPTER 5

Amernic, J. (1984). *Victims: The Orphans of Justice*. Toronto: McClelland & Stewart-Bantam Ltd. An engaging journalistic account of the rise of the Canadian victims' rights movement.

Canadian Federal-Provincial Task Force. (1983). *Canadian Federal-Provincial Task Force Report: Justice for Victims of Crime*. Ottawa: Minister of Supply and Services. A detailed government report that lays out many of the legal, administrative, and institutional concerns faced by Canadian victims of crime from around the time the victims' rights movement emerged.

Dickson, B. (1984). The forgotten party—the victim of crime. *UBC Law Review 18*, 319–334. A frank and thoughtful discussion by the late, former Chief Justice of the Supreme Court of Canada, following his own victimization, on the then limited legal response to victims.

Rock, P. (1988). Governments, victims, and policies in two countries. *British Journal of Criminology 28*(1), 44–66. Rock argues that, contrary to the image of populist activism, the Canadian federal government launched the victim initiative and spent money trying to prompt a relatively inert "private sector" into organizing itself.

Weed, F. (1995). *Certainty of Justice: Reform in the Crime Victim Movement*. New York: Aldine de Gruyter. Outlines the emergence, activities, social construction, and characteristics of the American crime victim movement.

CHAPTER 6

Elias, R. (1983). Symbolic politics of victim compensation. *Victimology 8*(1–2), 213–224. A classic study of the politically advantageous disconnect between style and substance in victim programs. Elias introduces and elaborates on the concept of symbolic politics in this area.

Erez, E., & Laster, K. (1999). Neutralizing victim reform: Legal professionals' perspectives on victims and impact statements. *Crime and Delinquency 45*(4), 530–553. Research illustrating that victim impact statements have little or no influence in criminal cases.

Landau, T. C. (2006). *Challenging Notions*. Toronto: Canadian Scholars' Press Inc. Chapter 7, "Everywhere and Nowhere: Contemporary Victims Policy in Canada" (pp. 117–128), provides an overview of victim policies and programs, questioning their substance and raising further issues regarding potential negative impacts.

Weed, F. (1995). *Certainty of Justice: Reform in the Crime Victim Movement*. New York: Aldine de Gruyter. An empirical discussion, in the American context, of many of the issues discussed in this chapter (i.e., the construction of various types of victim programs and policies, victim impact statements, compensation programs, and symbolic politics).

Winkel, F. W., & Renssen, M. R. (1998). A pessimistic outlook on victims and an "upward bias" in social comparison expectations of victim support workers regarding their clients. *International Review of Victimology 5*, 203–220. A good introductory discussion on the role of staff biases in victim support programs and their potential to inhibit client coping.

CHAPTER 7

Acorn, A. (2004). *Compulsory Compassion: A Critique of Restorative Justice*. Vancouver: University of British Columbia Press. A readable and engaging critique of restorative justice.

Harris, N. (2006). Reintegrative shaming, shame, and criminal justice. *Journal of Social Issues 62*(2), 327–346. Discusses an empirical test of the implications of Braithwaite's re-integrative shaming theory, suggesting that the emotional consequences of shaming in restorative justice are more complex than originally theorized.

Latimer, J., Dowden, C., & Muise, D. (2001). *The Effectiveness of Restorative Justice Practices: A Meta-analysis*. Ottawa: Department of Justice. A detailed overview of prior research and a generally favourable assessment of restorative justice. Urges study of the interactional processes underlying restorative justice.

Law Commission of Canada. (1998). *From Restorative Justice to Transformative Justice: Discussion Paper*. Ottawa: Law Commission of Canada. A key position paper outlining the potential rewards and pitfalls of restorative justice for resolving social conflict from both social and legal perspectives.

Umbreit, M. (2001). *The Handbook of Victim–Offender Mediation: An Essential Guide to Practice and Research*. San Francisco: Jossey Bass. A good source for those seeking to work as facilitators in restorative justice.

CHAPTER 8

Alvazzi del Frate, A. (2002). Criminal victimization in Latin America. In P. Nieuwbeerta (Ed.), *Criminal Victimization in Comparative Perspective* (pp. 110–115). The Hague: Boom Juridische uitgevers. A discussion of comparative data on Latin American patterns of victimization from the 2000 International Crime Victimization Survey.

Alvazzi del Frate, A. (2007). Victimization: An international perspective. In R. Davis, A. Lurigio, & S. Herman (Eds.), *Victims of Crime* (pp. 233–252). Los Angeles: Sage. A good review of comparative data on international patterns of victimization from the 2000 International Crime Victimization Survey.

Besserer, S. (2002). Criminal victimization: An international perspective. Results of the 2000 International Crime Victimization Survey. *Statistics Canada—Catalogue no. 85–002-XPE, 22*(4), 1–19. A comparison of Canada and other countries in relation to criminal victimization.

Mawby, R., & Walklate, S. (1994). *Critical Victimology*. London, Sage. A good outline of a critical, theoretical approach to victimology that both supersedes many earlier structural and micro-level approaches with its emphasis on reality construction and, in some respects, underlies the approach taken in the current chapter.

Nieuwbeerta, P., de Geest, G., & Siegers, J. (2002). Corruption in industrialized and developing countries. In P. Nieuwbeerta (Ed.), *Criminal Victimization in Comparative Perspective* (pp. 163–182). The Hague: Boom Juridische uitgevers. A comparative, international analysis of corruption in industrialized and developing countries, including attempts to test several law and economics hypotheses.

APPENDIX B

Websites

CHAPTER 2

Statistics Canada
www.statcan.gc.ca
Up-to-date information on patterns of crime and victimization in Canada.

Canadian Resource Centre for Victims of Crime
www.crcvc.ca/en/resources
Victim perspectives on the impact of various types of victimization.

National Organization for Victim Assistance (NOVA)
www.trynova.org
NOVA is the major US umbrella organization for crime victims. This site contains useful links, including NOVA's definition of a crime victim, various after-effects that may be associated with victimization, and information resources for victims and those seeking to help them.

Ontario Victim Services Secretariat
www.attorneygeneral.jus.gov.on.ca/english/ovss
Information on the official definition of "victim" that is applied to those requesting criminal injuries compensation. This definition was applied to many of the participants in this chapter. Other provinces have their own definitions and websites.

Shelternet
www.shelternet.ca
Outlines common ideas about the definition of "victimization" that are current among shelters, one of the groups studied in this chapter.

CHAPTER 3

Canadian Resource Centre for Victims of Crime
www.crcvc.ca/en/links
Numerous links to Canadian victims' groups, services, counselling, and other resources, some specifically targeted at men, women, or children.

Bereaved Families of Ontario
www.bereavedfamilies.net
An excellent Canadian resource for the bereaved.

Parents of Murdered Children
www.pomc.com
An American bereavement group that specifically focuses on helping the families of homicide victims.

National Organization for Victim Assistance (NOVA)
www.trynova.org/victiminfo/victimizationhelp/thetrauma.html
This page has an interesting discussion on the "social injury" of victimization.

Victim Assistance Online
www.vaonline.org
A non-profit information, research, and networking resource for victim assistance specialists, professionals in related disciplines, and all interested in the field of victimology. This organization has researched, reviewed, and published link directories on more than 40 victim-assistance-related topics, totalling more than 3,000 links to organizations, agencies, and services around the world. It also contains a virtual library: an index of online research-class articles, documents, handbooks, and guides, listed alphabetically and by topic category.

CHAPTER 4

Canadian Resource Centre for Victims of Crime
www.crcvc.ca/docs/A_Victims_Guide_to_the_Canadian_CJS_07.pdf
A booklet to assist victims of crime, and their families, in better understanding the Canadian criminal justice system. *A Victim's Guide to the Canadian Criminal Justice System: Questions and Answers* provides comprehensive answers to questions that victims may have about the justice system at the various stages of the process.

www.crcvc.ca/docs/HazelMagnussenpaper_victimadvocacy.pdf
This document gives Hazel Magnussen's views of the Canadian justice system following the murder of her brother.

Canadian Statement of Basic Principles of Justice for Victims of Crime, 2003
www.justice.gc.ca/eng/pi/pcvi-cpcv/pub/03/princ.html
Based on an October 2003 meeting of federal and provincial justice ministers, this statement outlines the basic principles that officially guide the development of policies, programs, and legislation related to victims of crime.

Correctional Service of Canada (CSC)
www.csc-scc.gc.ca/victims-victimes/index-eng.shtml
The official CSC website, detailing the CSC's position on victim issues and available services.

National Parole Board (NPB)
www.npb-cnlc.gc.ca/victims/victims_e.htm
The official NPB website, detailing the NPB's position on information available to victims and the procedures victims should follow to provide input at parole hearings.

CHAPTER 5

Canadian Resource Centre for Victims of Crime
www.crcvc.ca/en/links/#nonProfit
A list of links to contemporary Canadian, US, and international victim advocacy and service organizations.

Victims of Violence
www.victimsofviolence.on.ca
The present incarnation of the group discussed in this chapter, for many years operated by Gary and Sharon Rosenfeldt.

CAVEAT
www.caveat.org
The most prominent Canadian victims' organization during the 1990s, founded by Priscilla de Villiers and others following the murder of her daughter. The author once volunteered with this group.

Mothers Against Drunk Driving (MADD)
www.madd.org/About-Us/About-Us/History.aspx
The history of perhaps the best-known populist victims organization.

US Department of Justice, Office of Justice
Programs, Office for Victims of Crime
www.ojp.usdoj.gov/ovc/ncvrw/2005/pg4c.html
A detailed history of the crime victims' movement in the USA.

CHAPTER 6

Department of Justice, Policy Centre for Victim Issues (PCVI)
http://canada.justice.gc.ca/eng/pi/pcvi-cpcv/index.html
The PCVI, based in the federal Department of Justice, engages in legislative
reform, consultation, policy development, research, and project funding
in the area of victims of crime. The PCVI has a close working relationship with the provinces and territories that are tasked with victim service
delivery and the provision of criminal injuries compensation to victims of
violent crime, where such programs exist. This site provides an overview of
and links to services provided to victims of crime in provincial jurisdictions.

National Office for Victims
www.publicsafety.gc.ca/prg/cor/nov/nov-bnv-en.asp
Established in November 2005, the National Office for Victims is a central
resource for victims of offenders under federal responsibility. It provides:
- general information for victims and the public
- referrals to the Correctional Service of Canada (CSC) and
the National Parole Board (NPB) for specific enquiries
- a victim's perspective in national policy development
In addition, the office responds to complaints about the services provided to victims by the CSC and the NPB, once all other avenues for complaint have been exhausted.

The National Office for Victims is designed to complement several services offered by the CSC, the NPB and the Policy Centre for Victim Issues at
the Department of Justice.

www.justice.gc.ca/eng/pi/rs/rd-rr.html
The *Victims of Crime — Research Digest* is an annual periodical published
by the Department of Justice Canada during National Victims of Crime
Awareness Week, which occurs in April every year. Its aim is to dissemi-
nate short, accessible articles on current and completed victims of crime

research that is supported by the Policy Centre for Victim Issues at the Department of Justice.

Office of the Federal Ombudsman for Victims of Crime
www.victimsfirst.gc.ca
Created in 2007, the office claims to be a new, independent resource for Canadian victims. Headed by Steve Sullivan, a long-time advocate for victims of crime, victims can contact the office to learn more about their rights under federal law and the services available to them, or to make a complaint about any federal agency or federal legislation dealing with victims of crime. In addition, the office attempts to ensure that policy makers and other criminal justice personnel are aware of victims' needs and concerns, and identify important issues and trends that may negatively impact victims. Where appropriate, the Ombudsman may also make recommendations to the Federal Government.

Ontario Victim Services Secretariat (OVSS)
www.attorneygeneral.jus.gov.on.ca/english/ovss
The OVSS is a division of the Ontario Ministry of the Attorney General. It claims to work to ensure that victims of crime are treated with respect and receive the information and services they need. Various programs and services for victims of crime (e.g., criminal injuries compensation), grant programs, and general information on the criminal justice system are listed as links on this page.

Office for Victims of Crime (OVC)
www.ojp.usdoj.gov/ovc
The OVC is a US organization that was established by the 1984 *Victims of Crime Act* (VOCA) to oversee diverse programs that benefit victims of crime. Located in the Department of Justice, the OVC provides funding to state victim assistance and compensation programs and supports training designed to educate criminal justice and allied professionals regarding the rights and needs of crime victims. This site contains links to geographic lists of VOCA-funded victim service organizations. Each report contains summary data of all the state programs, followed by individual programs listed by city.

CHAPTER 7

Department of Justice Canada
www.justice.gc.ca/eng/pi/rs/rep-rap/2001/rr01_9/p1.html
A critical review of the literature on victim's experiences, expectations, and perceptions of restorative justice.

Nova Scotia Restorative Justice Program
www.gov.ns.ca/just/rj
A site that provides detailed information on the most institutionally complete restorative justice program in Canada, and perhaps in the world.

Correctional Service of Canada
www.csc-scc.gc.ca/text/rj/index-eng.shtml
Discusses restorative justice, specifically from a correctional perspective. It lists a variety of links and resources for those interested in this area.

Mennonite Central Committee
www.mcc.org/canada/restorativejustice/index.html
A faith-based group that pioneered Canadian restorative justice services in the 1970s. This group is still running programs in many provinces and partners with other community organizations.

The Centre for Restorative Justice
www.sfu.ca/crj/index.html
An initiative of the School of Criminology at Simon Fraser University, the Centre for Restorative Justice is at the forefront of research, education, program development and evaluation, and advocacy surrounding restorative justice.

CHAPTER 8

World Society of Victimology
www.worldsocietyofvictimology.org
A not-for-profit, nongovernmental organization that includes a world-wide membership of victim assistance practitioners, social scientists, social workers, physicians, lawyers, civil servants, volunteers, university academics of all levels, and students.

It aims "to advance victimological research and practices around the world; to encourage interdisciplinary and comparative work and research in this field; and to advance cooperation between international, national, regional, and local agencies and other groups who are concerned with the problems of victims."

International Victimology Website
www.victimology.nl
Aims to be "a global platform for everybody working in or associated with victimology, victim support, and allied disciplines and bring international research within reach and give the global victimology community a voice."

United Nations Interregional Crime and Justice Research Institute (UNICRI)
www.unicri.it
An international clearing house for criminological research and policy issues, "UNICRI's activities tackle major concerns in the field of crime prevention and criminal justice, such as corruption, security governance and counter-terrorism, [and] organized crime (in particular, trafficking of persons as well as illicit drugs and arms). Other areas of intervention [include] violence, both domestic and in the workplace; environmental- and cybercrimes; [and] protection of victims and cultural heritage. UNICRI also conducts major programs in criminal justice reform, with a special focus on juvenile justice."

NationMaster
www.nationmaster.com/index.php
A central data source that can be used to graphically compare nations. NationMaster compiles data from sources such as the *CIA World Factbook*, the United Nations, and the Organisation for Economic Co-operation and Development. With this website, graphical statistical representations can be composed to assess relationships between variables.

Human Rights Watch
www.hrw.org
Human Rights Watch says that it is: "One of the world's leading independent organizations dedicated to defending and protecting human rights. By focusing international attention where human rights are violated, we give voice to the oppressed and hold oppressors accountable for their crimes. Our rigorous, objective investigations and strategic, targeted advocacy build intense pressure for action and raise the cost of human rights abuse. For 30 years, Human Rights Watch has worked tenaciously to lay the legal and moral groundwork for deep-rooted change and has fought to bring greater justice and security to people around the world."

APPENDIX C

Qualitative Analysis of Victimization: Methodological Issues

Performing research on emotionally troubled (and troubling) participants has been little mentioned in the qualitative analysis literature. Nevertheless, qualitative sociologists frequently deal with serious topics and troubling individuals. One immediately thinks of the many classic studies of deviance that have been conducted through ethnographic inquiry. However, the topic is much broader and includes areas such as medical sociology, criminology, victimology, feminist studies, and media analysis. This appendix takes a preliminary look at the issues raised for qualitative researchers by emotionally troubling topics.

As noted, my first—and biggest—research project dealt with murder. I personally interacted with 53 participants, 32 in face-to-face interviews and then 22 in a less direct fashion through surveys (one person completed both). Participants included parents and family members of children who had been murdered. I also accessed 108 homicide files at the Ontario Criminal Injuries Compensation Board (CICB) (which included detailed psychiatric reports and victim impact statements), and conducted participant observation with an Ontario victims' support/advocacy organization. While my initial goal was to examine gender differences in active coping among such homicide survivors, it quickly became apparent that this group was troubled by far more than the crime itself. Indeed, there were a wide variety of issues to investigate (e.g., the often hurtful reactions of family, friends, and the community, and upsetting encounters with various "helping" agents and the criminal justice system). Previously, relatively little attention had been paid to such matters in this context (Kenney, 1998).

Performing qualitative research on such emotionally sensitive and explosive issues seemed the most appropriate strategy for several reasons. First, there has been very little research on such subjects, so I felt it necessary to explore the participants' own meanings and experiences through flexible, semi-structured interviews, ethnographic observation, and content analysis. I wanted to know their perspectives on these devastating experiences, not what others thought or assumed was important (Berg, 1995; Denzin, 1989). Second, there were difficulties in identifying the population because of the isolation and secrecy that surrounds emotional and sensitive issues, particularly in relation to the death of children. As such, it would have been very difficult to conduct a large, quantitative study (Berg, 1995; Lee, 1993). Third, due to the sensitive nature of the issues, many participants at first questioned my trustworthiness. I had to earn their trust, and face-to-face communication was the most appropriate way to do this.

ETHICS REVIEW

The literature shows that researchers are facing increasing difficulties with ever more stringent ethics review policies (Lee, 1993; Van den Hoonaard, 2000). With particularly emotional and sensitive topics, such as battered women, such difficulties are even greater due to concerns about exposing participants to stressful moments (Chatzifotiou, 2000). Hence, in studying homicide, I found the difficulties even more pronounced. As is standard, I obtained university ethics approval. In doing so, I initially faced the difficulty of creating instruments that were both sufficiently structured and sensitively worded enough to satisfy the ethics review board, yet open enough to enable flexibility and for participants to speak their own words.

Given the uniqueness of the issues being explored, problems also arose in making contact with potential participants (Lee, 1993). It was necessary to access organizations (e.g., victims' organizations, support and bereavement groups) and their representatives, who acted as gatekeepers. As part of this process, I had to submit a detailed plan of my proposed research and the questionnaire to a US victims' association for review by a staff physician before the research was approved. As for the content analysis of the CICB files, it goes without saying that the provincial government would not allow the viewing of such sensitive documents unless confidentiality was to be respected. A detailed written agreement was carefully negotiated between the myself and the CICB ensuring just that.

In seeking ethics approval to deal directly with victims, it was very important to emphasize that data would be collected only from willing participants who would be informed in advance about the sensitive nature of my research. Thus, detailed written notices were prepared for each organization regarding the nature of my study. I made it clear that research participants, whether being observed or later agreeing to interviews or mail-back surveys, would be well aware of my role. Indeed, I noted that immediately prior to conducting each interview, each participant would again be informed that there would be personal and potentially upsetting questions asked. I indicated that participants would be advised that they could decline any questions and withdraw from the interview at any time. Participants were further advised that their comments were confidential, that any records would be confidentially stored and destroyed following completion of the research, and that neither their names nor potentially identifying details would be used in any publication. Finally, I indicated that participants' written permission to tape-record interviews would be required on a form that reiterated all of the above matters.

One final note in this regard. I have conducted several other victim-related projects since obtaining ethics approval for this research in the mid 1990s (e.g., on public and private victim support services and restorative justice programs). My experiences with research ethics policies and the inevitable political elements in these contexts have sometimes left me wondering whether I would be able to have my homicide project approved were I beginning this work today.

ISSUES IN THE DESIGN OF RESEARCH INSTRUMENTS

With reference to interview schedules and questionnaires, the organizational structure primarily centred around thematic topics, while including many open-ended questions and opportunities for participants to speak about their own concerns. Both the interview schedules and the survey instrument followed the same basic structure. Following initial questions documenting demographic characteristics, participants were asked to describe their unique experiences in their own words.

Specifically, participants were asked to describe their reactions, feelings, and how, if they could, they would describe what it was like to lose a loved one in this manner. They were also asked what meanings this event disclosed for their present life. They were then questioned about what they viewed as helpful and unhelpful encounters with: (1) immediate family; (2) extended family and friends; (3) help agents, such as self-help organizations, counsellors, and the medical and psychiatric professions; and (4) various legal institutions. The issue of gender was examined in each of these contexts, particularly with regard to participants' coping responses.

The construction of these instruments was checked by having both academic colleagues and key members of the organizations read and comment before they were used. As well, rather than rely on only one question per issue, these instruments were constructed in such a manner that they generally utilized several different questions to measure the same thing. As such, problems with consistency in responses were reduced or negated.

ACCESSING PARTICIPANTS

It has long been noted that locating participants and gaining their cooperation are problems when researching sensitive subjects (Gelles, 1978; Lee, 1993). Recognizing this, I started by volunteering with a national victims' rights organization. This offered me the opportunity to participate and conduct fieldwork on many key events that crucially impacted "victims'" concerns. I learned a great deal about victims' issues by helping with some of this organization's projects, eventually working myself into a position where I was able to: (1) act as a delegate, distribute surveys, and conduct interviews at two national conferences; and (2) obtain information from courtroom observers and volunteers on the progress of a notorious murder trial. More than anything else, however, volunteering with this organization enabled me to have regular contact and network with many potential research participants.

It quickly became apparent that closer access to many key participants would not have been gained were it not for my ability to empathize or share a personal story. As a result, I shared my own experience of a murder in the family. This helped to establish a trusting relationship with my first, well-connected participant. The goodwill and word-of-mouth endorsements that followed enabled me to hear personal accounts from many key individuals. As a result of this success, I continued to share personal accounts with subsequent participants.

Indeed, without my prior knowledge of and experience with this topic, many participants indicated that they would probably not have felt comfortable enough to share the details of their experiences for fear that I would not be able to understand or be able to handle many of the shocking details (i.e., I'd simply be seen as one of the detached, less than sensitive "-ologists" that were often dismissed by many of my participants).

INTERVIEWING AND OBSERVING PARTICIPANTS

This was the core area where emotional upset on the part of participants and myself was most notable. By and large, the individuals I spoke with were glad to talk to someone about their experiences. Many participants had become socially isolated, losing friends and maintaining little contact with family (Kenney, 2002b). This was often considered the result of others' misunderstanding, uncertainty of how to act, or because of blame, indicating that labelling was at work (Kenney, 2002b). Indeed, many felt as though they were being avoided. As one woman stated, "It's been two years and I think you are the third person that's been in this house."

The interviews were very emotional for the participants as well as for myself. Still, I found that carefully gauging questions and responses to the moods of participants helped to prevent upsetting them too much or becoming visibly upset myself. Nevertheless, as the literature suggests (Chatzifotiou, 2000; Kinard, 1996), interviewer anxiety was an issue and there were many times when the interviews were very tense. During the interviews in which showing upset was appropriate or where the subject matter rendered it unavoidable, I personally found that the empathetic experience of mutual upset actually helped both the participants and myself.

Indeed, participants were able to express emotions that they hadn't often displayed because people were avoiding them. There were a few interviews in which I was especially concerned about having upset the participants, but was reassured that it was not my fault: it was their situation. In the words of one woman:

> "My friends are afraid to keep bringing it up, and they shy away because they're afraid they're going to 'Say something that's going to hurt you.' So they shy away. 'Cause, maybe they don't know that you want it. That it's all right to talk about it. They're afraid to. They don't understand that you can't be hurt any more than you already have been" (female, age 45).

Being able to share these emotions generally strengthened my rapport with participants. However, in situations where they were very upset I turned off the tape recorder and we would chat for a few minutes before resuming. There were a few exceptions that involved older men who adhered to more traditional gender roles and wouldn't show their upset. In these cases I took non-verbal cues such as finger-tapping on the table as a sign to change the nature of the dialogue or to wrap up the interview. Nevertheless, there was never a time where I or a participant could not finish an interview.

Because of the intensity and sensitive nature of the subject matter, I found that I had to plan the interview times carefully. I did not face the problem of doing many emotionally gruelling interviews in a short time because I rarely did more than two interviews a week. Nevertheless, I found it necessary to carefully accommodate participants' time preferences such that interviews were held at the most convenient time for them, often when participants felt it most helpful to talk.

The use of language was a constant challenge. I faced the problem of framing questions in such a way that they would be less likely to upset participants. For example, I was informed that the seemingly innocent demographic question "How many children do you have?" can be quite upsetting in this context.

Perhaps more significantly, asking people to describe (1) what it was like to lose someone like this and (2) whether they personally saw themselves as victims tended to provoke strong responses. While certainly evocative of a great deal of key data, these questions could be a touchy matter for some participants. Some responses were quite graphic. Many simply stated that the experience was indescribable, but then went on to use a variety of disturbing metaphors of loss to convey, insofar as possible, their lived experiences (Kenney, 2002a). Others, if they felt their victim status was in question, responded in a similar fashion to interactionally reinforce their position. One way or another, this metaphorical language was emotionally gripping.

Centred around the idea that "when you lose someone you love, you lose a part of yourself," expressions such as having one's "heart torn out," experiencing an "amputation," feeling "dead inside," "violated," "broken," and having "no future" were delivered with an emotional punch that nearly left me reeling. For example:

> "When they shot my son, they shot me. I felt such an emptiness. They killed my boy and they killed me inside. I'm not the same and I never will be" (female, age 45).

> "This was the most traumatic, violating event that I think could happen to anybody. I cannot imagine ever being more violated—not even by rape. My mother was a suicide, the rest of my family died of heart attacks and other various related things. There's no comparison. Absolutely no comparison" (female, age 51).

> "How does it feel? Well, it feels like someone reached into my heart, cut out a nice big chunk, filled it with blackness, and left me cold on the sidewalk" (male, age 24).

> "It's like sinking in quicksand, but never quite suffocating and dying oneself" (female, age 53).

I particularly recall one interview in which I interviewed the father of a young woman who had been murdered by her boyfriend. This man was evidently in a very emotionally fragile condition, particularly because he had once saved the life of the offender and now felt that it was his fault that his daughter had been killed. Many comments to this regard were made throughout, providing evidence that he was deeply embedded in a cyclical grief cycle (Kenney, 2003). This interview required considerable discretion, attention to the participant's non-verbal cues, and emotion management on my part to navigate the interview to a successful conclusion (Hochschild, 1983).

Upon experiencing such difficulties in the interviews, I found that I needed added safeguards for those participants farther afield who completed mail-back surveys. Thus, before sending out questionnaires, I informed all such participants in a cover letter about the subject matter of the survey, the nature of the questions, and confidentiality. I also gave them an opportunity to ask questions of me by telephone before proceeding. Indeed, I spoke at length to many of these individuals on the telephone before sending out questionnaires, and fielded several calls for clarification as the questionnaires were being completed by participants.

Perhaps the most disturbing aspect of the data collection for me was the fact that several participants used the term "my baby" with reference to the deceased. I particularly recall one incident early in my research when I was volunteering and conducting fieldwork at a victims' organization. I had been asked to help type up a handwritten letter to the parole board for my "gatekeeper." In that letter, she used the phrase "My baby was dead" in relation to her murdered daughter—something that triggered memories of my own cousin's emotionally intense funeral. "My baby" were the words that my aunt screamed over and over as she was escorted out of the funeral home after viewing his body. It was the saddest thing I have ever seen in my life, and hearing such words from another mother in a similar context was very difficult for me, necessitating a break for the day.

TRANSCRIPTION AND DATA ANALYSIS

Personally, I feel that the emotionally difficult part of this research only began with data collection. There were times in transcribing and reviewing the data when my own upset was triggered. Participants noted emotionally upsetting encounters in a number of contexts—things that shocked even me, a jaded sociological researcher who thought he had heard it all. For example, in addition to the common avoidance by others, one mother spoke of highly disturbing forms of telephone harassment.

I also recall one particularly difficult instance where I interviewed a woman about the murder of a five-year-old girl by a pedophile young offender. She described in grim detail how the little girl had died and the unspeakable things that were done to her. The participant and her family found this out in court, without any warning, through a video re-enactment by the offender.

Particularly disturbing in this case, the participants then gave me a picture of the little girl to keep. Needless to say, I found it very upsetting when I transcribed and reviewed these comments and saw the picture in the file. In situations such as this, I found that I had to take a break from work, sometimes for the rest of the day.

It could also be difficult to share such information with others I worked with. For instance, I had hired a student to assist with transcription. I was careful to consider her feelings when asking her to transcribe an interview. Despite this, at times she did not find this easy material to deal with. Also, as this research was for my PhD dissertation, I shared these data with my thesis committee. Writing up the data was one thing, but having to relay it was quite another. I know that some of these data upset my supervisor: she told me so. I was constantly aware of the difficulties these data presented to others who had to deal with them.

The sheer volume and complexity of qualitative data collected for this study required an intensive and organized approach to coding and analysis. Before data analysis began, all of the tape-recorded interviews and field notes, as well as the open-ended mail-back surveys and CICB files, were entered verbatim into separate files in WordPerfect. Paper copies were also made of these documents.

In time, as analysis progressed, I found that I gradually became less sensitized to the data when compared to the interview, transcription, and initial analysis stages. This was most likely due to the increase familiarity caused by repeated exposure through working with the data. Sometimes I still question whether that is a good thing.

PRESENTATION OF DATA

I was very concerned about how to present such sensitive and upsetting material. In giving my participants a voice, which is the intention when undertaking grounded-theory methodology, it is the responsibility of the researcher to ensure that the participants' meanings and perspectives are presented just as they were described. I have presented these data professionally in a number of contexts, including lectures at universities and academic conferences. All that I can offer on this account is that I try as sensitively as possible to prepare my audiences by informing them that the nature of the data is graphic and may be upsetting to hear. I always find there is a level of discomfort among even professional audiences, yet there is also much interest in knowing how I was able to manage such sensitive research.

In addition, I have provided summaries of my research to interested participants and organizations that I worked with during the process. For the most part I have received favourable responses. Indeed, I have been warmly received by several of my participants upon encountering them at conferences.

In all of this, I must again stress the importance of confidentiality, particularly in presenting the data in an anonymous fashion such that individuals cannot be identified. In my sample, many of the participants knew or were aware of each other and their circumstances. Safeguards such as changing names and omitting identifiable features were integral to the overall favour-able responses that I received.

ASSESSMENT

For the most part, I did not find the research particularly upsetting to do on the surface (with the notable exceptions above). Because I had experienced a murder in my own family more than a decade before, I had largely learned to deal with my emotions by the time I did the research. They were not so unfamiliar that I was shocked by them. Indeed, near the end of my disserta-tion, the disturbing feelings that had given way to de-sensitization started to slip into feelings of tedium and a heartfelt desire to get the whole thing fin-ished once and for all (a not uncommon feeling among students who spend years writing their theses!). I often noted to friends and colleagues that I was "sick to death of death."

Nevertheless, I did fear at times that constantly reviewing such shocking and depressing material would get to me "beneath the surface." In this vein, I suddenly realized a great irony some months after completing my research. Much of the data in this study focused on active coping strategies utilized by the participants. However, my own coping strategies, in dealing with this material, in some ways paralleled those of the participants. For instance, many participants found that in order to deal with their grief they had to bal-ance their time between focusing on their grief and other life activities that occupied their thoughts—to deal with it a bit at a time in "more easily digest-ible chunks." Upon reflection, I saw that this had proven to be a useful cop-ing strategy for many of my own activities in relation to this material. Writ-ing about the emotionally upsetting materials enabled me to work through my own upset in this regard (Francis, 2000), while balancing this with other activities (e.g., exercise, socializing, reading about other things) formed a useful strategy of emotion management (Hochschild, 1983).

Of course, this quickly became a useful insight in other ways, because finishing one's thesis is never really the end. Working in academia, I soon had to take this dissertation research and re-work it into a series of publica-tions—a process which, years later, is thankfully nearly complete. I have had to draw upon the coping practices noted above again and again to deal with the diverse feelings that are still evoked by this material. Moreover, now that I have two small children of my own, I have had to draw anew upon these coping skills in completing such endeavours, and feel that this has deepened my insights. All the same, I question whether I would personally have dif-ficulties conducting the same research today.

Clearly, working with sensitive and emotionally upsetting data raises many complex issues. In the end, it is ironic that those subjects who are so difficult to access and research, the very subjects that many in society shy away from, may prove to be the most rewarding and personally enlightening of one's research career.

REFERENCES

Berg, B. L. (1995). *Qualitative Research Methods for the Social Sciences* (2nd ed.). Needham Heights, MA: Allyn and Bacon.

Chatzifotiou, S. (2000). Conducting qualitative research on wife abuse: Dealing with the issue of anxiety. *Sociological Research Online 5*. Retrieved from http://www.socresonline.org.uk/5/2/chatzifotiou.html

Denzin, N. K. (1989). *Interpretive Interactionism*. Newbury Park, CA: Sage.

Francis, L. E. (2000). The health benefits of narrative: Why and how? Washington: American Sociological Association.

Gelles, R. J. (1978). Methods for studying sensitive family topics. *American Journal of Orthopsychiatry 48*(3), 408–424.

Hochschild, A. R. (1983). *The Managed Heart*. Berkeley, CA: University of California Press.

Kenney, J. S. (1998). *Coping with grief: Survivors of murder victims*. Unpublished doctoral thesis, McMaster University, Hamilton, ON.

Kenney, J. S. (2002a). Metaphors of loss: Murder, bereavement, gender, and presentation of the "victimized" self. *International Review of Victimology 9*, 219–251.

Kenney, J. S. (2002b). Victims of crime and labeling theory: A parallel process? *Deviant Behaviour 23*, 235–265.

Kenney, J. S. (2003). Gender roles and grief cycles: Observations on models of grief and coping in homicide cases. *International Review of Victimology 10*(1), 19–47.

Kinard, E. M. (1996). Conducting research on child maltreatment: Effects on researchers. *Violence and Victims 11*(1), 65–69.

Lee, R. M. (1993). *Doing Research on Sensitive Topics*. Newbury Park, CA: Sage.

Van den Hoonaard, W. C. (2000). *Research Ethics Review as a Moral Panic*. Paper presented at the 17th Annual Qualitative Analysis Conference, University of New Brunswick.

Copyright Acknowledgements

Index

accommodation, 43, 45, 51, 52

accused vs. state, "legal fiction" of, 81, 85, 215, 222n4, 237

acquaintances, labelling and, 46–50

activism, 68, 111, 120, 122;
    therapy and, 110, 115, 119, 126, 128

adherence vs. flexibility, gender and, 61

agency, human, 64–75, 237, 239

agency control, 189, 198

Alberta, domestic violence legislation in, 235

alcohol use, 52–53, 55

alternative dispute resolution, 173

Amernic, Jerry, 119, 123, 124;
    Victims: Orphans of Justice, 121, 125

anger, 68, 110, 115, 116, 120, 123, 124, 126, 173, 181, 187;
    displacement of, 55;
    male, 29–30, 56–58, 61, 100–101

anti-gang legislation, 232

anti-terrorism legislation, 233

assault, 13, 145, 219;
    common, 167n2;
    sexual, 13, 18, 86, 136, 145, 211–12, 219, 231, 235

assertive claims:
    offenders', 181–82;
    victims', 176–78

avoidance, 43–46, 72

bail process, 216, 233

bail reform, 110

"balance of probabilities," 135

battered woman syndrome, 13

Beccaria, Cesare, 104n1

Bentham, Jeremy, 104n1

bereavement, 21, 22, 25, 34, 58, 76, 94, 236–37;
    gender and, 61;
    homicide and, 20–33;
    parental, 22, 32;
    as test of masculinity, 22

Bill C-7, 231

Bill C-15A, 233

Bill C-16, 233

Bill C-37, 231–32

Bill C-41 (the "Hate Bill"), 232

Bill C-68, 232

Bill C-72, 232

Bill C-89, 110, 140, 141, 230

bills of rights, victims', 140–41

biological factors, 114

blame, 42, 45, 51, 68, 158, 260;
    restorative justice and, 175, 181, 188

blamelessness, 115–16

blaming, 49

break and enter/burglary, 13, 189, 211

British Columbia, parole system in, 234

bureaucratic equality vs. inequality, 219–20